Economics as Literature

A rich vein of economic writings which runs through the nineteenth century and beyond is now largely ignored because its authors were women or because they favoured literary over scientific forms. *Economics as Literature* re-examines some of the most interesting texts from within this tradition.

The works considered include:

- stories (by Maria Edgeworth and Harriet Martineau)
- dialogues (by Jane Marcet and Thomas De Quincey)
- 'imaginative' writing (from John Ruskin and Francis Edgeworth)
- John Maynard Keynes's *General Theory*, which is located within a nine-teenth-century 'tradition' of uniting science and art

Willie Henderson, using analyses based on rhetoric and literary form, demonstrates that these works have both analytical and literary merit, and challenges the accepted notion of a hierarchy of knowledge based on the superiority of science.

Willie Henderson is Senior Lecturer at the School of Continuing Studies, University of Birmingham. He works on African studies, and on education and language in economics. His previous publications include *Models and Economic Theory* (1977, with I. Papps), *The Language of Economics: The Analysis of Economics Discourse* (1990, edited with Tony Dudley-Evans) and *Economics and Language* (1993, edited with Tony Dudley-Evans and Roger Backhouse).

Routledge Studies in the History of Economics

Economics as Literature

Willie Henderson

Routledge
Taylor & Francis Group

LONDON AND NEW YORK

First published 1995
by Routledge
2 Park Square, Milton Park, Abingdon, Oxfordshire OX14 4RN

Simultaneously published in the USA and Canada
by Routledge
711 Third Avenue, New York, NY 10017

First issued in paperback 2014

Routledge is an imprint of the Taylor & Francis Group, an informa business

© 1995 Willie Henderson

British Library Cataloguing in Publication Data
A catalogue record for this book is available from the British Library

Library of Congress Cataloguing in Publication Data
A catalogue record for this book has been requested

ISBN 978-0-415-12908-4 (hbk)
ISBN 978-0-415-75656-3 (pbk)

To
Annalisa

Contents

Acknowledgements

Teaching economics to adults and to second language learners alerted me to the problem of language and economics. It was thanks to colleagues in the English for Overseas Student Unit, The University of Birmingham, that I started to appreciate that there were methods available to study language use within particular subjects. Tim Johns and Tony Dudley-Evans have provided me with support and encouragement over the years and I am grateful for this opportunity to thank them for the comments generously provided for this latest project. A debt of gratitude is also owed to Tony Davies, also of the English Department, who has commented most generously on each of the essays published here and in so doing has helped with the transition from a stress on language to a stress on literary appreciation. Similar thanks go to Valerie Sanders of the University of Buckingham for similar support. Roger Backhouse, Vivienne Brown, Peter Cain, Michael Goulder, Doreen Innes, Jo McDonagh, Greg Myers, D. P. O'Brien, Ron Speirs, Linda Thomas, David Whitehead, and D. N. Winch also provided useful comments on early drafts on one or more of the chapters. I am grateful to them all. Thanks also go to D.N. McCloskey who put 'rhetoric' on the economics agenda. I also express my appreciation to the anonymous commentator for comments made on Chapter 1. They were both generous and helpful. Errors and omissions remain my own responsibility.

The staff of the Heslop Room, University of Birmingham Library, helped provide access to the collection of papers on Harriet Martineau and the British Library provided a microfilm version of Jane Marcet's *Conversations on Political Economy*. Co-operation from both institutions made it so much easier to undertake the research. The School of Continuing Studies, The University of Birmingham, is thanked for providing me with some space, in each busy week, to undertake research. I appreciate, also, the work of Irene McKenzie, School of Continuing Studies, who helped with the word processing.

Chapter 3 was published with the same title in *History of Education*, December 1994 and Chapter 4 was published in the same journal in

Acknowledgements

December 1992. I thank the journal and its publishers, Taylor and Francis, for permission to republish.

The chapter on Keynes was read in an early version at a one-day conference on 'Rhetoric Ancient and Modern' held in March 1994 at the European Humanities Research Centre, University of Warwick. Participants are thanked for their supportive comments.

I express my gratitude to Kitty, Annalisa and Angus for their support and tolerance, especially when I worked on evenings and at weekends.

1

Economics as literature

An introduction to 'literary economics'

The contemplation of the nineteenth century in the history of economic thought is primarily focused upon the canons of political economy, i.e. for the period under examination here, works by Adam Smith, Thomas Malthus, David Ricardo and John Stuart Mill. Whilst there may be debate about the precise nature and significance of the canons, writing on the canons dominates the field and efforts to re-work the major writers in terms of later economic and mathematical insight abound. The method of analysis used has been described as 'canonization' (Brown, 1993: 67). When a canonical interpretation is made of what are seen as key texts, the tendency is to frame the texts in terms of the origins of modern-day economic ideas. Past texts are read in terms of current developments and an intellectual parentage established for recent trends. Such a framework, according to Brown, tends to restrict, over time, the meanings found in the text as the discipline, through academic discussion and negotiation, reduces the range of acceptable interpretations. Many possible voices in the text are, by the process, reduced to one voice. This process is the very opposite of that taken by scholars of literature to the fictive writing of the same era. Literary analysis accepts the 'many voiced' nature of a text, the possibility of ambiguity and the changes of meaning consequent upon the changing point of view of the reader and of protagonists in the narrative (Brown, 1994b: 4). The aim is to open-up rather than to restrict meanings.

A literary approach is potentially available for the study of political economy texts, and such an approach, backed by scholars such as McCloskey and Brown, challenges the 'single voice' results of canonical investigation. A concrete example will serve as a means of illustrating the problem. De Quincey is usually interpreted as a follower of Ricardo, and there is much in his writing that suggests pure hero-worship. In objecting to the social dangers of rent consuming all the available surplus De Quincey points out Ricardo's omission of technical change, and refers to

that great antagonist force for ever at work in Great Britain –

1

through skill, capital, and the energy of freemen; only by an antagonist law for ever operative in throwing back the descents – in raising the soil in case E, in the year 1700, to the level B as it was in 1500 – the soil of O, in the year 1800, to the level of E as it stood in 1600: thus and only thus, do we escape, have escaped, and shall escape, the action of rent; which action, by the just exposures of Ricardo, tends always to engulf us; which action, by the unjust concealments of Ricardo, ought long ago to have frozen us into dead lock – anything to the contrary notwithstanding which has ever been insisted on by that great master of economy.

(De Quincey, 1897e: 248–249)

This could be seen as simply a matter of exploring the consequences of technical change, De Quincey merely adding to the scientific model by shifting the production possibility curve, thus demonstrating his technical ability in political economy. Look again at the language, see how the economic agents are depicted in terms suggestive of free agents and conservative and sustained social values, rather than as mechanistic and value-free. Economic agents work consistently over-time, secure within the timelessness of English society, to counter the effects of mechanistic law. Such an understanding makes De Quincey's text critical, value-laden in senses different from those of Ricardo, ironic and potentially antagonistic towards some Ricardian ideas (McDonagh, 1994: 49). The passage illustrates a more general ambiguity towards Ricardo in *Logic*.

In canonical terms, the essays as written here are 'outside the field' both with respect to subject matter and with respect to style of analysis. Whilst there is inevitably summarisation and translation, the method of analysis attempts to integrate the economics and the linguistic expression, i.e. the concern is both with economic argument and the ways in which the argument is presented in literary form. The focus is sometimes upon the economics or on the economics education and sometimes on the ways in which ideas are expressed and developed. If framed by the literary approach to economics writing promoted by McCloskey's work *The Rhetoric of Economics*,[1] and pursued in the cross-over between literature and economics in Marc Shell's *The Economy of Literature* (1978) and Kurt Heinzelman's excellent *The Economics of the Imagination*, then these essays are attempting to bring to economists and economics educators some of the benefits of that alternative tradition. They are part of results of the process of paying more attention to the encoding and decoding of economics meanings. A careful consideration not only of what is written but how it is written changes the meaning and implications of text. In this context, the relationship between, say, Ricardo and De Quincey becomes problematic.

Canonical approaches have deepened knowledge of the origins and development of sets of economic ideas and forms a legitimate basis for making judgements on past and present economic argument. This knowledge has been purchased at a price. Economic texts have been cut off from their contemporary audiences; the impact of economics writing, for most of the century accessible to educated people in general, on contemporary values and ideas and the interaction between economics and education, economics and literature and literature and economics has not tended to be seen as part of the official histories. The canonical approach reconfirms the professionalisation of the discipline and justifies the compartmentalisation of knowledge. The works of Adam Smith, Thomas Malthus, David Ricardo and John Stuart Mill (for the period that the essays in this collection concentrate upon) are, and remain, key works – but they were not alone in the field. They, and the economic circumstances that they were engaged in analysing, gave rise to further works, including novels with socio-economic themes, which have their origins in the writings of Maria Edgeworth and Harriet Martineau, and to the imaginatively rather than scientifically constructed economic ideas of the Romantic poets. The earliest writings took the form of educational works in political economy. Later works, by the Romantic poets, inaugurated a criticism of economic ideas, culminating in the economic writings of John Ruskin. Francis Ysidro Edgeworth, nephew of Maria Edgeworth, blended the literary tradition with the scientific tradition and passed on to his contemporaries, including John Maynard Keynes, some of the cultural traditions of literary economics. The meaning to be attached to literary economics is explored below. What is emphasised here, for the time being, is the *self-conscious* 'literariness' of the texts (the term 'literariness' is borrowed from Brown, 1994: 368). The set of essays published here represent an attempt, using the original sense of the word essay, to apply insights that flow from a heightened awareness of literary criticism, rhetoric and language-use in economics to economics texts that have rarely been recognised as part of the literature of economics. These are not 'authorised readings' of authorised texts, but individual readings of writings which incorporate different discursive practices, which promote economics understanding within different, but related, genres and for different kinds of audiences.[2] The writings come from a period when intellectual culture was not yet split by academic specialisation, when literary figures could challenge or support economic ideas considered as part of the joint stock of knowledge of writers and thinkers. It would not have been possible to write this work without having the benefit of working within, and of reading works within, the growing literature on undertaking a literary analysis of economics. Although an individual reading, that reading has taken place within the growing discursive practices promoted by the 'rhetorical' turn in economics.

The essays do not constitute, however, an integrated study of nineteenth-century literary economics. That is a vast undertaking, demanding wide reading in a variety of subjects and genres. Currently such works are being pursued by the academics interested in the critical appraisal of English literature, McDonagh's work being a prime example. A close reading of individual texts remains a literary method even when it illuminates problems in the history of economic thought. There may be a need to integrate the study of major and minor economics texts as history with the insights achieved by literary analysis. The studies presented here are concerned primarily with individual texts, with re-establishing such texts as interesting and significant in terms of the contemporary audiences for them and only then, and retrospectively at that, for their interconnections.

The subject matter is different kinds of economic texts: economic stories for children written by Maria Edgeworth; Jane Marcet's economics textbook based upon dialogue; economic stories, by Harriet Martineau, written for adults; dialogues and an introductory text written by Thomas De Quincey; John Ruskin's emotive essays challenging popular economic values; and a blend of science and literature in the case of F. Y. Edgeworth. Keynes is included because he represents a late flowering of the tradition which the other writers represent. *The General Theory* (1936) was available to an educated audience (an audience whom he intended to re-educate) and not simply to economists. The level of reader awareness, the literary quality of the more rhetorical passages and the subtle references to a wider literary culture in Keynes's work suggests a link with Edgeworth and through him to the other authors examined here. Even although united by common interests in economics and in education, the implication of the variety of styles and purposes is that the type of literary analysis undertaken and personal responses to the readings vary from chapter to chapter. The question as to how these and other texts can be read is reflected upon in the section headed 'A Literary Reading of Literary Economics'.

The works examined, though from different time periods and written with differing problems and audiences in mind, are strongly linked through the loosely defined notion of literary economics. All authors had literary interests and all of the works display a talent for narrative writing involving the development or application of economic ideas. Most of the works examined here have been given scant attention by historians of economic thought.[3] It must not be forgotten, however, that canonical writing was also literary in a sense however. Adam Smith's texts were produced under the influence of notions of rhetoric and *belles-lettres*, while culture (in its modern and ideological sense) had a great significance in the work of John Stuart Mill. Both Smith and Mill are acknowledged as fine writers and so, in this sense, style is a concern of nineteenth-century economics. Ricardo is an exception, for his work is regarded by his contemporaries and others, for stylistic and structural reasons, as 'difficult'. The origins of the 'difficulty' of Ricardo needs textual exploration in a way which integrates the economics and its literary expression, though De Quincey puts forward in his *Logic of Political Economy* (1897) a convincing set of justifications for such a view. The examination of literary economics as both economics and literature, could equally be applied to Smith and to Mill as it is to the writers and texts examined here. Though the canonical works are rarely touched upon in this volume, in the section headed 'Smith, Ricardo, Malthus and Mill as Literary Economists', some thoughts on such key texts are set out.

Another strong link between the texts, which weakens only with the essay on the early work of F. Y. Edgeworth, is the concern for education with which the economics writing is infused. If the nineteenth century is a century of social and intellectual innovation, one of its key shifts was with respect to education. A prime shift in emphasis came with the concern, exhibited throughout the movement towards socio-political reforms, with the notion of appropriate education. Whilst the issues are complex, refined classical knowledge came to be increasingly contrasted with the notion of useful knowledge. The notion of useful knowledge was worked out by the middle classes for the working classes, the intelligentsia being taken-up with establishing cultural standards for Coleridge's 'cleresy', an intellectual class dedicated to the maintenance of classical culture in the context of aristocratic decline and the rise of the commercial middle classes. What constituted useful knowledge was the subject of considerable debate, particularly in the years leading to the Reform Act of 1832. Political economy, provided a method of communicating it to the 'lower orders' could be established, was, with its notion of social truths, one of the most significant subjects (though not, of course, the only subject). The primary examples of how an economics curriculum for the wider society could and should be developed are the works of three women, usually dismissed as popularisers and propagandists, but treated here as serious minded educators, operating with either explicit or implicit educational theories. Maria Edgeworth, working within the context of the reform of manners as well as 'practical education', led the field with works for children based as much upon Priestley's and Bentham's notions of utilitarianism as on the works of Adam Smith. Jane Marcet followed with *Conversations on Political Economy*, aimed at adolescents, particularly young women. She was in turn followed by Harriet Martineau, who wrote economic tales for adults. That Martineau was able to write for a living, for a period of more than two years, on economics education, is truly remarkable. Marcet also made money out of her writing, though her educational writing spread well beyond economics. Marshall, the leading figure in the professionalisation of neoclassical economics by the end of the century, had one eye on the economics profession and the other on the general public and disliked the contributions made by Marcet and Martineau. He argued that they peddled economics as truths without the framework of cautions and assumptions necessary for economic ideas to have such a status. Even Marshall admitted, however, that the belief in the truth of economics was widespread at the time and shared by some of the writers in the classical tradition. The view from the end of the nineteenth century ought not to be the final judgement on their texts. Re-reading in order to recapture the richness of the texts requires a focus that is not simply that of Marshall. The narrative element is strong in such examples of literary economics.

All of the essayists (save F. Y. Edgeworth) were also professional writers, engaged to some extent in deliberate educational activity. Keynes was a pamphleteer and the opening flourishes of *The General Theory* owe something to that genre. Most made a distinctive contribution to ideas concerning the nature of economics education as well as to the development of literary economics. Thomas De Quincey's *Dialogues* owe something to Marcet and share, as does his *Logic*, with Martineau a willingness to reflect upon the nature of audience (both explicitly and implicitly). Like Martineau, he wrote to earn a living. Extensive exemplifications in De Quincey's *Logic* are essentially vivid short stories uniting the art of description and narrative with analytical intention and share something of Martineau's purposes. De Quincey, unlike Marcet and Martineau is also explicitly concerned with furthering, and hence critically assessing, economic argument. However, it is important not to push the point too far: Marcet, through the character of the young student Caroline, puts forward numerous points, often of a moral nature, against conventional economics which the political economist, Mrs B. goes to great lengths to refute. Dialogue allows at least two points of view to be stated, although carefully constructed monologue (but not a catechism) can achieve similar results. An independent reader has the opportunity of agreeing with Caroline. If a comparison must be made, Marcet's two-way dialogue is simpler, clearer and more direct that De Quincey's three. Martineau also demonstrates an understanding, though not in the stories so much as in her morals, of the important role of government in the context of *laissez-faire*.

John Ruskin is misunderstood if his educational motives are not appreciated as being a significant part of his aims as an economics commentator. Ruskin wrote many things, but his lecturing and writing were primarily inspired by a desire to educate. Some, particularly those biased towards the genius of John Stuart Mill, will balk at the idea of Martineau and Ruskin being treated seriously as writers of economics. Ruskin's reputation as a socio-economic critic and reformer, in particular, is subject to bouts of attention and neglect, elaborate praise and acid criticism. The emotional basis of his writing (dismissed as 'hysterical' and 'feminine' in the view of many of his masculine contemporaries) makes many responses possible. Martineau was also regarded as having been 'un-sexed' by her writing and hence said to display 'masculine' character-istics. In writing as they did, each challenged accepted notions of the proper, i.e. gendered, division of labour. The switching of roles and of genres disturbs accepted notions of the textual division of labour, and hence of categories of appropriate knowledge. Ruskin's works, as products of emotion, were not deemed capable of carrying any scientific meaning.

It is, of course, a mistake to read Ruskin only for his prose style to the detriment of intended or possible meanings. It is as well to remember that the nineteenth century gave rise to a whole set of new words and concepts, identified by Raymond Williams (1960) as part of the set '*indus-try, democracy, class, art* and *culture*', many of which had their origins in the need to describe and construct a society based not upon agrarianism but on manufacturing and the social inequalities and change that it gave rise to (Williams, 1960: xv, xvii). Many of these terms and their changing significance have their origins in the need to understand the socio-economic problems of the early nineteenth century and are directly or indirectly related to the subject matter of literary economics. A concern for the meaning of words, something that Ruskin learned from Carlyle, that other great literary critic of economic modernism and *laissez-faire*, is, given the changes of meaning that were essential to further discussion of changing society, not out of place or trivial. Smith, Ricardo, De Quincey, Mill and Ruskin worked hard on the notions of 'wealth' and of 'value', providing elements of a discourse which helped shape their changing world. Ruskin was in the thick of such words, his socio-economic criticisms have their origins in the contemplation of the relationship between art and society and between art and the industrial arts, between 'labour' and 'work', between 'wealth' and 'value'. Exploring his images and his use of words reveals a poetically constructed discourse which is capable of yielding up critical and potentially scientific ideas.

Ruskin's paternalism shares, in its desire to see an ethical and respons-ible governing class worthy of the respect of working people, much with Martineau, though she was essentially a democrat. Where they differ is in the relationship between responsibility and political economy. For Martineau, political economy suggested a pattern for social reform. For Ruskin, political economy was itself the object of reform. By reforming ideas about the proper nature of a 'true' economy, the economic world itself would be reconstructed. Ruskin deliberately uses the powers of the imagination as an antidote to what he sees as a mistaken science.

F. Y. Edgeworth shared many of the literary interests of De Quincey and Ruskin and shows in his early economics writing an appreciation of the cultural and literary traditions, of literary economics, liberally larding his texts with subtle references to literary culture, in much the same way as De Quincey and Ruskin. There is textual (and other) evidence, in his early work that he had read both of these writers. F. Y. Edgeworth's writing, which seems in the history of economic thought, out of step with the general development of scientific economic writing is, in the context of De Quincey and Ruskin at least, part of the wider cultural and literary tradition of the nineteenth century. Edgeworth's text looks backwards towards that tradition; and forwards, in its mathematical reasoning, towards the economics argumentation of the middle decades of the twentieth century. As with Ruskin, a modern reader will typically struggle with Edgeworth. Keynes's major work illustrates, in its literary qualities, his links with Edgeworth.

Another significant theme running through all of the texts, save, perhaps, F. Y. Edgeworth, is the theme of economic agency. In neo-classical economics, model-building and the supporting language of model building has led, in introductory texts at least, but also in some higher-level theory, to the deletion of economic actors or agents, replacing them with equilibrating forces or rational expectations. But in the writing considered here the class orders of classical economics and the economic behaviour of members of the class tend to be individually identified as economic agents. Maria Edgeworth depicts economic actions within a network of social relations, either that of parent and child or of children amongst themselves. Children and adults of *all* social classes are brought within the net of rational economic motivation and discussion. Martineau sets agency in the context of individual lives and changing social relationships, drawing imaginatively upon domestic and village scenes to illustrate economic argument in a context that allows links to be made between principles and social practice. Marcet sees women as significant actors in the household economy and on the interface between the household and the wider world, requiring her student to draw upon her own economic understanding directly gathered from her experience as an economic agent. Women's agency is located in a gender role but need not be restricted to it. De Quincey is more interested in the abstractions of the theory of value, but in a passage directly concerned with economic story-telling he animates the consumer as a living person ('you', engaged in reading). Rather than manipulating a simple cipher, he provides a psychological depth generally absent from others operating within the Ricardian tradition. His model of consumer psychology is based upon his own experience of drug addiction.

Ruskin's concern for the economic agent as a three-dimensional human being, capable, like all human beings of answering back and animated as much by morality as by concerns about 'getting on', fills his version of economics with social and moral issues. In his public lecture, later published as 'Of King's Treasuries', Ruskin, in an amateurish attempt at descriptive ethics, directly asks, in the context of criticisms of his concept of economic 'virtue', whether his specification of human motivation is appropriate (Ruskin, n.d.: 14–15). Whereas Martineau exhibits themes illustrating the useful power of the market, Ruskin's notion of agency is intended to transcend the mechanistic market mechanism and in so doing lead to the creation of 'true' wealth and 'true' economy. Although their agents are literary creations and as much fictions as 'economic man', the imaginary worlds in which the fictions live and work are more like the worlds inhabited by ordinary readers.

If the coldness of Maria Edgeworth's 'The Purple Jar' is set aside, economic agents in much of this writing are recognisable rounded human beings, though standing in a series of differing relationships with the formal aspects of economic thought. Maria Edgeworth's characters are animated by educational, economic and moral considerations and set in the social dimension of improvement. Marcet's notion of individual reflection, guided by economics understanding promoted by discussion, provided a basis in women's lives for the development of a sophisticated economics, exposed to criticism from both the head and the heart. Martineau's agents are set within the social context of change and reform, lead by the (useful) destructive principles of *laissez-faire*. Agency in De Quincey, when constructed as story, helps shift the focus away from objective to subjective notions of value. The agent in Ruskin is capable of moral action and more and more capable, through a process of consumer education, of reading the socially harmful aspects of market activity. Ruskin's agent is not an economic monad or a mechanistic automaton but a member of society enmeshed in moral responsibilities and duties.

A common theme in the treatment of agency is found in the way in which exemplification is vividly constructed within an economic narrative that can often be construed as parable. For such authors, economics was 'a social process', and their writing unites formal and substantive economy sometimes along lines similar in intent to those of the realist novel (McCloskey, 1994: 333). This notion is especially true for the writing of Keynes who feels very intensely, and certainly as vividly as Ruskin, the tension between received economic theory and the economic world and behaviours to which such theory points. When read together with the canonical texts, our authors can provide us with insight into how the notion of economic agency grew and developed, in theoretical, practical and normative terms in the course of the nineteenth century. Today's economic agents, in much theoretical literature, are assumed to possess a psychological life consistent with the notion of equilibrium or rational expectations, a point of view mocked in a recent paper by Rector (Rector, 1990: 195).

These texts can be profitably explored using a variety of techniques derived from literary studies to reveal their persuasive structures and intents in the context of their contemporary popularity. As with the other writers, what we bring to the texts is likely to influence what we find. It would be misleading to suggest that the chapters were achieved in the order that they are published here. The work evolved and, indeed, started with F. Y. Edgeworth and Harriet Martineau. If I were to rewrite the chapter on F. Y. Edgeworth there is little doubt that his work would be better integrated into the literary economics tradition of uniting economics and the imagination, a tradition which Edgeworth, I feel, helped pass on to Keynes. Keynes is included as a kind of epilogue, for, although *The General Theory* is a major text, it is self-consciously literary and persuasive and uses a variety of devices in common with the literary economics of the nineteenth century. The papers are set out here in chronological historical order rather than the order in which they were worked upon.

A LITERARY READING OF LITERARY ECONOMICS

There are many different ways of approaching the reading of literary economics and differing problems to be faced. It is hard to re-read the works of Marcet and Martineau without outfacing Marshall whose own reading was undertaken with knowledge of what their writings had come, in the fullness of time, to support. Marshall's concerns for an economics 'understanded of the people' nevertheless illustrates that he too was concerned with the nature of public understanding. The difference between him and those considered here was that he wished the public understanding of economics to be guided by those also responsible for the professionalisation of the discipline. Ruskin is another writer towards whom contemporary readers must struggle. If Ruskin is approached with canonical writing in mind, his *bravura* passages are likely to seem wild and out of place and even as a barrier to understanding rather than as stimulants for the development of an economics imagination that could reach beyond existing conditions. Ruskin's failure was also a failure of the imagination in the sense that his preference for paternalistic medievalism could not provide a positive vision capable of sustaining alternative approaches to substantive economic activity. His text, like Edgeworth's and Keynes's, raises the question of the role of the imagination in the development of economics understanding and of the role that reading places on achieving an imaginative understanding of economics. All the writers used their imagination to present pictures of economic life and all felt it essential that others came to know and understand economic issues and economic argument on a creative and imaginative basis. There is a strong visual element in the texts from Edgeworth, Maria to Edgeworth, Francis, whether descriptively or metaphorically based.

In contemporary analysis, the problem of audience holds some significance. It is an assumption, common to all save F. Y. Edgeworth, that the canonical texts were beyond the reach, in some sense, of the readership selected. Even with F. Y. Edgeworth, the relationship with the audience is ambiguous in this respect. The authors' constructions of their intended readership is interesting. Maria Edgeworth's readership is not simply children, but also their parents. Economic lessons given are given to parents and children and parental behaviour, particularly with respect to economic issues, is patterned almost as much as is the behaviour of the children. Parents are constructed in terms of utilitarianism and 'practical education'. The images of parental behaviour and the associated economic values of the growing middle class of the early nineteenth century are depicted in terms of the educational practices of the aristocratic Edgeworths, who came from a social class that had the expensive leisure time to make the labour-intensive methods work. But the stories worked and formed an important element in children's reading for at least one hundred years.[4] Experience and co-operation are the educational foundation for economics learning. Marcet's intended readers are young, essentially middle-class, persons of either sex, though she concentrates upon young women. Like Edgeworth she depicts women's education as a matter of activating economics understanding gained through ordinary social experience and reflecting upon it in a co-operative way in the company of a sound guide and supplemented by resort to examples and counter-examples from ancient texts, contemporary political economy and literature. A model of economics education is set out for the targeted reader, whose own experience of economics and learning is reconstructed by the text and whose interests are not constrained by assumptions about what is conventionally thought suitable for women to know.

Martineau's intended readership is slightly more complex. She rejects canonical text, with its cold picking-over of disputed points, as an inappropriate starting point for those new to economics, and interested novices are her primary intended audience. However, in attempting to make the governing classes worthy of the respect of the poor and the moral character of the poor known to the governing classes, her novices are intended to come from all social classes. The imaginary economic world that she constructs is, however, with some notable exceptions, the social world of her own experience, albeit supplemented by extensive reading. Although her sales were enormous there is some dispute concerning the nature of the actual readership and the uses to which the 'lessons' were put. The texts can be seen as both literature and lesson and could as a result be read by different readers for different purposes and points of view. The domestication of economic agency made it possible for poorer members of Victorian society to read them with pleasure as mini-novels, reconstructing and even ennobling their own experiences. Martineau intended not to sugar the economics pill but may have in a sense over-sugared it and so achieved the very opposite.

De Quincey, though also writing for other political economists, consistently constructs his readership in terms of the novice and sees Ricardo's *Principles* as unsuitable as a starting point not because of any emotional coldness in the text (he intellectually approves of picking over bare bones) but because of the way in which topics are sequenced. He criticises the 'flying reader' and attempts to come to terms with the changing perception of the reading process by alternating between closely argued scholasticism and lighter and more imaginative passages. As far as the economics is concerned, he is at his most liberated in terms of value theory when he imaginatively constructs the economic agent and draws the reader into the text on that basis. His target reader, like that of F. Y. Edgeworth, is clever enough to appreciate De Quincey's rhetorical flourishes, his classical learning and his direct and indirect references to English literature.

With Ruskin, the notion of audience must encompass both readers and listeners for much of his work has its origins in the large, public lecture and whole passages of his writing retain the original sense of oral delivery. In his most declarative passages he often resorts to cumulating parallelisms, a technical device that is also found in the early writings of F. Y. Edgeworth. Such parallelisms are better spoken than read. Ruskin aims to move an audience, in the sense both of heightening their emotional experience of the topic and of changing their attitudes towards it. Ruskin's texts, unlike conventional political economy, cannot be described as cold. If his audience read Ruskin, Ruskin always attempted to 'read' his audience: 'I never can go on with an address unless I feel, or know, that my audience are either with or against me: (I do not much care which, in beginning) but I must know where they are' (Ruskin, n.d.: 14–15). When he was there in person, face-to-face, so to speak, he could control the situation by carefully adjusting the rhetoric to achieve the desired mood, even if the material had been carefully worked over beforehand. When he challenged economic values in print, at a distance which any text implies, his intentions could lead to anger rather than change.

The construction of the intended reader in Edgeworth's *Mathematical Psychics* is also problematic. Marshall, always intent on being in charge of professional economics and of the public understanding of economics, felt that F. Y. Edgeworth needed to take greater care of his readers. Edgeworth's intended reader is no novice as a reader nor as a literary critic and as a mathematician, sometimes is, and sometimes not, suitably skilled. However, in the tradition of literary economics, as represented by De Quincey and Ruskin, Edgeworth's approach seems less singular than is depicted in the paper as published. Edgeworth shares with Ruskin and De Quincey the desire to construct a creative reader who is imaginatively involved in the economics that is being developed in the text. Keynes identifies and constructs (reconstructs) his imaginative reader in terms that share something with Edgeworth's attempts without generating the same reputation for stylistic obscurity. De Quincey complained about the 'flying reader'. There has been a tendency, inspired by Marshall, to see Edgeworth as the 'flying writer'. Edgeworth looks back to the literary reader of the earlier part of the century and forwards to the fully professional reader of the opening years of the twentieth century.

An unusually high level of 'reader awareness' is found in *The General Theory*. Keynes constructs the reader in terms that would reflect the views of Bloomsbury: modern, questioning, alive and (potentially) free of the restricted vision of the nineteenth century. Such a reader is both critical and imaginative and capable of working alongside Keynes in pursuit of the goal of sloughing off the ideas of 'the classical economics' in order to construct an economics that is closer to shared 'actual' experience and understanding of contemporary economic circumstances. Keynes's level of reader awareness shares much more with De Quincey, Ruskin and F. Y. Edgeworth than it does with the orderly and restrained writing of J. S. Mill.

As there has been a tendency to downgrade most of the texts and authors presented here, as, for example, mere 'tyros' or slavish followers of 'the masters', I have attempted to demonstrate that 'richer' readings are possible. A means of undertaking a richer reading implies taking an approach to reading that is eclectic. Each of the texts, even that of the simple story by Maria Edgeworth, can be looked at from a number of points of view – interpretation is not simple or straightforward. Maria Edgeworth, even in the simplest of stories, is working with philosophical ideas. The discursive framework that has been applied has differed from the one text to another. With Marcet and Martineau, for example, an educational framework changes the works from 'mere capitalistic propaganda' to 'sophisticated curriculum development', subsequent investigation revealing instances of interesting educational 'moves' that do not constitute elements of a catechism. Throwing off the label of catechism and exploring *Conversations on Political Economy* (1816) as (albeit contrived) conversations, yields richer returns to reading. Approaching Ruskin through Heinzelman's *Economics of the Imagination* (1980) reveals scientific possibilities made possible by working upon the grasping of reality through the fancy. An awareness of metaphor, of classical rhetoric and parable as well as of the sources of literary allusions, enriches the reading of the economics writing of De Quincey and F. Y. Edgeworth, and helps, in the case of De Quincey, to reveal a critical oscillation in *Logic* between an objective and subjective account of value, between hero-worship for Ricardo and rejection of the mechanistic view of economy that Ricardo implies. Narrative and imagination challenge the notion of a single, given economy that can be directly apprehended by one straightforward act of interpretation. The notion of an active nineteenth-century tradition integrating and challenging scientific narrowing provides an interesting discursive context for re-reading *Mathematical Psychics*.

The aim of all this has been to persuade readers that each of the texts are worthy of another look, for their own sake (though through different lenses) and for what they can tell us about problems and prospects in the interpretation of varieties of economics. The approaches taken here are not secured within the canonical tradition of interpretation but grounded in the idea of alternative frames of reference or rhetorical approaches, based upon the interests and point of view of a particular reader or reading. Each of the readings is preliminary in the sense that further reading will undoubtedly reveal other aspects to the writing and other ways of framing and interpreting the economic ideas.

SMITH, RICARDO, MALTHUS AND MILL AS LITERARY ECONOMISTS

It would be inappropriate to give the impression that Smith, Ricardo and Mill were not also part of a literary tradition. The mere fact of them writing in English, rather than in the specialist language of mathematics, means that they must, by necessity, be part of a literary tradition. This is, perhaps, not too wide an idea for writing in English opens the way for literary analysis, along lines argued by McCloskey and actively pursued by Brown. But does it suggest a literary tradition? Literary economics, in the sense that it is used here, implies more than a sense of the author as literary figure, though even in these terms it would be difficult to set up any hard and fast division between text types. A simple genre distinction (i.e. fiction/non-fiction) does not work, for the literary authors use a variety; De Quincey in *Logic* uses both. Also the selection of a genre does not imply anything about the status of the argumentative context, e.g., whether or not the texts support or criticise a mechanistic approach to economic agency and to the nature of economic knowledge.

So far, the term literary economics has merely implied a self-conscious awareness of the fictive element of economics discourse (i.e. of 'the logic of fiction'), of melding reason and the imagination; of the significance of metaphor or the role of narrative in the development of economic argument. The very identification of such a tradition is a challenge to subject epistemology, an epistemology consistently criticised by McCloskey, which insists upon a barrier between the two elements or, if not that then upon a hierarchy in which the literary efforts are placed below those of the scientific. Any distinction would be hard to maintain, for an argument for a literary analysis of economics is one that accepts that reasoned argument operates with and through such rhetorical devices.

All are mixed in this sense. Both literature and economics create and use fictions. Smith wrote, as far as we know, no purely fictional works in the sense of novels or critical essays upon novels, though in the *Lectures on Rhetoric and Belles-Lettres*, he undertook literary criticism. He was, however, both well-read and well-travelled and exhibits in the *Lectures on Rhetoric and Belles-Lettres* a command of questions of style and rhetoric and its associated literature (what he called the 'very silly books' of classifications of rhetorical devices).

In terms of a self-awareness of technique, Smith is not without what Gide and Rist refer to as 'literary charm' (1948: 70). The application of such literary analysis to key texts is already under way. Smith is a teller of economic tales, either directly or indirectly. Smith's exemplification of the pin factory, as a way of illustrating the concept of the division of labour is the source, filtered through Rousseau's idea of a mother's need to protect her child in a garden, of Maria Edgeworth's 'The Cherry Orchard' (1776). Smith's fictive pin factory could be seen as a kind of social realism, based upon observation, or what we could consider to be a field method. Edgeworth's fictive cherry-orchard is Utopia. Edgeworth's socially motivated division of labour is undertaken as a journey towards a utopia and reminds us that economics is rarely an end it itself, but, in the utilitarian tradition, a means towards an end, happy and fulfilled human beings. Suddenly, Maria Edgeworth shares insights with both Adam Smith and John Ruskin! Smith's use of concrete examples embedded and picked over in the *Wealth of Nations*, and subsequent canonical texts, are directly and indirectly (through the development of teaching by example within the work of Edgeworth and Marcet) the inspiration for Martineau's teaching of economics through extended exemplifications which became mini-novels. Smith's examples became in this sense Martineau's fictive case-studies, just as Malthus's *Essay on Population* and Ricardo's theory of rent are extended by the story of *Ella of Gaverlock*. Martineau's incidental comments on the misrepresentation of Malthus in social discussion and her awakened understanding of what she found in the *Essay on Population* when she started to read it reveal the kinds of energy with which the middle classes received and discussed economic ideas, as does Marcet's comment on the 'veneration' of Adam Smith. In literary terms, Martineau's tales become examples of 'continuations', possible readings of the original story beyond the original text. Continuations attest to the reality of different interpretations, to the possibility that 'meanings can never quite be contained and confined but seem to overflow the boundaries of a text' (Brown, 1994a: 370).

What Marcet or Martineau saw in the works of Adam Smith differ from what others might have seen. Their discursive frame gave rise to continuations which, in turn, frame the original in new ways. They change our understanding of the original by illustrating what happens to the argument in a changed context. Continuations may seem to be continuations within the same genre, e.g. Martineau's *Life in the Wild* is a development of *Robinson Crusoe*, but this is in turn an outcome of Selkirk's authentic experience of shipwreck. Her whole economics project translates ideas from one genre to another, and, with the economic epilogues, back again! Smith's economics, viewed through the *Lectures on Rhetoric and Belles-Lettres* would look different from his economics viewed through the canonical process of interpretation, as criticised by Vivienne Brown, or through the continuations practised by his literary followers (Brown, 1994a: 370). Brown specifically rejects the *Lectures* as a useful frame for reading Smith's economics. The interpretation proposed by a literary approach to economics writing stresses, amongst other things, the significance of inter-textual relationships. It occasions the breakdown of the simple category of 'literary economics' as used earlier in this chapter.

Ricardo's writings, to which Jane Marcet's *Conversations on Political Economy* and De Quincey's *Dialogues* and *Logic* are linked, are often described as 'difficult'. Certainly the *Principles of Political Economy and Taxation* (1817) were held, by others, to give rise to problems for the reader. Ricardo's fictions (e.g. his 'trade-minded savages') are well known. Marcet's work, it ought to be remembered, pre-dates Ricardo's. De Quincey justifies his own activities as an economics writer with respect to the organisational structure of Ricardo's work and its use of terms. If his is a sequel, and Marcet's a prequel, two additional frameworks for the interpretation of the difficulties or alleged difficulties of Ricardo become available.

Mill is the other giant, for his work on economics and other issues set a standard of clarity and dominated the middle years of the nineteenth century. Raymond Williams, in analysing Mill's essays on Bentham and Coleridge, talks of his 'reasonable' tone and his 'professional skill in summary and distinction' (Williams, 1960: 49). Blaug refers to the way in which Mill's authoritative economics writing and sense of style set the standard for the *Principles* text for the next generation of writers to overcome (Blaug, 1986: 101). Mill brought together style, literary and imaginative understanding and reasoned and restrained argument. Those who are prepared to read his *Principles* text will find clarity and care to be key elements of his writing. It is possible to make too much of Ruskin's attacks on Mill and there is little doubt that Ruskin overstates his case, for Mill too can be construed as reading beyond the market and reading beyond economics to a wider set of possibilities of social science. Heinzelman (1980) locates these in both the full-title of the work, *Principles of Political Economy With Some of Their Applications to Social Philosophy*, and in textual realisation. In Heinzelman's terms, Mill works upon both the formalist and mechanistic aspect of economics and upon the substantivist notion of economics as a study of how wants are expressed and satisfied in a given society (Heinzelman, 1980: 77). Mill's reader is expected to read beyond the formalist economics towards an imaginative social philosophy (Heinzelman, 1980: 76–94). Ruskin's reading of Mill is certainly superficial, for he seems to concentrate upon the formalist aspect of Mill. Ruskin is on surer ground with respect to reading how Mill and the other political economists translated into a wider set of social values and assumptions.

McCloskey has recently suggested various reasons for undertaking a rhetorical analysis of the economics text: 'to understand it, to admire it, to debunk it, to set it beside other works of persuasion in science, to see that science is not a new dogma but is thoroughly and respectably part of the culture' (McCloskey, 1994: 336). The present essays are not primarily concerned with adding to the literature on the *theory* of text analysis in economics. The various chapters contain approaches that are at times 'new', and at other times 'old fashioned'. The biographical emphasis will, to some, seem particularly 'old-fashioned'. Whilst accepting the hermeneutical concept of distanciation, and the associated notion that meaning is created in the interface between the reader and the text, the fact that the writing is the product of a given author, working in given circumstances, remains of interest. If nothing else, it explains the choice of genre, and conventionally at least this shapes the potential responses. Genre in this sense is not neutral. Whilst accepting that the act of interpretation is reader-based and not author-based, it is still possible to make an argument about authorial intention based upon textual evidence. It is legitimate to explore the nature of the intended readership as revealed by textual evidence or the degree to which the author is committed to the ideas expressed, whilst at the same time accepting that the textual evidence being presented is subject to interpretation.

I have enormously enjoyed reading and analysing the literary economics set out in this small collection. The category 'literary economics' does not yield a confined set of works or even of genres, but has none the less provided an interesting starting point for exercises in the literary analysis of economics. My motivation for making the analysis was as mixed as McCloskey's list suggested, as were the methods used in the promotion of the activity. There is no doubt that I wished to work in the field of the history of economic thought but found the standard process of summarisation and translation of literary ideas into mathematical formula unappealing. It was primarily in an effort to see what was possible to achieve by way of economics understanding through different approaches to the educational problem of enlightening the public on economic issues that I took to the texts selected. What I found challenged my notions of the nature of economics and of economics understanding, of the relationship between economic fact and economic fiction. Although the difficulties with the notion of 'literary economics' have been set out above, there does seem to be a body of writing on economics, of which only a sample has been provided, that self-consciously brings together 'science' and 'art'; that links economic argument and literary allusion and that insists upon the creative role of narrative, metaphor and the imagination. Whilst talk of a tradition of literary economics is probably unhelpful, there does seem to be something in the idea of a nineteenth-century approach to economics being carried forwards into the twentieth century by Keynes's *General Theory*. What makes the *General Theory* part of the tradition of literary economics, in the loose sense in which the term has been used here, are not only the links Keynes makes with literary culture (Ibsen's *Wild Duck*, De Mandeville, Shakespeare) and his *bravura* passages but the way in which the reader is imaginatively constructed and incorporated into the text. I find that I need to reflect further on the role of economic imagination, particularly when teaching introductory courses on economics. There is no doubt that by framing the works within contexts and questions other than those which we would routinely apply to the standard canons my own enjoyment of, and enthusiasm for, the texts has increased enormously. The results are set out here in the hope that others might share in this and feel able to use the skills required to undertake a literary analysis of literary or any other economics, for their own analytical purposes. One major use of the (flawed) notion of a literary tradition of literary economics could be to rework Mill's *Principles* in terms of it, another could be to rework the reading of Keynes's *General Theory of Employment, Interest and Money*.

The rhetorical and literary techniques of undertaking a literary analysis of literary economics have not been explored in detail, the question of narrative and economics is, for example, hardly explored at all. However, a range of possible techniques are demonstrated within each of the essays as published. The devices range from an understanding of classical and modern notions of the nature of rhetoric; an awareness of metaphor and other features of classical rhetoric; a sensitivity to allusion either directly or indirectly to English literature; the construction of the reader; an awareness of the relationship between economic ideas and the language used to clothe them. The attitude of mind must be to attempt to remain 'open' to the texts themselves, whilst maintaining that critical faculty which is essential for all interesting and rewarding reading. Brown talks of the text as something given, 'as a complete entity with no missing parts' and compares this to the economy in which the text has to be 'compiled, sifted and sorted' (Brown, 1994a: 375). The notion of the economy as an incomplete text is a useful one. The notion of texts, particularly historical texts, as complete in themselves, though reasonable, is not without difficulties. Ruskin's suggestion that a horse is not much good to someone who does not know how to ride would seem to apply to anyone coming new to a literary reading of literary economics. If we do not know literature in English, if we are not certain of the strength

18

or force of the allusions or the sense or senses of the metaphors (for example, the barely noticed preference De Quincey has for the language of cosmology as a way of talking about the inter-connectedness and recurrence of key elements in economic argument),[5] if we cannot struggle towards an integrated stylistic and argumentative culture then despite a textual whole, all we can have access to are fragments to be sifted. What is seen in a text is partly determined by what we are capable of seeing. No single method of 'seeing' has been used or demonstrated either here in the introduction nor in the various chapters. The 'seeing' has been both promoted and constrained by a desire to explore economics writing originally aimed, largely, at interested non-professionals. The aim has been 'to read with understanding' (McCloskey, 1994: 320). When taken together, however, the chapters which follow give some idea, however imperfectly, of what is required in undertaking an analysis of this type. If further guidance is needed there are numerous sources, both within economics discussion and literary criticism, to which interested readers can turn.

NOTES

1 For a list of McCloskey's works on rhetoric see the bibliography section to his 'How to Do a Rhetorical Analysis, and Why' in Backhouse, 1994: 319–342.
2 For a discussion see Vivienne Brown 'The Economy as Text', in Backhouse, 1994: 368–382.
3 The exceptions are, of course, Creedy, 1986: and Mirowski, 1994 who have worked on Edgeworth. Keynes is given enormous attention.
4 I was read the story of Jem and Lightfoot as a child in a Glasgow primary school in the 1950s.
5 It was pointed out to me by Tony Davies.

REFERENCES

Blaug, M. (1986) *Great Economists Before Keynes*, Brighton: Wheatsheaf Books.
Brown, V. (1993) 'Decanonizing Discourses: Textual Analysis and the History of Economic Thought', in Henderson, W., Dudley-Evans, T., and Backhouse, R., (eds) *Economics and Language*, London: Routledge, 64–84.
Brown, V. (1994a) 'The Economy as Text', in Backhouse, R. E. (ed.) *New Directions in Economic Methodology*, London: Routledge, 368–382.
Brown, V. (1994b), *Adam Smith's Discourse: Canonicity, Commerce and Conscience*, London: Routledge.
Creedy, J. (1886) *Edgeworth and the Development of Neoclassical Economics*, Oxford: Basil Blackwell.
De Quincey, T. (1897) 'Logic of Political Economy', in Masson, D. (ed.) *De Quincey's Works* IX *Political Economy and Politics*, London: A & C Black, 248–249.
Gide, C. and Rist, C. (1948) *A History of Economic Doctrines*, 2nd ed. (trans. R. Richards), London: Harrap & Co.
Heinzelman, K. (1980) *The Economics of the Imagination*, Amherst: University of Massachusetts Press.

McCloskey, D. (1994) 'How to Do a Rhetorical Analysis and Why?' in Backhouse, R. (ed.) *New Directions in Economic Methodology*, London: Routledge, 319–342.

McDonagh, J. (1994) *De Quincey's Disciplines*, Oxford: Oxford University Press, ch. 2, 42–65.

Mirowski, P. (1994) 'Marshalling the Unruly Atoms: Understanding Edgeworth's Career,' in *Edgeworth on Chance, Economic Hazard and Statistics*, Totowa, New Jersey: Rowan and Littlefield, 1–78.

Rector, R. A. (1990) 'The Economics of Rationality and the Rationality of Economics', in Lavoie, D. (ed.) *Economics and Hermeneutics*, London: Routledge, 195–235.

Ruskin, J. (n.d.) [1865] 'Of King's Treasuries', in *Sesame and Lilies*, London and Glasgow: Collins Clear-Type Press.

Shell, M. (1978) *The Economy of Literature*, Baltimore: Johns Hopkins University Press.

Williams, R. (1960) *Culture and Society 1780–1950*, London: Chatto and Windus.

2

Child's play

Maria Edgeworth and economics education

The end of the eighteenth and beginning of the nineteenth century saw the development, on a serious and sustained basis, of education in political economy. The movement leading to this development had its origins both in the political economy of the day and in the growth of ideas about education itself. An engaging aspect of the movement is the extent to which it was pioneered by women. The three women concerned were Maria Edgeworth (1767–1849), Jane Marcet (1769–1858) and Harriet Martineau (1802–1876). In two further chapters I illustrate the special contribution of Martineau, engaged in the informal education of all ranks in society, but particularly of adults, through economic stories, and of Marcet, who taught economics to young people, through the use of dialogue. This chapter concentrates on the contribution made by Maria Edgeworth who aimed her economics writing at the very young.

The intention is to explore Edgeworth's economics writings, developed within an educational approach that synthesised the ideas of Locke and Rousseau, for insight into how non-canonical literature interpreted economics ideas and values to an audience of children and their parents. The paper is therefore divided into two parts: the first deals with Edgeworth as an interpreter of economics themes for an audience of children, the second draws out from these the principles which guided her approach to economics education and outlines their influence upon Marcet and Martineau. The paper will not be concerned with a suggestion made by Millhauser that, in her adult novel *The Absentee*, Edgeworth produced the first socio-economic novel (Millhauser, 1938: 205). This claim would shift, of course, if justified, the origins of this favoured nineteenth-century genre away from Harriet Martineau.[1]

THE ECONOMIC STORIES

Maria Edgeworth is mentioned in the history of education, particularly in terms of her 'partnership' with her father, Richard Lovell Edgeworth. Biographers and feminists differ on the significance of the relationship for the development of Edgeworth's writing. The main issue, and one that has persisted over the years, has been the usefulness or otherwise of Lovell Edgeworth's involvement. Speculation developed early. Lawless puts the negative case very well: 'that he was in essentials one of the best intentioned of fathers is certain, yet few bad, few merely indifferent fathers, have inflicted upon a gifted son or daughter worse injuries from an intellectual point of view than he did' (Lawless, 1904: 38–39). According to Lawless, Lovell Edgeworth stunted Edgeworth's imagination. Harriet Martineau, whose sharp observations are of considerable interest in this respect, got in first. In a letter to Fanny Wedgwood, she is very forthright in her response to reading the 'Edgeworth Memoir'. She praises Maria Edgworth's 'spirit and temper' and domestic 'generosity' but complains about 'the dreary worldliness and lowness in which she was held down, in spite of all possible capacity for aspiration, and of a temperament made up of enthusiasms' (Arbuckle, 1983: 286).[2]

According to the biographer Clarke, Lovell Edgeworth planned and promoted Edgeworth's interest in writing and possessed 'the imagination, the ideas, the fruitful mind that could help her' (Clarke, 1965: 95). Little wonder that feminists have encountered difficulties in making an analysis of Edgeworth's writings. Kowaleski-Wallace (1991) analyses the relationship within the context of patriarchy. The answer to the question of Lovell Edgeworth's influence remains open. Although the economic stories have a moral purpose, the improving moralising, usually associated with Lovell Edgeworth, is covert rather than overt, at least in those stories which have an economic dimension. The indirect influence is evident in the development of educational insights which led to the publication of *Practical Education* (1798). Here the mixture of influences is complex for the observations of childhood behaviour on which the work is partly based were initiated by Maria Edgeworth's step-mother in collaboration with Lovell Edgeworth. Maria Edgeworth took over the partnership after her step-mother's death. There is no evidence that Lovell Edgeworth had any direct interest in economics education and the writing skills upon which Edgeworth herself built in this respect were her own. Her ideas on economics she learned from the works of Adam Smith and, see below, from David Hume, though the utilitarian aspects she probably owes to Lovell Edgeworth and his contact with Priestley. Her educational theory developed within the partnership between herself and Lovell Edgeworth and through independent reading of educational works.

Edgeworth is only briefly mentioned in the social context of the history of economic thought, for, on her (later) visits to London she moved in the circles frequented by the political economists such as Malthus, Ricardo and Marcet. She is depicted as someone who had 'once played charades with Ricardo', and who had correspondence with him on the subject of Ireland and the potato.[3] Her elegant and humorous comment

Maria Edgeworth

on the working relationship between Ricardo and Malthus is mentioned by Heilbroner: 'they hunted together in search of truth and huuzzaed when they found her, without caring who found her first' (Heilbroner, 1955: 141). Reference is made to her on works on Francis Ysidero Edgeworth because she was his 'aunt'. She receives less attention than Marcet and Martineau and they are only treated, I suspect, because of Marshall's dislike of their efforts. Nor is her work much considered in the (somewhat underdeveloped) history of economics education. With respect to economics, she made no original contribution to the development of economic doctrines, though, as will become apparent, Edgeworth is interesting in terms of the particular interpretation she puts upon economic ideas and the impact of her writing on Marcet and Martineau. Her economics education is incorporated into her 'wee-wee' stories developed in the context of life within the family circle at her home at Edgeworthstown.

Practical Education[4] is the immediate educational context within which the specifically economic tales are developed. Prefaces to collected editions of the stories make frequent reference to its ideas. The stories carry the message into the wider world. The work concentrates upon education within the context of the upper-class family, the stories extend the interest to the middle classes: 'that great multitude of society who are neither high born or high bred'.[5] The review correctly spots the domesticity of the stories, which offer the middling classes 'a picture of their own condition'. Lovell Edgeworth was brought up by his mother in an educational regime influenced by the ideas of Locke. Lovell Edgeworth, in turn, brought up his eldest son with an educational regime suggested by Rousseau, though the experiment was later abandoned.[6] Kowaleski-Wallace argues that Lovell Edgeworth's approach to Edgeworth was contained in an ideology of patriarchy supported and justified by Lockean notions of education. This system both promoted and constrained her freedom. Lovell Edgeworth explored educational issues with friends within the Lunar Society so, despite the note of sourness with which he is often treated in the literature, his ideas were generally progressive. The observations of children's behaviour in the context of educational development logged over the years by Maria and Lovell Edgeworth must have greatly assisted Maria Edgeworth develop observational skills, essential to the writer's craft.

The general tenor of the work is that education can take place within the practical concerns of everyday life. Science for example can be discovered in a snowstorm: snow-covered clothes become sodden and heavy in front of the fire, why? Observation and experience will lead the child towards an answer. Steam from the tea kettle can give rise to further lessons. Solids, liquids and gases can be thought about in the context of mundane experience. The introduction of science and the drafting of a

23

simple curriculum based on small-scale experiments is one of the innovations.[7] Adults must be aware of the educational resources and possibilities created in the environment of everyday: in the situations encountered, in the toys that are bought and in the books that are read. Lessons are to be interesting, involving, varied and short. Rote-learning, a persistent element in eighteenth-century education, is to be avoided.[8] Reason is to be supported and sustained and punishment and boredom banished. The mixture is an interesting synthesis of Locke (to whom it owes the concern for experience), Rousseau (to whom is owed the notion that childhood, and associated learning, ought to be happy), and ideas discussed with friends in the Lunar Society and domestically generated.

Erasmus Darwin's notion of 'virtue', which consists in sympathy, veracity, prudence, fortitude and temperance, is, as will be seen, exemplified in the stories constructed to support *Practical Education* (Cutt, 1979: 4). It is not as singularly based on Lockean notions as Kowaleski-Wallace suggests.[9] The morality that is urged by the Edgeworths' educational project is not evangelical Christian, in the style of a Mrs Trimmer, but a practical morality based on secular principles such as utility. An essential feature of the system of education set out in *Practical Education* is that it was just that, an educational system worked out in terms of curriculum, teaching methods and approaches. Critics have pointed out that in terms of resources, it was far from practical and that it could not, and did not, provide a model for working-class education in the course of the nineteenth century (Butler, 1972: 172; Paterson, 1914: 111). Such criticism fails to understand that the term 'practical' implies a system in which philosophical ideas are embodied within a curriculum based upon mundane experience and carefully selected toys and reading materials, rather than an abstract system of philosophical principles.[10] Children can learn from everyday experience provided adults give the required framework. These insights are transported straight into the economic stories in which children learn under their own steam, as in 'The Cherry Orchard' or within the structure of experience created by the adult in co-operation with the child, as in 'The Purple Jar'.

Edgeworth's children's stories are interesting in themselves. They were highly regarded throughout the nineteenth century. Harriet Martineau, for example, in researching *The Playfellow* during September 1840, asks Fanny Wedgwood's daughter Julia to comment on *The Parent's Assistant* in terms of how she likes the 'book itself' and 'the separate stories in it' (Arbuckle, 1983: 36). The stories became a standard for judging the contributions made by others to children's writing, as well as to economics education.

Several stories carry specific economic content. Special attention will be given to three stories which illustrate the range of relevant economic themes and philosophical influences: 'The Cherry Orchard' (a tale illustrating the benefits of the division of labour); 'The Purple Jar' (a tale about rational consumer behaviour) and 'Lazy Lawrence' (a tale of work and thrift). These were developed and published under the rather dull title *The Parent's Assistant* (Edgeworth would have preferred 'Friend') as well as in 'Rosamond' and *Early Lessons*.[11] Edgeworth's titles remind us that the key actors in the rapidly growing market for children's books were the parents rather than the children themselves. The lessons illustrate amongst other things appropriate educational behaviour for parents pursuing the Edgeworths' method of instruction. Her market advantage was that she had tested out her fiction on a ready-made group of children, for she had been gathering anecdotes and evidence for seven years prior to the publication of *Practical Education*. In addition she could also justify her approach through the provision of an educational theory which gave parents an important role. She could thus appeal to the purchaser as well as the final consumer![12] However, although the stories are simply and clearly written, they have more than one dimension and alternative interpretations are possible. Each story is presented and analysed in turn.

'The Cherry Orchard'

The story is focused upon the 'remarkably good-tempered' Marianne and her cousin, the 'ill-tempered' Owen. Marianne liked the short-cut to school which went by the lane, Owen preferred the high-road 'because he liked to see the carts and carriages, and horsemen' (Edgeworth, 1990: 54). At the start of the story Owen insists on all the children going to school by the main road. Marianne and the others object since they had followed Owen's wishes over the previous three days. After a dispute, they decide to go along with Owen but only 'to please Marianne' who was intent upon preventing a quarrel. Owen continues to be fractious: kicking up dust and trying to bend Marianne to his will. In the end she and the others leave Owen at a turnstile which they bar against his entry. Owen is furious but is unable to overcome the combined strength of the forces against him and he turns for home in a huff. Marianne, ever the peace-maker, gives Owen one more chance and convinces him to rejoin the children in a better mood by promising something that Owen 'likes very much', ripe cherries. He rejoins the children. He is asked to keep his word about not kicking up any dust. He is allowed through because 'he was a boy of truth; and he always kept his promises' (p. 71).

The cherries are being sold by an old woman and there is just enough for each. All the children, save Owen, are willing to give the ripest bunch to Marianne. Owen complains about his cherries and, when faced with the anger of the others, grabs the stick upon which the cherries are tied, throws it to the ground and crushes them under foot. As a result he is banished from the company of the children. They go their separate ways to school where Owen performs well. As a reward he is allowed to read to the class the advertisement for the opening of the cherry orchard. The entry fee is sixpence. The excited children ask how money may be earned for all their money went on the cherries that Owen crushed. The suggested activity is 'plaiting straw for hats'. In undertaking the activity, none of the children would work with Owen. Owen is certain of his skills; 'I shall have done my work long before any of you finished yours; for I can plait quicker and better than any of you' (p. 86).

Although Owen is capable of hard work, he soon discovers that he is wrong. The main group of children have all been helping one another. Owen requests a reason for their success but no answer comes. He simply watches and discovers that 'one picked the outside off the straws; another cut them to their proper length; another sorted them, and laid them in bundles; another flattened them' (p. 89). Owen sees that 'Each did what he could do best, and quickest' (p. 90). Owen's own experience was of doing each stage by himself so that 'When he had done sewing, he found out that his hand was out for plaiting' (p. 93). Owen's plight is now clear: if he is to go into the orchard then he must rejoin the group. He apologises and declares that he will 'never be cross any more' (p. 94). The children debate the change in mood. He is still left out and it is only near the hour of going to the cherry orchard that they think about relenting. Proof of changed behaviour is wanted and Cymon tests Owen by pulling apart some plaiting. Owen does not object. His lesson has been truly learned. All help, and Owen can then go to the cherry orchard where he reflects upon his actions.

Comment

The series of events that take place around the plaiting of the straw is intended as a concrete example, well within the experience of many children, of the division of labour. The stages in development of the activities parallel Adam Smith's description of the pin factory in the *Wealth of Nations*. There can be little doubt that a main purpose of the story is to illustrate the principle. Edgeworth had read Smith's *Theory of Moral Sentiments* and works on political economy (Butler, 1972: 150, 153). Owen is not given an explanation of the group's motivation nor of the principles upon which the work was organised. He has to work these out from his observation and experience. No mention is made of the 'principle of the division of labour' as it would be mentioned (later) in a *Principles* text or in the Martineau tales. Furthermore, when Owen concludes the story with a summarisation of his learning, the moral is not economic but social: 'I hope I shall never be cross to any of you again, whenever I feel inclined to be cross, I will think of your good-nature to me, and of **The Cherry-Orchard**'. The title is in bold and the implication is that children, when thinking about being cross, will also recall the cherry orchard as a model of social harmony, a Garden of Eden. The utopian enclosure carries a very strong hint of Rousseau's advice to mothers: 'Form an enclosure around your child's soul at an early date. Someone else can draw its circumference, but you alone must build the fence' (Rousseau, 1816: 38). The overtly stated moral is about the value of co-operative behaviour in terms of both work and leisure. The specific economic lesson, that of the division of labour, is taught within a wider context and, indeed, takes up less than half the story. Jane Marcet, in talking about the story, takes it to be primarily an economics lesson, illustrating an economic concept, as did the reviews in the *Edinburgh Review*, where Edgeworth was a long-standing favourite, and the *Quarterly Review*, in 1833.[13]

But the wider economic and social lesson is that too much individualism is socially disruptive and, in the end, ineffective. Owen, the lad who prefers the dust and bustle of the high-road to the green of the lane, is, according to Myers, a symbol of the individualistic and (potentially) disruptive male (Myers, 1990: iii–xiii). Marianne is the peace-maker, in charge of her feelings, capable of monitoring her own behaviour and influential in the group by social negotiation, and example, rather than by coercion. The *Edinburgh Review* suggests that many of Edgeworth's plots have a character like that of Marianne:

> there is not a tale, we believe, in which there is not some wife or daughter who is generous and gentle, and prudent and cheerful: and almost all the men who behave properly owe most of their good actions to the influence and suggestions of their lovely moni-tresses. If the pride of our sex would permit us, we might perhaps confess, after all, that this representation is not very far from the truth.
>
> (*Edinburgh Review*, 1804: 337)

And it is this kind of complicity that some commentators on her work find objectionable.

For Marianne, feelings and negotiation are the significant factors in the dynamics of the group and hence of society. The journey along the road and down the lane is a metaphor for moving towards a better future, though if read in the light of Rousseau, the contrast between the road and the lane could be seen as standing for the corrupting nature of civil society and the harmony of nature. Marianne's companion, the boy Cymon, is more sceptical than Marianne whose feelings can, and do, triumph over experience. Cymon represents a balancing force of sceptical reason. The main actors are, however, more than just symbols. They are, despite the slight over-drawing of their attributes, believable as children. Owen kicking the dust, Marianne organising the distribution of the cherries and Cymon unpicking Owen's work as a test of his changed mood, are the product of acute observation of behaviour. Owen is not all bad: he is 'truthful', clever and capable of hard and effective work. Marianne is, perhaps, just a little bit too good and needs to be balanced by the sceptical Cymon with whom she shares a leadership role.

Although the canonical texts in economics were to stress individualism, Edgeworth stresses the *social* nature of production. Production is embedded in a co-operative society in which negotiation rather than coercion, say, through the price mechanism, is the desired or ideal state of society. The children co-operate by choice. Owen is excluded by his own unco-operative actions. It is interesting that Jane Marcet, through Caroline, the young student in *Conversations on Political Economy*, often objects to economic ideas by reflecting upon social implications. Harriet Martineau is taken to task, later, for stressing, uncritically, the idea of economics as automatically leading to social harmony. Is there a gender difference, resulting from social experience, in the way in which all three women thought about social and economic life? Myers, developing the theme of rural idyll, argues that Edgeworth is offering up the qualities that can lead a community to a better future in which renewal blends 'reason with feeling, an ethic of care and community taking precedence over individual self-assertion' (Myers, 1990: vii). According to Myers, the story is primarily one of male and female values and leadership. This may well be the most satisfactory explanation, though it ignores the rational, sceptical and balancing role of Cymon and the (disapproving) laughter of 'the turnpike-man'. According to Lamb, Adam Smith used two methods of analysing society, 'the individualist and the social', and any full interpretation of the *Wealth of Nations* must be incomplete if this is not recognised (Lamb, 1974: 672). In a sense, Edgeworth embodies in the tale two aspects of Smith's ideas concerning the nature of economics and society, Owen is shaped by his 'passions' and self-interest but is also modified by social conditions and the 'sympathy' demonstrated by Marianne. If such readings are justifiable, Edgeworth's tale is philosophically rich.

The laughing turnpike-man and the other adults in the story do not take any part in shaping and resolving the dramatic tensions and the learning outcomes. The children in the story learn by and through their own contrasting experiences. From the point of view of the development of economics education, the socialisation of political economy, in the context of a morality of social improvement, is of considerable significance.

'The Purple Jar'

Rosamond, aged 'about seven', and in London shopping with her mother, expresses delight in every 'pretty thing' she sees in the shop windows.

She wants all, but her mother responds in terms of the usefulness of the items: 'but what use would they be of to me?' (Edgeworth, 1818: 3). Her excitement reaches a high point on seeing beautiful coloured jars in a chemist's window. Her desire for a purchase brings forth the adult response: 'What use would they be of to me, Rosamond?' (p. 4). Rosamond invents a use – a flower-pot. Despite her mother's caution, she insists that it could be used as a flower-pot. The mother then says: 'Perhaps if you were to see it nearer, if you were to examine it, you might be disappointed' (p. 4).

Rosamond continues to be highly attracted by the purple jar and asks if her mother has money. On discovering that there is money, Rosamond launches into a list of possible purchases, only to be distracted by a stone in her shoe. The mother establishes that there is a hole in the shoe. Rosamond is then anxious for a new pair of shoes and readily uses her mother's utilitarian argument in support: 'You know shoes would be really of use to me' (p. 6). The shoemaker's shop is dull, unattractive and smelly, quite unlike the shops that attracted Rosamond's attention earlier. Rosamond sees a pair that she is certain will do nicely. Her mother's response is 'Perhaps they might, but you can not be sure, till you have tried them on, any more than you can be quite sure, that you should like the purple vase *exceedingly*, till you have examined it, more attentively' (p. 7). Rosamond is then offered a choice: the shoes or 'that jar'. The mother refuses to give advice other than that Rosamond should 'choose what will make you the happiest'. Rosamond chooses the flower-pot. The 'flower-pot', still unexamined, is duly purchased and brought home by a servant. Rosamond's excitement soon turns to horror on discovering that the awful liquid inside the jar is responsible for the colour. Her mother holds her to her bargain, no new shoes till the month is over. Her problems do not stop there: she is unable to go to a 'glass-house' with her father and brother because she is 'walking slip-shod' (p. 16). The story ends with a summarisation by Rosamond of the utility moral.

Comment

This is a story about consumer awareness and choice. In essence it consists largely of dialogue between the bubbly child, Rosamond, and an adult schooled in the principles of Edgeworthian educational practice. The structural moves in the story are set out with an almost economic efficiency. The gaudy world of consumerism is set before the child who sees the wonder of it all: Rosamond is all 'wants'. The mother is concerned with use-value, with placing the range of wants within a context of utility. If the child is all 'wants', the mother is all 'needs'. The utilitarian approach is one Edgeworth herself considered with respect to the purchase of a tortoise shell: the shoe-maker wanted a guinea, Maria

Edgeworth considered that 'at the utmost it would not give Sophy above half a crown's worth of pleasure'. She declined to buy and left 'the shoemaker in quiet possession of his African tortoise' (Hare, 1894: 25). The core of utilitarianism (often misleadingly characterised by 'the greatest good for the greatest number') is to be found in the notion that actions are to be judged by consequences. The best actions make people better off than the available alternatives. Three elements are at the core of utilitarian thinking: actions are to be judged teleologically (i.e. by outcomes); the process of making judgements about society as a whole is based upon aggregation; and the outcomes are sensual (based upon the enhancement of pleasure and/or the avoidance of pain) (Lincoln, 1990: 3). In Edgeworth's story the concern is with the individual and so only the teleological and sensuous aspects are present.

The simple utilitarian argument is wasted on the child who, because of her highly developed imagination, readily invents a use for the purple jar. Rosamond remains committed to this use, even to the extent of collecting flowers to put in the vase while waiting for the servant to bring it home. Choice exists in the present between two objects but the consequences of choice are felt over time.

Although only 7 years old, Rosamond understands that money is involved in purchase. She shows, however, that her actions are not based upon any sense of the need to allocate scarce money over a number of different possible purchases, when, on discovering that there is money, she reels off her shopping list. Rosamond does reveal that she understands an aspect of the argument based upon utility when she recognises that she needs shoes and suggests that shoes ought to be purchased. However she is very miserable in the shoe shop: she dislikes the smell and finds it dull and unattractive so her mother offers her a choice, either the shoes or the purple jar. This is a surprising but essential move in the story. The child has shown an inability to think in terms of constraints that operate through budgets.

The experiment in economics education requires the experience of choice within the framework of budget limitations. Rosamond must decide and her mother repeats the point about examination but, and this is undoubtedly an unfortunate part of the story, she advises Rosamond to consider in terms of 'happiness' (p. 10) (not 'usefulness' which has been the tenor of the tale thus far). The move is unfortunate since Rosamond cannot be expected to understand the dependence of 'happiness' upon 'utility' or the need to calculate happiness as the second-order effect of utility. She innocently chooses 'happiness'. The 'authentic' utility of the shoes is rejected in favour of the 'false' utility of the imagination. In accordance with Edgeworthian ideas, disappointment with the jar is not enough, the lack of the useful service of the shoes must also be experienced.

This aspect of the story brings Edgeworth unexpectedly close to the Gradgrinds and delivered there by the 'deification of the great goddess Utility' (Lawless, 1904: 39).[14] The contrasts are made between 'useful knowledge' and 'fantastic visions' – recurrent themes in Edgeworth's stories: 'But why should the mind be filled with fantastic visions, instead of useful knowledge?' (Edgeworth, 1818: xii). As with Locke, this tale reveals Edgeworth's notion that the imagination in children does not need any stimulation other than can be derived from everyday life (Ezell, 1983–1984: 139–155). Locke gave his approval to *Aesop's Fables*, but the Edgeworths did away with fairies and talking beasts in favour of assisting the development of 'the inventive power' by a consideration of daily occurrences. Rosamond's inventive power, here at least, leads her astray.

It is easy to be annoyed with the mother in the story who, despite talk about careful investigation before purchase does not encourage Rosamond to make an actual investigation before the purchase was made. This is how many readers no doubt feel, but to feel like this is to misunderstand the moral purpose of the tale. The adult is acting appropriately in the context of the approach of *Practical Education* and the teleological principles of utilitarianism. The moral tale as a format, and the educational principles that Edgeworth accepts, both suggest that the child can, and will, learn from experience. It is from the child's own progressive reinterpretation of this experience that true learning springs. Rosamond is given an experimental framework: the intended readers (both parent and child) participate in the process vicariously but both will also have experience to draw upon in discussing and evaluating the story. The example of the purple jar is one that parents and children of the time could readily identify with. Despite the dialogue format, the parent's intervention in the story is only to sustain the economic experiment: an experiment, which if conducted in real life, would be both heartless and costly. If Maria Edgeworth, often identified as Rosamond, actually experienced treatment such as that described in 'The Purple Jar', then it really is a vindictive tale. However, experiential learning, even today, when it is a well-understood teaching method, can be painful. In this sense, acquiring knowledge has a value divorced from simple pleasure. Such a view would make Edgeworth an 'ideal utilitarian' rather than a 'hedonistic utilitarian' (Smart and Williams, 1974: 13).

The problem of educating children in appropriate consumer behaviour exercised Edgeworth again in 'The Bracelet of Memory', a story which, despite Edgeworth's condemnation of fairy tales, verges onto the edge of magic when a traveller brings forth from his case fantastic, life-like automatons taken at first by Rosamond, and the reader, to be authentic animals. The traveller or, rather, his bag of tricks, is very attractively presented, the writing glows. The quality of the description of the mouse, caterpillar and bird suggests that Edgeworth could have become a fine writer of fairy tales had her educational method, and Lovell Edgeworth's philosophical predispositions, allowed it.[15] Edgeworth here strayed into the margins of Johnson's fairyland, against which she in fact fervently objected. Once again she is deliberately filling the reader's mind with 'fantastic visions' only to contrast these with 'useful knowledge'. Too much must not be made of her playing with 'magic', for Edgeworth is a writer who consistently demonstrates her keen understanding of many different ideas and the imaginative and analytical power that enables her to communicate them without damaging their intellectual integrity is worthy of appreciation.

Rosamond is set with a choice, the superficial glamour of 'the bracelet of memory', which the traveller pushes, or the young horse that her father wishes to purchase for her. The link with 'The Purple Jar' is made explicitly in the text as well as through Rosamond's careful consideration and re-examination of the bracelet. In recognition of the progressive nature of economic understanding Rosamond is given, in a sense, two lessons.[16] In this one she chooses the horse, clearly intended, on utilitarian grounds, as the 'right' choice. The parents do not direct, but merely hope!

'Lazy Lawrence'

Jem Preston's mother is hard-working, honest but poor and, as a result of her illness, is unable to pay her rent.[17] To raise money the horse, Lightfoot, is to be sold. Jem is very fond of the horse and decides to raise the money through work. He undertakes various kinds of tasks willingly and, gradually, raises a small sum of money. As a result of one activity he is given, in addition to fair payment, a silver penny. The penny is destined to play a significant part in the outcome of the story. His acquaintance, Lazy Lawrence, dull, indolent and spoilt, has many childish wants for sweets and fine things. He is unwilling to work for money and worms it out of his father (usually when his father has been drinking). Lazy Lawrence is negligent and his father punishes him by refusing to give him any more money. He finds out about Jem's little store of wealth which is being saved, a bit at a time, to save Lightfoot from the market. In trying to raise money to spend on some fine nuts to eat, Lawrence discovers 'pitch-farthing', a simple form of gambling.

Once hooked on easy ways of raising money, Lawrence falls into bad company and is sucked into rough language and criminality. He conspires, somewhat reluctantly, with the stable boy, to steal Jem's hoard. Jem is rescued by a lady who had employed him in the garden but only after she has proof that the money was indeed stolen and not squandered by Jem. The money is recovered as a result of a milk-woman, wife of he who gave the silver penny to Jem with the advice that it was lucky and

Maria Edgeworth

ought never to be sold, having found it on the track. The culprits are discovered. The father realises that his indulgence and lack of direct interest have led Lawrence into trouble and resolves to change. Lazy Lawrence, after a short stay in Bridewell, is restored to physical and moral health: he becomes willing and industrious.

Comment

In economic terms, 'Lazy Lawrence' is about the work ethic and entrepreneurship. The writing is clear and simple, but it ought not to be dismissed as unsophisticated, for it incorporates ideas on the nature of economic motivation. What is displayed is the economic and moral potential of the poor, in line with philosophical ideas of the nature of economic motivation pursued by Adam Smith and, more consistently, by David Hume. Jem, in living-out creative economic activity, illustrates the social universality of reasoned economic action. The story is aimed at older children and it could, of course, have been read and enjoyed by an adult reader. The story is primarily about economic values and beliefs rather than about concepts such as use-value or the division of labour, though such ideas are also present.

'Lazy Lawrence' is also about the responsibility of adults towards young people: Jem's mother and Lawrence's father each contribute significantly to the quality of the environment surrounding the children. Edgeworth was aware that in educating the children, there was an opportunity for educating the parents. The values are carried both in the characters themselves and in their deeds. Jem is frequently described as being 'good' and 'industrious' or as a 'fine industrious little fellow', not easily discouraged (Edgeworth, 1838: 2, 5). Persistence at tasks, particularly economic tasks, is the hallmark of his nature: 'a boy not easily discouraged'. In short, Jem is a (Humean) problem-solving individual with a natural desire to achieve. Although he does meet obstacles such as the old lady who, not wishing competition, does not tell him where to find the stones that she sells, he tends to generate 'so much good will' (p. 6) that others are predisposed to help him in his projects. Jem has a goal and works steadily towards it. He is capable of work but more than this, he is capable of entrepreneurial activity. When he sees a market opportunity such as selling fossils, being useful or making mats, he takes it. His goal adds structure and meaning to his life, he is the entrepreneur as hero, made noble by the virtue of his goal and the social usefulness of his labour. When he has made only 'four and seven-pence' of the two guineas that he must raise, for, in accordance with Humean ideas, Jem is allowed to contemplate 'the daily increase of his fortune' (Hundert, 1974, quoting Hume: 142) Lawrence asks him what he intends to do with the money. Edgeworth provides him with the following response: ' "That's

33

a secret," said Jem, looking great' (p. 11). This is the greatness of nobility rather than of smugness.

His persistence is demonstrated by the mat-making episode. His mistress discovers a need for a mat and Jem decides, privately, to make one.[18] Edgeworth's picture of the entrepreneurial imagination is engaging:

> And all the way home, as he trudged along whistling, he was thinking over a scheme for making mats, which, however bold it may appear, he did not despair of executing, with patience and industry. Many were the difficulties which his 'prophetic eye' foresaw, but he felt within himself that spirit, which spurs men on to great enterprises, and makes them 'trample on impossibilities'.
>
> (Edgeworth, 1838: 15)

In 'thinking out' a scheme, the character gives example to Hume's contention that in working towards overcoming financial difficulties and towards future reward: 'The mind acquires a new vigour; enlarges its powers; and by an assiduity in honest industry, both satisfies its natural appetites, and prevents the growth of unnatural ones, which commonly spring up, when nourished by ease and idleness' (Hundert, 1974, quoting Hume: 141). Edgeworth, like Hume, accepts that the psychological characteristics of the poor are, in economic terms, no different from that of other classes in society.

He goes to the common land, collects the raw material and struggles for several hours a day over six days: 'But still he persevered. Nothing *truly great* can be accomplished without toil and time.' Labour could, in the rural society that Edgeworth depicts, still be turned into capital. The consequences in the tale are two-fold. Jem is allowed the chance to develop his skills; the mistress recognises that others could be persuaded to buy a mat and provides the opportunity for Jem to exploit the situation:

> Spend your time no more in weeding my garden, you can employ yourself much better; you shall have the reward of your ingenuity as well as your industry. Make as many mats as you can, and I will take care and dispose of them for you.
>
> (Edgeworth, 1838: 16)

The mistress, in sympathetically supporting Jem embodies elements of Smith's *Moral Sentiments*. The working economic concept here is one of absolute advantage rather than of comparative advantage. Jem then experiences further benefits which flow from what we would call 'learning-by-doing': he quickens the pace of production. As in 'The Purple Jar', the opportunity for further learning is created by the interaction of the adult and the child, but it is Jem that learns from his own experience. Earlier in the story the mistress, in accordance with Edgeworth's notions in *Practical Education* of life as a lesson, points out to Jem that her initial generosity with respect to the prices she is willing to pay for the stones was both economic reward and incentive but that it could not be repeated in such generous terms: '*That*, instead of encouraging you to be industrious, would teach you to be idle.' Repetition of a tried and tested formula is not allowed to Jem who must seek out new opportunities in accordance with the entrepreneurial theme.

Lawrence's character is quickly sketched and his ultimate fate hinted at early: he 'saunters', 'lounges' and 'yawns' and has already been advised that 'idleness was the root of all evil' (p. 5). He has no vision of a better future and wheedles and fawns on his drunken father (not an Edgeworthian parent) for money, for nuts and gingerbread. Unlike Jem, he lives listlessly, neither quite awake nor quite asleep, in the present. He is lazy as a result of parental neglect and indulgence. The ideas of Hume are, again, not far from the surface of the text, Edgeworth's picture of Lawrence embodies Hume on the economic consequences of 'indolence': 'Indolence or repose, indeed seems not of itself to contribute much to our enjoyment; but, like sleep, is requisite as an indulgence, to the weakness of human nature, which cannot support an uninterrupted course of business or pleasure' (Hundert, 1974, quoting Hume: 141). The outcome of Lawrence's lack of 'serious occupation' is also Humean, for the lad 'runs restless from one amusement to another' towards 'ruin'.

Learning can be both positive and negative and Lawrence 'though a *lazy*, had not yet learned to be a *wicked* boy'. According to the theory, the young readers had to be 'shocked with the representation of vice'. After making contact with the stable lad, through gaming, he goes to the yard often, where he sits, 'the spectator of wickedness'. In contrast to Jem's ennobling future orientation, Lawrence is bent upon short-term acts of consumption, too lazy even to open nuts by himself. In response to Jem's 'secret' plans, Lawrence outlines his own:

> I can guess, I know what I'd do with it if it was mine. First I'd buy pocketsful of gingerbread; then I'd buy ever so many apples and nuts; don't you love nuts? I'd buy nuts enough to last me from this time to Christmas, and I'd make little Newton crack 'em open for me; for that's the worst of nuts, there's the trouble of cracking them.
>
> (Edgeworth, 1838: 11)

His education in wickedness results in theft though his punishment is lighter than that of the stable lad because of his remorse and of the element of coercion that led him into crime. Lawrence is both redeemable and redeemed thanks to Jem.

Edgeworth knits the narrative together using a number of commonplace, almost proverbial, expressions to further the moral and point towards the intended outcome: 'one good turn deserves another' (p. 5);

'idleness was the root of all evil' (p. 5) (which can perhaps be seen as a neat amendment of the biblical phrase 'Love of money is the root of all evil', since it is love of other people's money which brings Lawrence down); 'honesty is the best policy'; 'better . . . Bridewell now, than . . the gallows by and by'. But the economic interest of the tale is to be found in the structure and content of the work-related episodes. The work ethic is not a sole point: after all, the stable lads are in work (though no doubt with long spells of idleness). It is Jem's vision of the future and willingness to respond to, and to create, market opportunities that form a significant part of the narrative. The unity of nature and nurture and the articulation of early nineteenth-century economic values are complete in Jem, as Edgeworth was well aware for she intended that the tale 'separate as much as possible, the spirit of industry and avarice' (Edgeworth, 1838: Preface). Lawrence has no vision of the future, has a drunkard for a father and no sense of prudence. He is adrift in the present, with nothing to structure his life. What could have been a dull tale of work becomes an ennobling capitalistic adventure, reflecting middle-class economic values and all of the elements of Erasmus Darwin's notions of 'virtue' and Hume's notion of the fundamental nature of the drive towards creativity through work. The 'lucky penny' carries a hint of fairy, but the adventure of Jem's economic project is grounded in, albeit idealised, social experience. The educational interest in the narrative comes from the enlightened actions of adults, who are responsible for shaping an environment within which young people can experience growth.

MARIA EDGEWORTH AND ECONOMICS EDUCATION

Edgeworth's efforts in economics education are packed full of morality but they are not dull and neither are the children, even if they wear their virtues and vices rather too openly. Nor are they devoid of economic meaning: her philosophical influences for economics are undoubtedly Smith, Hume and Bentham, and, for education, Locke and Rousseau. Edgeworth, (nor Marcet nor Martineau, all described by Thomson as 'Adam Smith's Daughters'), did not derive her economic ideas from a single source. Edgeworth is interested in the development and communication of economic ideas. Reasoned economic behaviour is available to children and to the lower orders, an idea that is later taken up and developed by Martineau. That Edgeworth could simplify complex economic ideas without destroying their integrity as ideas, whilst making them accessible to children, is a major intellectual achievement. The range of economic and other notions illustrated in the four stories analysed is wide. The fact that she prefers realism to fairy-land could be seen as an imaginative failure but in the context of literary economics it is an enormous source of strength. To render complex ideas in simple form requires both analytical clarity, and a well-developed imagination.

Her fictional children, as is often stated, are animated, and interesting as children. The clear delineation of character and behaviour found in the stories is also found in Edgeworth's letters and her capacity for short, telling descriptions (she was very conscious of appearances) stayed with her throughout her life. It is also clear that for Edgeworth herself, life was an education. This comes across in her private letters, where she is voicing her own, rather than her father's, opinions. Education was not a peripheral activity, a concern of childhood, but the essence. This precise observation of people and places, but particularly of people, together with the care in which the economic incidents are woven into the narrative, gives a gentler edge to the moral than might otherwise have been the case. The child-focused nature and setting within a 'safe' adult world of concerned parents gives then, on the whole, a softness lacking (the chillness of 'The Purple Jar' not withstanding) in some of Martineau's writings. As with Martineau's writings, both positive and negative aspects of nineteenth-century economic values are carried in the stories. For Edgeworth, humankind remain social beings and economic activity is constructed as an integral part of a wider social and philosophical view of the world.

Maria Edgeworth, in dealing with small children and their learning, cannot assume much experience: it needs to be created with the narrative. The situations are usually ones that children can identify with, such as in 'The Purple Jar'. A constant assumption is that children can learn from experience. When a moral is made, the child makes it. The developing understanding of the child, as well as the child-centred articulation of the learning, limits the level of abstraction achieved in the narrative. The stories that are concerned with economics education illustrate, however, in their structure and content, that Edgeworth's economic awareness was highly developed in terms of the growing discipline of political economy, insights derived from estate management (to which her father contributed by sharing his business approach with members of the family circle) and knowledge of the world. The economic world that she creates is, largely, idyllic and benign, though not without its hard knocks. The adults assist in the construction of experience and, although a right answer is intended, children are credited with an ability to work out implications and so learn. Educational philosophy takes priority over the economics, but the economic motivation is founded upon a broad understanding that the creative urge to economic life can be found in children of all social classes. For the stories to be successful they must first succeed as stories. If practical education is to win converts, it requires child readers and the willing reconstruction of parents. What is uppermost then is Edgeworth's skill as a writer: the stories prospered long after the didactic introductions, written under Lovell Edgeworth's influence and gradually removed in editions published later in the century, had been abandoned. Parents need to see believable children, for they, rather than the introductions, had the persuasive power crucial to the success of the educational project. Comments on the natural and unforced style of her economic tales are made, to the detriment of those of Harriet Martineau, in 1833. By that date, some of the economics stories had been in circulation for more than three decades and yet they still commanded considerable respect.[19]

Jane Marcet, in contrast, in developing a strategy for the economics education of the young adult, can assume an experience of getting and spending as well as a knowledge of writing in subjects other than economics. Marcet encourages the young person to reflect on her existing knowledge, derived from social experience, as a way of approaching new ideas to be learned though, in her work too, a right answer is intended.[20] Edgeworth's reputation, and her command of the infant market, made her the natural starting point for Jane Marcet who takes up economics education where Edgeworth left off. By the time that Marcet comes to write *Conversations on Political Economy* (1816) the subject was well established in intellectual London society but not as a subject in the developing educational curriculum. In establishing political economy as part of the curriculum, she acknowledges Edgeworth's educational standing. Marcet also adopts in Mrs B., the diligent governess in *Conversations*, a stance that is similar to that of the rational parent found in the economic tales and justified in *Practical Education*. If a model is to be found for Mrs B., then Marcet herself, and the Edgeworthian parent, are the two most likely sources. Although Marcet's work on political economy is a direct result of her own attempts to learn the subject through conversation, there is little doubt that she understood the methods set out by the Edgeworths.[21]

Edgeworth's influence on Harriet Martineau is, at first sight, indirect. Martineau claims that she was inspired to write her economic tales for adults through reading Jane Marcet. When working on Martineau's economics writing, I took this to be a general inspiration. However, Martineau developed a specific justification for her approach. She decided to supply both story and overtly stated economic principle or moral. This can be read as a response to Marcet's comment about 'The Cherry Orchard' in *Conversations on Political Economy*. Marcet supports the lack of an overtly stated economic principle, or moral, in Edgeworth's story, on the grounds that such ideas 'abstractedly laid down' are little understood by children. The implication is that it would be appropriate to formulate the economic principle in abstract terms when educating adults. Martineau's claim to be the first to use the method of writing economic lessons as stories, is strictly correct, for her published work contains a coda in which the

Maria Edgeworth

relevant economics is set out. However, her stories look less original when viewed through 'Lazy Lawrence', Edgeworth's economic story which most approaches writing for adults. In educational terms, they are certainly less subtle. Edgeworth's moral does often emerge naturally from the story whereas Martineau's is often imposed upon it.[22] This is certainly the conclusion of the *Quarterly Review* of 1833 which insists upon preferring 'Miss Edgeworth', basing the justification of the preference on the relationship between the narrative and the political economy:

> But the difference between the two writers is, that the moral of Miss Edgeworth's tales is naturally suggested to the reader by the course of events of which he pursues the narrative; that of Miss Martineau is embodied in elaborate dialogues or most unnatural incidents, with which her stories are interlarded and interrupted, to the utter destruction of the interest of all but detached bits of them.[23]

However, Martineau's approach is an extension into the adult field of that adopted by Edgeworth for the child. Her work, like that of Edgeworth, is set in the context of social reform, and her concerns are with the practical and moral improvement of society, through the publication of economics stories which provided 'pictures of what those principles are actually doing in communities' (Martineau, 1834: Preface). Her debt to Edgeworth tends to be understated, something which Martineau herself may have contrived in order to differentiate her approach. In this respect, Martineau is influenced by Marcet, who taught technical economics, and by Edgeworth, who wrote stories. The economics takes priority over the plot because the object is to teach formal economics through story. The *Edinburgh Review* understood this dual nature of Martineau's texts and judged them accordingly.

Such a reading establishes a direct line from Edgeworth through Marcet to Martineau in terms of the development of the methodology of economics education, and justifies the earlier reference to an educational movement. It also suggests that Edgeworth's writing made it easier for first Marcet and then Martineau to establish their niche in the new subject. Edgeworth, Marcet and Martineau were women entering a field which, though 'new', was heavily male-oriented. The concept of women as teachers and writers in the educational field had been established in continental and English society as a result of the success of the female followers of Rousseau, and of efforts women had made in support of their own education. Edgeworth, by entering the world of economics through the nursery, made it easier for Marcet to enter through the classroom and Martineau to enter through non-formal education. The political economists, after Adam Smith, were more concerned with talking to each other than they were with talking to a wider public. The women talked to the public so powerfully that Marshall objected to their

39

influence, felt even towards the end of the nineteenth century, and tried to convince his followers to write clearly in order to shut out popularisers. Their longer-term success as educators ('popularisation' under-estimates the extent to which their work was informed by educational strategies) may have suggested to him the need for economists to talk in language 'understanded of the people' (Marshall, 1881: 457).

The economics education corpus that their works collectively represent, contains many insights into how students can be helped engage in learning economics. Edgeworth was, first and foremost, a writer and educationalist: her economic tales are, though delightful, few. Her influence was, nevertheless, extensive. Edgeworth's work, to a greater extent than that of either Marcet or Martineau, needs to be placed against the development of literature for children as such literature developed throughout the eighteenth century. Edgeworth is the most involved in the theoretical and practical consideration of education. Marcet is more involved in the direct teaching of technical political economy and Martineau in extending the understanding of what economic agency was accomplishing in society within the social context of reform.[24] None the less, Edgeworth's educational thinking, as exemplified by the economic stories, challenged both Marcet and Martineau to develop their own educational strategies with respect to economics teaching. In this sense too, Edgeworth's work made Marcet's and Martineau's possible.

NOTES

1 Millhauser was no doubt unaware that he was echoing the sentiments of the *Quarterly Review* of 1833 which argued that Edgeworth's works were both prior and superior to Martineau's because 'Political economy is far more ingeniously as well as justly illustrated in the "Absentee" and "Castle Rackrent", than in "Ireland" ', (Millhauser, 1938: 152).
2 I am very grateful to Valerie Sanders for drawing my attention to Martineau's correspondence with Fanny Wedgwood.
3 For details of the correspondence, see *The Economic Journal*, 1907.
4 Ideas in *Practical Education* are generally held to have had a greater impact on the continent of Europe than in Britain. However they are likely to have been both directly and indirectly influential in the turn away from classical towards 'useful knowledge' with which the early to middle years of the nineteenth century were so much concerned.
5 Review of '*Popular Tales*, by Maria Edgeworth, author of Practical Education, Castle Rackrent, &c. &c. 8vo. 3 vol. Johnson, London, 1804', *Edinburgh Review*, July, 1804, pp. 329–337.
6 Rousseau's work *Emile* was not intended as a literal model for educational activity. His work is concerned with philosophical principles of education rather than a practical educational regime.
7 Science became a theme in the *Harry and Lucy* stories.
8 Another literary figure interested in economics, Thomas De Quincey, was as

a child asked to learn a dictionary by rote, during the course of his early education. De Quincey refused.

9 Rousseau owed a considerable amount to Locke, particularly with respect to the role of the senses in the shaping of the mind and in the process of learning. See Introduction in Boutet de Monvel (1972).

10 It seems to be the case, judging from the reception given to the Edgeworths during a visit to the Continent, that the work had a greater impact in Europe than it did in Britain.

11 Rosamond is thought to be based upon Maria Edgeworth as a child.

12 Though in the preface to *Harry and Lucy* there is a slight hesitation about the effort required to be made by parents.

13 See the chapter on Harriet Martineau for a discussion of the views.

14 Lawless, on the same page, claims that 'even the deification of the great goddess Utility, and the chanting in season and out of season of her arid and scraggy perfections' is forgivable if only Lovell Edgeworth had resisted involving himself with Edgeworth's writing. Utility reigns supreme in 'The Purple Jar'.

15 The high quality of the description of the mouse and of the other devices does carry a very strong hint that Maria Edgeworth could have been challenged to write glowing imaginative tales rather than morals grounded in mundane reality. Here, Lawless and others may well be right about the dreariness of Lovell Edgeworth's influence. However, caution must be exercised for it must not be forgotten that her stories for children were read with delight throughout the nineteenth century.

16 We would now accept that economics understanding of the very young only develops over time. Research in this field is now well developed. (See Berti and Bombi, 1988.) The observations made by the Edgeworths were not based upon psychological or developmental principles.

17 The name 'Jem' sounds like 'gem': is this accidental?

18 The image of the mistress, busy about the house and garden, hints at Maria Edgeworth's own domestic preoccupations.

19 We must not, however, overlook Byron's comment, inspired by didactic elements, that 'Miss Edgeworth's Cupid must be a Presbyterian'. Quoted in Armytage (1946: 251).

20 For a detailed analysis of the educational moves in Marcet's *Conversations on Political Economy*, see Chapter 3.

21 Jane Marcet was a friend of Maria Edgeworth and was aware of the Edgeworths' educational writing.

22 This judgement must be treated with care. 'The Purple Jar' does superimpose an 'economic' structure on the narrative but even here this is less than the way in which worked out economic doctrines impinge upon the story line in much of Martineau's writings.

23 See Chapter 3. The review on which Henderson's comments are based is found in *The Quarterly Review*, XLIX, April–July 1833, pp. 136–152.

24 Her concern for economic agency has recently attracted some attention. In much neo-classical economics, the economic agent is removed. As a result of criticism of 'scientism' in economics, there is currently a turn towards a less abstract, more sociological approach to economics agents.

Maria Edgeworth

REFERENCES

Arbuckle, Sanders E. (ed.) (1983) *Harriet Martineau's Letters to Fanny Wedgwood*, Stanford: Stanford University Press.

Armytage, W. H. G. (1946) 'Little Woman', *Queen's Quarterly*, 56, 248–257.

Berti, A. E. and Bombi, A. S. (1988) *The Child's Construction of Economics*, Cambridge: Maison des Sciences de l'Homme and Cambridge University Press.

Boutet de Manvel, A. (1972) *Emile*, London: Dent.

Butler, M. (1972), *Maria Edgeworth: A Literary Biography*, Oxford: Clarendon Press.

Clarke, D. (1965) *The Ingenious Mr. Edgeworth*, London: Osbourne.

Cutt, M. N. (1979) *Ministering Angels: A Study of Nineteenth-century Evangelical Writing*, Richmond: Five Owls Press.

Edgeworth, M. (1818) [1801] *Early Lessons in Two Volumes*, 6th ed. ('Rosamond', Vol. II), London: R. Hunter.

Edgeworth, M. (1838) [1796] 'Lazy Lawrence', in *Edgeworth's Parent's Assistant*, London: Simpkin, Marshall & Co.

Edgeworth, M. (1990) *The Little Dog Rusty; The Orange Man; and the Cherry Orchard Being the Tenth Part of Early Lessons* (ed. M. Myers), Los Angeles: University of California, The Augustinian Reprint Society, William Andrews Clark Memorial Library, no. 263–264.

Ezell, M. J. M. (1983–1984) 'John Locke's Images of Childhood: Early Eighteenth Century Responses to *Some Thoughts Concerning Education*', *Eighteenth Century Studies* 17, 139–155.

Hare, A. J. C. (ed.) (1894) *Life and Letters of Maria Edgeworth*, London: Edward Arnold.

Heilbroner, R. L. (1955), *The Great Economists*, London: Eyre and Spottiswoode.

Hundert, E. J. (1974) 'The Achievement Motive in Hume's Political Economy', *Journal of the History of Ideas*, 35, 139–143.

Kowaleski-Wallace, E. (1991) *Their Father's Daughters, Hannah More, Maria Edgeworth and Patriarchal Complicity*, New York and Oxford: Oxford University Press.

Lamb, R. B. (1974) 'Adam Smith's System: sympathy not self-interest', *History of Ideas*, 35.

Lawless, E. (1904) *Maria Edgeworth*, London: Macmillan.

Lincoln, A. (ed.) (1990) *The Utilitarian Response: The Contemporary Viability of Utilitarian Political Philosophy*, London: Sage.

Marshall, A. (1881) 'Review of *Mathematical Psychics*', The Academy 457, reprinted in Whitaker, J. K. (ed.) (1975) *The Early Writings of Alfred Marshall*, London and Basingstoke: Macmillan, 265–268.

Martineau, H. (1834) *Illustrations of Political Economy*, London: Charles Fox.

Millhauser, M. (1938) 'Maria Edgeworth as a Social Novelist', *Notes and Queries* clxxv, July–December, 205.

Myers, M. (1990) 'Introduction', in Edgeworth, M., *The Little Dog Rusty; The Orange Man; and The Cherry Orchard Being the Tenth Part of the Early Lessons*, Los Angeles: University of California.

Paterson, A. (1914) *The Edgeworths: A Study in Later Eighteenth-Century Education*, London: W. B. Clive.

Smart, J. J. C. and Williams, B. (1974) *Utilitarianism: Pro and Con*, Cambridge: Cambridge University Press.

Thomson, Lampen D. (1973) *Adam Smith's Daughters*, New York: Exposition Press.

3

Jane Marcet's
Conversations on Political Economy
A new interpretation

It is not easy to view economics education at the beginning of the nineteenth century without considerable interference from what it became during the whole course of that century. The influence of the object lesson, well illustrated by Charles Dickens in *Hard Times*, and the subsequent pressing of economic ideas into a rigid, mechanical catechism inevitably leads to a judgement of earlier ideas in terms of their later development. Frequent repetition of Alfred Marshall's opinion of the works of Jane Marcet and others – that they simplified economic principles 'without the conditions required to make them true' – clouds our understanding of the pioneering works of the early part of the century.[1] Unfavourable comment obscures the educational originality of the texts themselves and clouds our judgement concerning Marcet as political economist and educator. Literature designed to remind us of her achievements tends merely to rework what is known of Marcet's life. It also tends to treat her economics work descriptively, illustrating her method by lengthy and essentially unanalysed episodes from the dialogues.

The usefulness of subjecting nineteenth-century educational dialogues to analysis is illustrated by Myers, who has examined the dialogue in popular science.[2] Myers points out that the dialogue form, a long-established method for rehearsing a new and difficult argument, when applied to scientific discourse allows the modern reader the opportunity to explore the language of scientific discourse, the role of the reader and the relationship between scientific ideas and such popularisations that have fictional frames. Myers is not concerned with the revaluation of any particular text. Rather he traces the ways in which popularisation of science, over time, changed the activity away from that of genuine science towards a diluted version of science suitable for 'women and children'. However, as Myers himself states, Marcet, through her *Conversations on Chemistry* (1806) is credited with introducing Faraday to the study of chemistry. He also points out that Marcet's works were essentially textbooks. Furthermore, in the USA, according to Armstrong, she popularised the experimental method as the definitive method of scientific teaching; a consequence which places her work within the educational field.[3] There is therefore a duality in her works that is worthy of textual exploration. Her early work was aimed at young people but based on scientific activity. Her economics writing was also enormously influential in the USA as well as in the UK. Marcet's work in economics as much as in chemistry requires individual analysis, for the educational impact of her discipline-based works was, in my view, beneficial as well as profound. With respect to *Conversations on Political Economy*, 'serious education' rather than 'popularisation' may be a more appropriate lens through which to view her work.

After a brief introduction to Marcet and the corpus that she created, this chapter examines *Conversations on Political Economy* as the first textbook in economics education. It makes a textual analysis of key areas of the work in order to present an analysis of the educational strategy pursued by Marcet, as suggested by the way in which the text is constructed. It also has a secondary concern, which is with setting the text within the framework of the economic thinking of the day as well as with establishing its relationship to subsequent approaches to economics knowledge in the first half of the nineteenth century.

JANE MARCET'S LIFE AND WORKS

Jane Marcet, née Haldimand, was born into a wealthy, London-based, Swiss family in the year 1769. Her father, A. F. Haldimand, was first a merchant and, later, also a banker. Although little is known of her early education, there can be little doubt that the household was one in which education was valued. William, her younger brother, who later became a director of the Bank of England and a member of Parliament, was given 'a plain English education'.[4] As girls of the middling classes in society were educated at home with their brothers, it is very likely that Jane was subject to the same educational regime. The family was one which, given its business connections, was likely to have had extensive contact with English society as well as with the Swiss community living in London. Jane was fluent in French as well as English (evidence here comes directly from the first edition of *Political Economy* in which she inserts several lengthy passages in French). At the age of 30, which might have been considered late at that time, she married a distinguished physician, Dr Alexander Marcet, who was, like her father, also Swiss born. Speculation as to what she did until the age of thirty is unlikely to be particularly fruitful, though we can imagine an industrious Swiss household in which she would be expected to play a significant part, her mother having died when Jane was 15. For at least some of the time she must have continued to read widely and evidence from her later writing suggests a skilled and careful reader. She had a close and significant relationship with her father, and it is certain that he encouraged her to continue to develop both educationally and socially.[5]

Although his practice was successful, Alexander Marcet's great passion in life was chemistry, particularly the relationship between medicine and chemistry. Jane and he married in 1799 and, although Alexander continued to run a distinguished medical practice, he became more and more involved in the study of chemistry. As a member of the Geological Society of London, he had contact with other intellectuals of a scientific bent. In Alexander Marcet's company, Jane Marcet was brought into contact with the leading members of the scientific community of the day. The social ambit in which she operated was thereby extended, and Jane Marcet was drawn into an intellectually rich scientific circle from which she was to benefit enormously.

It is important not to overestimate Alexander Marcet's influence in this respect. Acting as hostess in her father's house had already brought her contact with a wide range of people in the artistic world, and she had been, for a time, 'friend and pupil of the celebrated Reynolds and of Thomas Lawrence'.[6] This talent for drawing was put to unexpected good use when Marcet worked on her *Conversations on Chemistry*. The line drawings of apparatus which accompany the experiments are of an economy and clarity that is at once efficient and beautiful, preserving both a simplicity and a sense of three-dimensional space that suggest an accomplished artist. Because of the Haldimands' banking business, contact with Ricardo came both through the family and through the intellectual activities of Alexander Marcet. In the introduction to her published work on *Political Economy* she talks of her 'literary advisors' in the plural, so Alexander Marcet and some of their intellectual friends are likely to have been involved. Malthus and his wife dined with the Marcets in 1813 and we know that Jane Marcet had read Malthus's works.[7] Her intellectual debt to him is acknowledged in the preface to the first edition. David Ricardo, who is specifically acknowledged in the second edition of her *Conversations on Political Economy*, but not in the first, was a member of the family circle and was certainly involved in commenting on the plans for the first and second editions as well as on the 'sheets' of the second edition when they were produced. Ricardo, in a letter to Malthus dated 1817, shows that he well understands the nature of the relationship between Caroline, Mrs B. (pupil and teacher in *Conversations on Political Economy*) and Jane Marcet:

> Mrs Marcet will immediately publish a second edition. I have given her my opinion on some passages of her book, and I have pointed out those which I know you would dispute with me. If she begins to listen to our controversy, the printing of her book will be long

delayed; she had better avoid it, and keep her course on neutral ground. I believe we should sadly puzzle Miss Caroline, and I doubt whether Mrs. B. herself could clear up the difficulty.[8]

It is interesting that Harriet Martineau, writing on economics topics from 1832, adopts the same approach and keeps clear of controversy. Today's economics textbooks have been criticised for failing to mention disputed points within the discipline.[9] In works that are self-consciously textbooks the avoidance of controversy would seem to be a very long tradition indeed!

Alexander Marcet retired from his practice in 1819 and, partly supported by his wife's inheritance, removed to Switzerland, where he continued to lecture in chemistry, drawing on his experience of lecturing on the subject developed in Guy's Hospital in London. He had published material on chemistry, including his syllabus and a well-received essay on 'The chemical history and medical treatment of calculus disorders' in the years 1816 to 1819. He died whilst visiting London in 1822, at the age of 53. Jane Marcet, already a much published author by this time, decided to make London her home once again, and soon re-established herself in London society. She maintained and developed her contacts after her husband's death. Maria Edgeworth records in her letters that, for example, she met Babbage, 'white as tallow candle' at Marcet's house in 1841.[10] Jane Marcet lived on to the age of 89 (she died on 28 June 1858). Although not a great deal is known about the details of her life, her personality is recorded by Maria Edgeworth (1767–1849), in various letters that she wrote, and by Harriet Martineau: close reading of both reveal much about Marcet's personality and lifestyle. Marcet, of course, mentions Maria Edgeworth's economics stories written for young children, in 'Conversation I', and Harriet Martineau was inspired by Marcet's own work. She too was a friend of Jane Marcet and it is fitting that the two women, so prominent amongst the distinguished ranks of women educators, should have had contact with Jane Marcet as a point in common.

Edgeworth, ever sensitive to the appearance of others, describes Marcet as 'plain' and of being in possession of neither 'an agreeable voice or a fashionable appearance'.[11] In the same letter, she reveals that her father had given Marcet's *Conversations on Chemistry* to a 9-year-old to read, an act that surprised Jane Marcet, who considered her works to be aimed at young persons rather than children. Edgeworth also gives a picture of a caring mother, agreeable children and a sociable household, whose activities, during Alexander Marcet's lifetime and thereafter, included hosting breakfasts, giving and receiving afternoon visits, providing dinners and, intriguingly, a talent for theatricals: 'Father and mother went out to buy some colors to paint a scene for Mrs. Marcet's play which is to be acted tomorrow . . .'.[12] We know that the friendship lasted and that Edgeworth thought of Marcet as: 'dear, good, agreeable ever-the-same and never tiring Mrs. Marcet . . .'.[13] She mentions Marcet's measured approach to knowledge and information of all sorts and her unwillingness to speculate. She also provides some information concerning her energy and desire for knowledge. In March 1841, when Marcet was already of a considerable age, she went with her daughter and Edgeworth to visit a pauper school at Battersea where they discussed educational methods together. A picture of an active, warm, restless human being with a sense of her own limitations emerges from Edgeworth's comments.

Martineau also gives some insight into Marcet's restlessness, a restlessness that found its outlet, thanks to the support of Alexander Marcet, in writing. Martineau also (perhaps) suggests a troubled and confused old age:

> A constitutional restlessness which always troubled her existence, and became at last an insuperable malady, indicated the employment from which she derived the greatest solace and relief the case admitted of. It was under her husband's counsel and guidance that she applied herself to authorship; and he witnessesd her first successes before his death in 1822.[14]

Marcet herself acknowledges Alexander's support. In *Chemistry* she quietly states the importance of 'conversing with a friend' as an important source of her own learning. She may have been helped into writing by Alexander but her lifetime's output, for she continued to write long after Alexander's death, was enormous: the entry under 'Marcet (Jane)' in the British Library catalogue covers almost three full columns. The numerous editions of both *Chemistry* and *Political Economy* are included, as well as her writing for children.

Martineau reinforces Marcet's own interpretation of her achievements:

> Mrs. Marcet never made any false pretensions. She never overrated her own books, nor, consciously, her own knowledge. She sought information from learned persons, believed she understood what she was told, and generally did so; wrote down in a clear, cheerful serviceable style what she had to tell; submitted it to criticism, accepted criticism gaily, and always protested against being ranked with authors of original quality, whether discoverers on science or thinkers in literature. She simply desired to be useful; and she was eminently so.[15]

Although a clear-headed observer of people and events, Martineau in this instance underestimates the work that Marcet herself puts into her own learning, for conversations 'with a friend', if they are genuine conversations, must have some basis in equality of effort. Jane Marcet actively pursued her knowledge of chemistry and directly performed experiments. This undoubtedly helped her set out with great clarity steps required for setting up experiments. Martineau, a hard judge on herself, is also a hard judge on others, and although she owed an intellectual debt to Jane Marcet, was not unaware of her faults. She comments on Jane Marcet's 'conventional life' and on the fact that her 'good sense' could be obscured by the:

> atmosphere of complacency and mutual flattery, and bookish gossip, and somewhat insolent worldliness in which the Whig literary society which surrounded her revelled during her most sociable years.[16]

Martineau, who had suffered at the hands of both Whig and Tory reviewers in 1833, had reason to criticise the Whig literary establishment and is here viewing the circle through her own experience. Almost immediately, however, she modifies this judgement by reminding us of Marcet's 'humble' heart and 'generous' spirit. She confirms Maria Edgeworth's opinion and what we can suspect from her writings, particularly her writing for children, that: 'no fine speeches from great men could spoil her as a companion for children'. In the closing sentences of her appreciation, Martineau again hints at a difficult old age: 'Though we may not regret her death, under her burden of years and infirmity, we may well be thankful for her life and services'.[17]

EDUCATIONAL STRATEGY AND
CONVERSATIONS ON POLITICAL ECONOMY

Conversations on Political Economy adopts the format already proved successful in *Conversations on Chemistry* and a common understanding of an educational strategy suitable for 'young persons' informs both. The introductory moves that initiate the conversations, as well as the prefaces that justify the approach, are similar in both publications. Marcet herself provides evidence that her 'advisors' did not think dialogue a suitable form within which to discuss political economy. She persevered with her own judgement, no doubt fortified by the very favourable reviews that had received *Chemistry* with respect to style and suitability for beginners, and by the fact that the work had already gone into three editions. The dialogue form was adopted, though without too much effort in maintaining consistency of character between the two publications.

Myers points out that dialogues had been used in numerous works in previous centuries and mentions, in the context of scientific writing, works by Galileo and Robert Boyle. The dialogue idea no doubt traces back to the various Socratic dialogues set down by Plato. Quoting Multhauf, Myers suggests that Boyle chose the dialogue form as a rhetorical device that eased the introduction of new ideas into a field rigid with orthodox thinking.[18] Marcet, who may have read the Socratic dialogues – for there is evidence that she had considerable knowledge of classical texts – is not, however, operating in such a context. Her writings adopt a style of her own making and are carefully constructed to lead the reader down the path of recently established knowledge. For Marcet, the dialogue is a teaching method, a means of conveying established knowledge as well as of helping young people to reorganise their own thoughts and experiences.

Although there is no evidence that Marcet had read David Hume's *Dialogues Concerning Natural Religion*, in that work he also says useful things about the dialogue as a method of writing which might help us explore the purpose and motivation behind the dialogue form.[19] He sets out, in the introduction, a justification of the dialogue in two very different circumstances: where a point of doctrine is 'so obvious that it scarcely admits of dispute, but at the same time so important that it cannot be too often inculcated, seems to require some such method of handling it'; and 'Any question of philosophy, on the other hand, which is so obscure and uncertain that human reason can reach no fixed determination with regard to it – if it should be treated at all – seems to lead us naturally into the style of dialogue and conversation'. As it is clear that Marcet was temperamentally unwilling to enter into controversial subjects and that Ricardo and others specifically advised her not to, then the dialogues fall into the first category in which the 'vivacity of conversation' is intended to 'enforce precept'.[20]

Although it would appear that 'The Catechism', as set out in *The Book of Common Prayer*, is a dialogue in this sense, it fails in many respects as a model for an educational dialogue since it is wholly lacking in the vivacity of 'normal' conversation. Not only does The Catechism contain a predetermined set of questions and answers but the initiator and respondent are cast in fixed roles. This is not the case in any of Jane Marcet's dialogues, in which intellectual activity is shared between the pupil and the teacher. The dialogue as presented in *Conversations on Political Economy* is not in any sense, as Marcet states in the preface, 'confined to the mere intersection of questions and answers, as in common school books' though questions and answers are certainly to be found therein. Caroline is allowed to be sceptical and questioning of the material being presented to her. There is, as we shall see, an essential part of Marcet's educational method. If there were established ideas as to what constituted educationally useful dialogues, The Catechism was not one of them. In fact, Marcet is unlikely to have had any model to follow for her project of bringing political economy to the attention of 'young persons of either sex'. She says as much in her preface: 'no English writer has yet presented' the subject 'in an easy and familiar form'. Furthermore, later in the preface she states that she had:

scarcely any other guide in the popular mode of viewing the subject, than the recollections of the impressions she herself experienced when she first turned her attention to this study.

The experience that was at her disposal was that of writing *Conversations on Chemistry* and her own experience of trying to assimilate the economics writing available to her. The dialogue format gave her the chance 'of introducing objections, and placing in various points of view questions and answers as they had actually occurred to her own mind . . .'. In reflecting on her own learning, Marcet felt that she has a good insight into the processes that others might be involved in when approaching political economy.

Marcet's reflections are, educationally, far from naïve and there can be no doubt that her work put political economy on the educational curriculum for young people of the middling and upper echelons of society. To discover their insights, both preface and 'Conversation I' must be considered in detail. Marcet's objective was to introduce the subject to adolescents on the understanding that such an introduction would be a useful way of 'diffusing useful truths' through society. A letter from 1816 reinforces the commitment to 'useful truths' and sets out her motivation:

> the hope of doing good by the propagation of useful truths amongst
> a class of people who, excepting in such a popular and familiar
> form would never have become acquainted with them.[21]

This aspect of the work is one that is consistently shared by those interested in political economy in the period after the Napoleonic Wars and up to and beyond the reforms of the 1830s. The adoption of such an attitude has tended to be labelled 'propaganda' when viewed from the end of the century and later. What must not be forgotten is that the notion of practical implications and the desire to pursue practical ends in education were to become widely held as was a search for principles with which the movement towards reform could be guided and judged. Marcet was part of a wider educational movement, which pioneered the trend away from 'polite learning' (Latin and Greek, high culture) towards that of 'useful knowledge' (Benthamite notions of education to inform social and economic practice).[22] Although the movement was not to get fully under way with respect to political economy until slightly later, and Marcet herself, in 1816, suggested her unwillingness to teach political economy 'to the labouring classes' (p. 158), her work stimulated the notion of the possibility of such instruction. It inspired Harriet Martineau to publish from early in 1832 her monthly tales directed towards all classes in society. By this date, Marcet had herself started to develop fictional approaches to the teaching of political economy, and Malthus is known to have appreciated her efforts in this respect. *Political Economy* is a text which must be seen in this very important context if we are to evaluate its educational significance. Indeed, Adam Smith's *Wealth of Nations*, itself, is one of the contemporary texts upon which a turn towards useful knowledge is likely to have hinged. Marcet was equally concerned with the importance of educating women and of making sure that young persons, including young women, could have access to subjects not normally thought suitable for them. This is seen at its strongest in *Chemistry* but there is clear textual evidence in both works of its significance to her. In her choice of career as writer as well as in her choice of subject matter, Marcet, despite Martineau's judgement on the conventional nature of her lifestyle, was innovative.

Her image of the young female is one of active intelligence, vulnerable to the fluctuations 'between the impulse of her heart and the progress of her reason'. Young people are pictured in the preface as operating under 'feelings of uninformed benevolence' or, as we would say, idealism. Whilst such words can cause a shudder when considered in the light of (later) excesses of *laissez-faire* argument, Marcet's illustration of 'uninformed benevolence' involves an analysis of ideas about actions beyond the first impact; in other words a realisation that action in the world has an immediate impact, followed by secondary impacts, and in the contemplation of such actions, the range of impacts needs to be considered. Such a view was, and is, acceptable to economics.

The conversations take place between two people: the patient and wise Mrs B. (Mrs Bryan in *Chemistry*) and her appreciative pupil, Caroline (also a character in the earlier work). As Marcet drew heavily on her own experience, it is tempting to see Mrs B. as Marcet after studying political economy and Caroline as Marcet before a study of political economy. There is something to be said for such an interpretation, and, as it in no way underestimates Marcet's educational insight, it will be adopted here. The suggestion will provide a useful way of organising the investigation of the relationship between Marcet and the political economists.

'Conversation I', designed to stimulate Caroline's interest in political economy, tackles the subject indirectly at first and arising out of an analysis of a classical text. The particular text is commenting on economic conditions, and Mrs B. and Caroline engage in a spirited argument about the correctness of the views about the relationship between town and country put forward in it. The term political economy is not mentioned by name until page five, and the discussion of economic ideas in the context of another subject is taken up again when Volney's reports of his travels in the Middle East are mentioned. This indirect approach is an example from 1816 of the notion of teaching economics awareness, catchphrase for wider economics education in the 1990s, through the economic dimension present in other subjects in the curriculum. Caroline balks at the idea of economics, mentions the reverence, 'almost religious veneration' with which Smith's name is mentioned within her family and talks of her experience of examining the book:

> I was so overwhelmed by a jargon of unintelligible prices, that after running over a few pages I threw the book away in despair.

Mrs B. then attempts to show that feminine interests such as dress have an economic dimension. Mrs B. does not accept her pupil's rejection of political economy willingly for in her eyes it is 'intimately connected with the daily occurrences of life' and ignorance of its principles can lead to 'serious practical errors'. Caroline uses many arguments to evade Mrs B. and hits upon the following: 'ignorance of political economy is a very excusable deficiency in women', arguing that since women are unlikely to become legislators, then 'a happy ignorance' is acceptable. But to Mrs B. ignorance, especially in women, is unacceptable. Jane Marcet, through the character of Mrs B., sets out another aspect of her educational theory: 'childhood is spent acquiring ideas, adolescence in discriminating and rejecting those which are false'. Education can help reduce the effort by trying to ensure that 'errors imbibed' are limited and 'such ideas only as are founded in truth' inculcated. Mothers need to educate their children and cannot afford to be ignorant. Mrs B. goes on to subscribe to Maria Edgeworth's use of stories to develop economics understanding amongst small children. Modern-day discussion of economics education for the very young has sometimes made heavy weather of the need to find a suitable method. Marcet simply gets on with it, holding that, with the right approach, even difficult subjects can be treated with the youngest of children. When Caroline objects that children can read without understanding the morale purpose of the story, Mrs B. responds in a way which illustrates her conceptual understanding of the problem:

> the moral is the only part of a fable which children never read; and in this they are perfectly right, for a principle abstractedly laid down is beyond their comprehension.

It is in the progression through later life that the applications will be made.

Caroline is convinced, but shows herself unwilling to study on her own:

> For as to studying scientific books, I am discouraged from the difficulty of the terms; which the language as well as the subject is new, there are too many obstacles to contend with at first setting out.

What modern-day economics educator would not understand this sentiment? Marcet herself resorted to the 'masters' in order to check and improve her understanding. But in Mrs B.'s response, the sophistication of her educational understanding is further revealed. Mrs B. agrees that the 'language of science is frequently its most difficult part', reassures her pupil that there are 'few technical terms' and continues:

> Indeed you have already a considerable stock of information on this subject, but your notions are so confused and irregular, such a mixture of truth and error, that your business will rather be to select, separate, and methodize what you already know, than to acquire new ideas.

If Caroline is Jane Marcet before, and Mrs B. after a course of political economy then she not only understood something about her own learning process, but hit upon an important element of adult education, the exploration of new ideas through challenging and reorganising existing experience. Of course, a generalisation from the experience of one, in terms of a justification for Marcet's approach to education, is not enough, but Marcet has the experience of watching her younger brother learn as well as dealing with her own children. We also know that she was good with children and young people in general, so her experience was not so limited as it might appear at first sight. The fact that the ultimate authority of established political economy stands firmly behind Mrs B., as Myers has pointed out, ought not to obscure the educational moves that fundamentally inform Marcet's writing.

The implications which flow from the approach are that the pupil's previous knowledge can be usefully involved in the learning process and that such previous knowledge can be specified, discursively explored, challenged and reorganised. Since economics, according to Marcet, informs all aspects of life, then other subjects as well as experience can be pressed into service; the exercise of imagination is needed to see the economics dimension in other subjects, including ideas expressed in poetry. The object is to develop insight into political economy, so references can be expected to primary sources. The other implication concerns the relationship between the teacher and the taught: Caroline is to be expected to be an instrument of her own learning rather than a passive recipient. An interesting aspect of this, and again one which relates directly to the notion of active learning, is that Caroline is expected to monitor her own understanding as it progresses:

> How very much you have already extended my conception of the meaning of wealth! And yet I can perceive that all these ideas were floating confusedly in my mind before.

Caroline is not expected to proceed by rote memorisation, essential to the successful conclusion of a catechism, but rather through a development of an understanding of the validity and usefulness of the underlying economics. The expression of the idea is rhetorically contrived, for Caroline is a model pupil rather than a realistic portrait of the young person.

Nevertheless, the point remains that, as a pupil, she is expected to be active rather than passive, and as an active personality she is convincing.

Two further questions on Marcet's educational methods can be asked. Is her approach consistent over the rest of the work where the main elements of political economy are discussed? Did she derive her educational insight from her own attempts to learn new subjects or was she helped by the works of others?

There are several ways of illustrating that Marcet's approach is consistent. In 'Conversation II', evidence for a desire to start from the pupil and work outwards is easy to find: Mrs B., in initiating a discussion on wealth, asks: 'what do you understand by riches in general – in what does wealth consist?' and Caroline responds: 'Oh, I suppose you mean money? – I should say that wealth consists in gold and silver'. When Caroline requests further help, at the beginning of 'Conversation III', Mrs B. makes it clear that she expects Caroline to be an active student:

> Do not leave everything to me, Caroline, I have told you that you were not without some general notions of political economy, though they are but ill arranged in your mind. Endeavour, therefore, to unreel the entangled thread, and discover for yourself what are the principal causes of the production of wealth in a nation.

This is a key element in her educational strategy, and the concluding episode in 'Conversation III' calls upon Caroline to summarise what she has learned: the emphasis on Caroline's summarisation here echoes the statement at the opening that the work ought to be undertaken by Caroline herself.

The above example suggests a carefully constructed and consistent approach to the educational development of the ideas over the length of a whole conversational episode but it can find ample support elsewhere in the writing. Caroline is expected to be willing and able to ask questions: 'By the necessaries of life, do you mean such things only as are indispensably necessary for its support?' (Conversation VIII); exemplify definitions: 'But the cotton-mills we have lately seen are a much more wonderful example of the effect of machinery...'; clarify misunderstandings: 'But to which kind of capital should the farming cattle be referred?' (p. 102). And she is permitted to defend her own understanding until shown to be wrong: 'you must show me where my error lies before I can consent to relinquish it' (p. 38). In a variety of different ways, then, Caroline is expected to be a partner in the learning process. Although political economy's victory is in the end complete, no matter how independently minded Caroline is, Myer's judgement that young people have all the questions and adults all the answers is extreme. His judgement must not close our minds to the educational richness of Marcet's writing.

Marcet's commitment to activating previous knowledge either from

54

lessons learned in other disciples or from experience of social life is also found at various points in the text. Volney is pressed into service as are Macpherson (*Annals of Commerce*) and Paley (on subsistence) and numerous other respected writers of the day. References to Classical Studies are also used frequently to explore economic points. Two of Goldsmith's poems (likely to have been part of the English curriculum) are explored in the second and third conversations, the 'Deserted Village' as an example of good poetry but of poor economics and the 'Traveller', from which a quotation concerning human motivation and satisfaction is used with effect. This attempt to integrate knowledge and to challenge ways of looking at the world in history, geography and fictional literature involves educational ideas that are very far from the spirit of a catechism! The integration of passages from other texts into the Conversations, an idea used to open the work as a whole, is later used to introduce the student directly to passages from Adam Smith, Sismondi and Say, once adequate preparation has taken place in advance. Mrs B. states, for example: 'Here is a beautiful passage in Adam Smith, the merits of which you will now be able to appreciate'. The end is to understand political economy; the conversations are a vehicle towards that end.

Later conversations yield up similar kinds of examples. Even given Marcet's understanding that Caroline has attitudes and propensities that are, perhaps, beyond her years, what we have in *Conversations on Political Economy* is the modelling of an educational relationship which, although it is clear where final authority rests, sees teacher and learner engaged in an active, even if unequal, partnership. It is in its clearly worked out and consistent educational approach that the strength of the work is to be found and it is time that it is appreciated in its own right for what it is: a pioneering work in economics education in which economics teaching is supported by educational insight.

The question of possible sources for Marcet's educational notions has been raised by others interested in Marcet's work, though none has subjected the educational moves in the text to the kind of analysis set out here. Thomson raises the question and points towards Mary Wollstonecraft as a possible source.[23] Wollstonecraft's belief that women were not well prepared for life and responsibility certainly finds echoes in Marcet's approach to educational provision. This insight, however, could just as well have grown out of Marcet's own social experience, in the sense that she had to look after her father's household when her mother died and so, hurriedly, enter the adult world. Equally, she wanted to operate within the same sphere as her husband, and found herself to be disadvantaged in the sciences. We have evidence that she reflected on her own learning and this could have been the case in terms of both formal and informal learning. In my view, Thomson supplies firmer, but again not conclusive, evidence, by drawing attention to Wollstonecraft's *Original Stories from Real*

Life in which two girls, Caroline and Mary, are instructed by a Mrs Mason.[24] Mrs Mason, according to Thomson, 'undertook her task with intense seriousness devoid of any humor'.[25] This is not a model for Mrs B., who is based on Jane Marcet herself, and Marcet has an undying reputation for easy and rewarding communication with younger people. However, Thomson explores further and finds in Wollstonecraft's work the following sentence: 'The elements of religion, history, the history of men, and politics, might also be taught by conversations in the Socratic form'. We now know that Harriet Martineau was inspired directly, in her educational approach to political economy, by two key passages in Marcet. Thus it seems plausible that Marcet in turn drew on the ideas of Wollstonecraft. Such a view, however, does not detract from Marcet's educational insight: it suggests a dialogue form but does not suggest in detail how this form is to be made educationally viable and valid. Marcet's originality remains intact. I am sceptical about this alleged source: Marcet fixes her own learning, particularly *Chemistry* from which the format for *Political Economy* is derived, within the context of 'conversing with a friend' and the view that the work is constructed to model her own useful conversation is still a strong contender as a primary influence.

The other place to look is towards the educational ideas of Maria Edgeworth and her father, Richard Lovell Edgeworth. *Political Economy* was inspired by *Chemistry* and *Chemistry* was the indirect product of a movement led by members of the Lunar Society that moved science away from its origins in academic and aristocratic society towards the middling classes in society. The educational writings of individual members of the society was prodigious with Priestley, Erasmus Darwin and Richard Lovell Edgeworth making significant contributions.[26] The direct link, and here the ground is sure, with the educational ideas of the members of the Lunar Society is Maria Edgeworth, daughter of one of its members.[27] Father and daughter had written on educational themes and Maria Edgeworth applied those themes to political economy before Marcet wrote *Political Economy.* We know directly from *Political Economy* that Marcet had read Maria Edgeworth's economics work. Jane Marcet knew of Lovell Edgeworth's reputation as an educator and knew what he could accomplish inside his own household, educating his numerous children, and beyond. On responding to the news that he had given *Political Economy* to a 9-year-old and that he had approached it 'bit by bit', Marcet exclaimed: 'Ah, who but Mr. E. would or could do that?'[28]

The main link would have come through the *Conversations on Chemistry* but, despite the fact that the two Edgeworths in their *Practical Education* spend time on setting out a chemistry curriculum for children based on very simple experiments and observation, it is difficult to see any direct link with the text of *Conversations on Chemistry*.[29] Marcet is concerned with the learning of the young adult, rather than with the very young, so the target group is not the same. The experiments and observations of that work derive directly from the experimental work of the day, and are very much based on subject knowledge worked out in collaboration with Alexander Marcet. Once again, it is the relationship with the subject and with Jane Marcet's attempts at understanding it that seems to be the prime source. Jane Marcet's syllabus as set out in the contents of *Chemistry* has a very clear relationship with Alexander Marcet's published syllabus of his lectures at Guy's Hospital as set out in 1817.[30] Since Jane Marcet published in 1806, it is as reasonable to assume that they devised the syllabus together as it is to assume that Jane derived the syllabus directly from Alexander. However in both *Chemistry* and *Political Economy* there is a commonality of understanding explicitly stated in the Edgeworths' work and implicit in Marcet's approach: an emphasis on stimulating the desire to learn; a commitment to not overloading the student (sometimes not entirely fulfilled in Marcet); a stress on the pleasure of success; a certain amount of trusting the student's judgement; responding to and shaping the student's own understanding resulting from social experience; a commitment to reworking experience and past knowledge; a limited role for rote memorisation. These commonalities do not imply strongly that Marcet had read *Practical Education*, but merely hint at it. They can equally imply that Marcet had thought hard about what kinds of attitude support learning in much the same way that the Edgeworths had. A provisional answer, then, to the question must be that Marcet thought hard about the conversations and the learning that she had been engaged in and, in the context of a wider understanding of good education, used these to model an educationally sound relationship with her chosen subjects. Her two greatest educational works were original in inspiration and design.

WHAT DID RICARDO SAY TO JANE MARCET?

We cannot know in detail how Ricardo and the other political economists advised Jane Marcet with letters or manuscripts to verify speculations. However, if Caroline is the version before or during initial discussion with political economists and Mrs B. the version after such discussion, then it is a reasonable proposition that, between the first and second edition, Caroline's questions will remain substantially unchanged but Mrs B.'s responses will reflect the advice received or criticisms made. Naturally, Marcet will have wished to make changes under her own steam so what is said here can only be indicative of the areas in which it is worth looking. The next stage is therefore one of comparing the first and second editions from the perspective of changes in the contributions made by Caroline and by Mrs B. What follows is indicative of the changes rather than the analysis of close details.

We know that the second edition followed quickly upon the first. Changes are limited but there is some textual evidence that they were carried out with some care. 'Conversation II', for example, is subjected to a very simple but nevertheless significant revision as follows:

As soon as these savages begin to apply themselves to pasturage . . .

(p. 19, 1816)

If these savages begin to apply themselves to pasturage . . .

(p. 19, 1817)

The substitution of 'if' for 'as soon as' in Mrs B.'s contribution reflects the highly problematic nature of the transformations within simple societies. Someone has clearly read the text with great care. The speed with which the second edition appeared does not in itself suggest lack of attention to detail.

In most cases the alterations involve a lengthening of the contribution by Mrs B. rather than any fundamental change in the questions asked by Caroline. For example, in 'Conversation ii', Mrs B.'s response to Caroline's 'most alarming attack on political economy' is increased from twenty-six lines to fifty-eight lines. The additional space is used to further justify the significance of generating wealth. Mrs B. shows considerable sensitivity in the two editions in responding to Caroline's moral objections to issues of wealth and distribution, and this sensitivity is increased in the second edition. There are, also, a small number of modifications in what Caroline says. These are usually made to maintain the continuity of conversations, for example in the opening section of 'Conversation X'. Some are stylistic, as in the substitution of 'you must shew me where the error lies, before I can consent to relinquish it' (p. 39, 1817) for 'you must shew me that it is erroneous before I can consent to relinquish it' (p. 38, 1816) and do not require investigation. There are, however, two which stand out, in my judgement, as significant. In 'Conversation VI', 1816, Caroline's attention is drawn to the emergence of rich and poor to which she responds: 'This, alas! is the dark side of the picture. The weeds spring up with the corn' (p. 83). The final sentence is deleted from the corresponding passage in the 1817 edition (see p. 88). This minor change in Caroline's utterance leads to a greater change on the part of Mrs B., who defends inequality in terms of its impact on the notion of industry. The 'weeds' in the 'corn' suggest something undesired and useless, but the dark side of the picture is beneficial, it forces indigent humankind to work. If Caroline is Jane Marcet before a study of political economy, then Marcet's questions are far from naïve, particularly those dealing with questions of justice. In the same area of the text we find Caroline's response to the privatisation of land: 'but the land cannot become private property without injustice to others who are thus deprived of their natural right to it' (pp. 37–8, 1816). This is clear, bald and reasonable. In the 1817 edition, this statement is modified to: 'but the land, it appears to me, cannot become private property without injustice to others . . .' (pp. 38–9, 1817). Again, the slight modification in Caroline's utterance is followed by a major modification in that of Mrs B. Justification of inequality through appeal to the 'dispensations of Providence' (p. 42, 1817) and private ownership of land as 'of necessity a preliminary step to cultivation' takes up an enhanced amount of space. Caroline's naïve view is strongly hedged by the addition of 'in my opinion' and doubt thereby thrown upon it. In the concluding part of the conversation, Caroline's conversion is, in both editions, complete; 'An institution of such evident general utility cannot then be considered as unjust' (p. 44, 1816). It may be not so much that young people have all the questions and adults all the answers but that all lay people stand in such a relationship to the new discipline. I suspect that in both these areas of the text, she received adverse comments from the political economists. However, Mrs B. is bound by the need to justify by argument and the revisions in the section which follows the initial question are extensive.

The other major revision, dealing with the vexed question of 'Wages and Population', is all on the side of Mrs B., with revisions in Caroline's summary at the opening of the next conversation, simply reflecting the changes that have been made. Here the additions are so extensive with respect to the economic content that outside influence is again suspected. As with other revisions, it consists of some minor textual modification, more than likely the result of Marcet's own dissatisfaction with the material, plus extensive additions. The tenor of the changes continues to be that of beneficial Providence, in other words what looks like a disadvantage is, in fact, a device to stimulate human ingenuity. Detailed textual analysis is not essential, since the textual revision is limited to stylistic concerns. The awkward negative sentence that opens the discussion is replaced by a positive sentence:

> You are quite mistaken if you imagine that I do not consider a great population as highly advantageous to a country where there is a capital which will afford wages sufficient . . .
>
> (p. 141, 1816)

> A great population is highly advantageous to a country, where there is a capital which will afford wages sufficient . . .
>
> (p. 146, 1817)

The revision simplifies greatly the appearance of the sentence without any major alterations to the meaning. The changes simply confirm Jane Marcet's commitment to a 'clear, cheerful, serviceable style'. The significant alteration is in the form of a lengthy addition to the text, which puts Caroline's growing sense of gloom into a more positive light: pressure of population upon subsistence is to be seen as a significant spur to economic and technical innovation.

CONCLUSION

Marcet's reputation suffers when viewed in terms of what economics education became later in the nineteenth century. Alfred Marshall, in reflecting on early economics education, argued that the catechism was the model. Recently Myers has shown that, in terms of *Chemistry*, it is possible to see in Marcet the origins of an educational movement in science in which children have all the questions and adults all the answers. Whilst there is something to be said for such views, they must not be allowed to obscure the educational originality and complexity of Marcet's work. *Political Economy* is based on a sound educational process, which is informed by Marcet's own attempts to learn new and difficult subjects. The conversations can be viewed as modelling an educational relationship whose foundations are 'conversing with a friend' and Marcet's own reflections on the educational significance to her of such conversations. The moves made by Mrs B. and Caroline, despite the strong element of authority, founded upon a view of the discipline based on the notion of 'truth', reflect a mature understanding of educational methods suitable for adults and young adults. The ideas that are implicit in such textual moves reflect essentially modern ideas of the nature and origins of economics understanding. Although we cannot be certain whether Marcet arrived at these ideas simply by reflecting on her own educational experiences or whether she had read and assimilated the ideas of other educators, her work is of greater educational significance than is normally assumed to be the case. The only element of a catechism in the work is the belief in the truth of the doctrine being expounded. This is a problem that all textbooks based on the primacy of a set of principles face and, in the context of the wider development of the economics textbook, where principles remain very much in command, Marcet's work is no more at fault than any others of its kind.

The relationship between Marcet and the political economists is equally interesting and complex. If both Caroline and Mrs B. are Jane Marcet, Caroline before and Mrs B. after economics education, then Marcet was undoubtedly an interesting personality, possessed of a lively intellect and interesting views concerning education and the nature of economic justice. Caroline's naïve questions could be troublesome. With regard to Mrs B., what is interesting is not only how few changes were made between the first and second editions, but also that the changes were essentially in the form of additions, suggesting that the text was basically acceptable as political economy. Martineau's notion that Marcet's work was entirely

Jane Marcet

derivative in the sense that she 'sought information from learned persons...' underestimates the effort that she put into her own learning and the way that such efforts informed the writing in respect of the roles of both Caroline and Mrs B. Marcet had to work with both diligence and skill in order to develop the economics curriculum. *Conversations on Political Economy* deserves further textual analysis of the duality in order to restore it to both education and economics as something other than a curiosity.

NOTES

1 Alfred Marshall, *Principles of Economics*, 9th (Variorum) edn, London, 1961, vol. I, p. 763n. Quoted in Robin Gilmour, 'The Gradgrind School: political economy in the classroom', *Victorian Studies*, December 1967, pp. 207–224. Gilmour analyses the object lesson in Dickens's *Hard Times* and presents evidence of the approach from a report on teaching at the Williams' Secular School (Edinburgh) from 1851.

2 Greg Myers, 'Science for Women and Children: the dialogue of popular science in the nineteenth century' in *Nature Transformed: Science and Literature 1700–1900* (eds John Christie and Sally Shuttleworth), Manchester University Press, 1989.

3 Eva V. Armstrong, 'Jane Marcet and Her "Conversations on Chemistry"', *Journal of Chemical Education*, 1938, pp. 53–7.

4 Dorothy Lampen Thomson, *Adam Smith's Daughters*, New York: Exposition Press, 1973.

5 B. A. Polkinghorn, 'Jane Marcet: Adam Smith's eldest "daughter"', unpublished paper, Department of Economics, California State University, Sacramento, undated, p. 4.

6 Eva V. Armstrong, op. cit., p. 54.

7 According to Maria Edgeworth, James Mill also breakfasted with the Marcets in March 1819, some time prior to the 24th. See Maria Edgeworth, *Letters from England: 1813–1844* (ed. Christine Colvin), Oxford: Clarendon Press, 1971.

8 David Ricardo, *Letters of Ricardo to Malthus, 1810–1823* (ed. James Bonar) Oxford, 1887, pp. 132–3.

9 Arjo Klamer, 'The textbook presentation of economics discourse', in *Economics as Discourse: An analysis of the language of economics* (ed. Warren J. Samuels), Boston/Dordrecht/London: Kluwer, 1990, pp. 129–65.

10 Maria Edgeworth in Christine Colvin (ed.), op. cit., letter dated ? February 1841.

11 Maria Edgeworth in Christine Colvin, op. cit., p. 62.

12 Maria Edgeworth in Christine Colvin, op. cit., letter dated 31 May 1813.

13 Ibid., letter dated 29 March 1831.

14 Harriet Martineau, 'Mrs. Marcet' in *Biographical Sketches, 1852–1875*, 4th edn., Macmillan, 1876, pp. 386–92. Martineau also informs us, in her autobiography, that Jane Marcet suffered from asthma.

15 Harriet Martineau, op. cit., p. 338.

16 Harriet Martineau, op. cit.

17 Harriet Martineau, op. cit., p. 392.

18 Greg Myers, op. cit., p. 172.

19 David Hume, *Dialogues Concerning Natural Religion*, New York: Hafner Library of the Classics, 1948.

20 Hume thought that the choice of dialogue made in order to avoid an author/reader relationship merely substituted a poorer one, the teacher/pupil relationship. This latter is the relationship that Marcet set out to model.

21 B. A. Polkinghorn, op. cit. Letter from Jane Marcet to Pierre Provost, 21 September 1816.

22 James Burns, 'From polite learning to useful knowledge', *History Today*, April 1986, pp. 21–9.

23 Dorothy Lampen Thomson, op. cit.

24 Mary Wollstonecraft, *Original Stories from Real Life*, London, 1791.

25 Dorothy Lampen Thomson, op. cit., p. 12.

26 R. E. Schofield, *The Lunar Society of Birmingham*, Oxford: Clarendon Press, 1963.

27 Richard Lovell Edgeworth married four times and had several children from each marriage. His total number of offspring was twenty-two. Four died in childhood. Richard Lovell Edgeworth was involved with the education of the remaining eighteen over most of his adult life. See Schofield, p. 405.

28 We would be tempted to answer, 'James Mill'. The quote is from a letter from Maria Edgeworth dated 18 May 1813, in Colvin (ed.), op. cit.

29 Richard Lovell Edgeworth and Maria Edgeworth, *Essays on Practical Education*, London, 1798.

30 Alexander Marcet, William Babington and William Allen, *A Syllabus of a Course of Chemical Lectures Read at Guy's Hospital*, London, 1816.

4

Harriet Martineau or 'when political economy was popular'

The significance of Harriet Martineau in the intellectual history of economics is beginning to be reappraised. Shackleton first raised the issue in a survey of women in economics in which Maria Edgeworth, Jane Marcet and Harriet Martineau are mentioned together with Rosa Luxemburg and Joan Robinson.[1] The relevance of Edgeworth, Marcet and Martineau might be summed up as 'economic thought and social consequences'. Of the three, Harriet Martineau is probably the most significant, having made a tremendous impact on the popular discussion of political economy from 1832 to 1834 with the publication of her monthly *Illustrations of Political Economy*.[2] Shackleton, in a later article, claims that Martineau's reputation as an economics writer has been undermined by hostile critics in the later history of economic thought.[3] In making this claim, Shackleton is substantially correct, though there are some exceptions.

In terms of intellectual history more widely defined, Harriet Martineau has a distinguished position in her own right. Her *Autobiography* has recently been republished by Virago and, over the years, she has been the subject of several biographies and scholarly works.[4] In the context of the development of the social novel and of Benthamite[5] and anti-Benthamite writing, Martineau is, in terms of the *Illustrations* at least, also given growing recognition.

In the intellectual history of economics, Martineau has been acknowledged as a friend of Malthus's last years and as a supporter of reform, *laissez-faire* and free trade. Her writings are considered to have shaped public understanding of *laissez-faire* both in the UK and in the USA.[6] Nassau W. Senior called on her during her morning visiting period in the 1830s and also attended at least one of her dinner parties.[7] Her presence at the dinner party at which Harriet Taylor first met John Stuart Mill also gets her mentioned in the context of the social ambit of the Political Economists. As she was fond of discussing the first meeting publicly, she eventually earned Harriet Taylor Mill's dislike. John Stuart

Mill also came to dislike her but more because of what he saw as her opinionated personality.[8]

In terms of her *Illustrations of Political Economy*, she has been acknowledged by writers such as Blaug,[9] and Sowell. Sowell sees her as a populariser but not as a member of the Classical School, who reached an audience untouched by the more illustrious economists (thus begging the question of the contemporary popularity of such economists).[10] Routh stresses the role of Martineau as propagandist.[11] Keynes,[12] though critical, is, in *Essays in Persuasion*, where his target is the success of the nineteenth-century Political Economists and their insistence on individualism and *laissez-faire*, willing to give Martineau a place: 'we should not think as we do, if Hobbes, Locke, Hume, Rousseau, Paley, Adam Smith, Bentham and Miss Martineau had not thought and written as they did'. Martineau's stories helped fix *laissez-faire* in 'the popular mind as the practical conclusion of political economy'.

Marshall is usually held to be critical and Keynes, in making use of Marshall's assessment of Martineau for his own purposes, quotes from Marshall's article of 1896: 'Never again will a Mrs Trimmer, a Mrs Marcet, or a Miss Martineau earn a goodly reputation by throwing economic principles into the form of a catechism or of simple tables, by aid of which any intelligent governess might make it clear to the children nestling around her where lies economic truth'.[13] This selective quote is repeated in the work of others and the governess image persists. But, as will be shown, Martineau's works were read by all classes of society, including those who regularly commented on economic ideas, and her relationship with the ideas of the Classical School is by no means simple.

It is hard to imagine why Keynes should be so snobbish about Martineau. Much of his popular writing was motivated by a desire to influence change, for reasons not dissimilar to those that motivated Martineau. Marshall's paragraph dealing with Martineau begins as follows: 'Thus general economic principles had to justify their existence before a court which no longer had any bias in their favour, and perhaps had some little bias against them. Consequently they became less dictatorial, and more willing to admit their own limitations. Never again . . .'. This paints a somewhat different picture of where Martineau might stand in relation to the Classical economists. Schumpeter, in contrast, shows himself to be consistently sympathetic to both Martineau and her contemporary economics writer friend, Jane Marcet.[14]

Although Martineau, as Keynes indicated, was unread by later generations, we know that at least one of his contemporaries read her. Martineau was 'the first political economist' that Austin Robinson, Professor of Economics at Cambridge and husband of Joan Robinson, ever read, 'not because of any particular interest in the subject-matter of her writings' but because of his descent from David Martineau, surgeon of Norwich.[15] Robinson suspected that Martineau's work was reading recommended by one social class for the benefit of another.

This chapter reviews the writing of *Illustrations of Political Economy*, the comment that it gave rise to and the way in which the material and the surrounding events are treated by economists, then and since. I will argue that Martineau's concern with 'painting a picture' of political economy, and the execution of the project, marks her as a brilliant economics educator (rather than 'mere' populariser or naïve propagandist) and that her work struck a chord with those frustrated by the abstract nature of existing economic thinking. Harriet Martineau was lionised by London society as a result of the publication of her work, but, with respect to the status of her *Illustrations*, she maintained her educational purpose and declined direct comment on analysis itself and on what she thought of as 'temporary questions', a view about controversy over policy that illustrates the strength of the Ricardian hold over participants in economic debate.

This stand is made explicit in the Preface to *Berkeley the Banker* in which Martineau shows that her object is 'less to offer my opinion on the contemporary questions in political economy which are now occupying the public mind, than, by exhibiting a few plain, permanent principles, to furnish others with the requisites to an opinion . . .'. And later in the same preface, 'I trust, for example, that some of my readers may not look altogether in vain for guidance from the story of *Berkeley the Banker*, though it contains no allusion to the Currency Controversy at Birmingham . . .'.[16] The controversy at Birmingham is likely to be reference to the public debate that took place between Thomas Attwood, banker and critic of Ricardian economics, and Cobbett in Birmingham in 1832. The allusion suggests that Martineau kept herself well informed of economic discussion. Attwood and his supporters were underconsumptionists who argued for a mildly expansionary monetary policy.[17]

ILLUSTRATIONS OF POLITICAL ECONOMY – MARTINEAU'S STORY

The origins of Martineau's interest in writing on political economy are to be found in her education as well as her particular circumstances. The evidence here comes from Harriet Martineau herself, as set out in her *Autobiography*, written at great speed when she thought she was dying and not published until after her death some twenty years later. Her *Autobiography* depicts her life as a 'stage by stage pilgrimage from darkness to enlightenment'.[18] Although her *Autobiography* remains the main source of any investigation of Martineau's life, and has been drawn upon by all subsequent biographers, the publication of Webb's biography of Harriet Martineau in 1960, of Pichanick's work in 1980 and Valerie Sanders' work on her letters and on her contribution to the development of the social novel in England are steps forward.[19] A sounder understanding of Martineau's relationship with the ideas of Priestley, Bentham, Adam Smith, Ricardo and Malthus and the notions of population and subsistence, *laissez-faire* and the role of education and good government than that held by historians of economic thought, is beginning to emerge.

Harriet was a bright child who, around the age of 12, succumbed to deafness. Growing up in a Unitarian household of some gentility in Norwich, she had access to ideas, argument and books. From the age of 12 she had four years of schooling, two in Norwich itself and a further two in Bristol. Her love of composition was developed by Mr Perry, an Orthodox dissenting minister converted to Unitarianism and who, as a result, lost his pulpit and most of his schoolboys. The loss of pupils created a space for Harriet and her sister. And with Mr Perry, she discovered elementary principles of composition: the Proposition, Reason and Rule, the Example (ancient and modern), the Confirmation, and the Conclusion.[20] A disciplined approach to the process as well as the structure of writing remained with her throughout her life. The young Harriet also found, in a geography book, passages relating to the National Debt and the Sinking Fund and took these subjects to heart.

It was her desire to write that came first and this desire was encouraged by her family. The interest in political economy developed within the confines of the world as she knew it, in Norwich, in Unitarianism, in the family business interests and in the pages of the *Globe* newspaper. It was the newspapers that provided an outlet for radical views, such as those of John Francis Bray, published first in a series of letters to the *Leeds Times* in December 1835 and January 1836 and much later as *Labour's Wrongs*.[21] The more radical literature and independent working-class explorations of socio-economic issues have to be considered in any full assessment of the reaction of the society of 1833 to Martineau's success. This issue will not be considered here. Once the first of her *Illustrations* were published, Martineau, clear about the value of newspaper publicity, wrote the following to her friend W. J. Fox: 'People ask me why the Series is not noticed in the *Globe, Sun* and *Chronicle*. Cd. it be managed?'[22]

Martineau's comments on economic ideas of the society of her school days are worth noting. Of the *Globe* newspaper and its writings on economic subjects she holds that: 'in its best days, when, without ever mentioning political economy, it taught it, and viewed public affairs in its light'. As a *Globe* reader she is likely to have seen McCulloch's Ricardian lectures reported on in the newspaper during 1824.[23]

Martineau also provides evidence for the manner in which formal ideas of Political Economy were discussed in more popular journals and in provincial circles. Of Malthus and his ideas of population, she holds forthrightly that:

> I was sick of his name before I was fifteen. His work was talked about then, as it has been ever since, very eloquently and forcibly, by persons who never saw so much as the outside of the book.

It must have been with delight that she revised her opinions reading the work and could share her earlier misunderstandings with Malthus when she later formed a friendship with him.[24]

Her earliest writings were on Unitarian and religious themes, but almost without knowing it she had started to drift on to topics treated by those interested in political economy, including addressing herself to the problem of machine breaking. This was of concern at the time and explored, much later, in Charlotte Brontë's novel *Shirley* (1849, but referring to a much earlier period). Martineau developed her earlier economic experience in the preparation made for the writing of her *Illustrations* and, in linking economic content with domestic circumstance, predates the social novels of the 1840s, written by Brontë, Dickens, Mrs Gaskell, Charles Kingsley and Disraeli. These novels, whilst a reaction against economic individualism, do not advocate state intervention but, rather, a sense of 'social solidarity'.[25] Family misfortune caused by the slump of 1825–26, the death of her father and the final failure of the family business interest, prompted Martineau towards the project that became the *Illustrations*. Her successes with earlier writing helped stimulate her ideas for something more substantial.

She started down the path of formal political economy on reading Jane Marcet's *Conversations on Political Economy*, a text first published in 1816, addressed to the education of young women and based on question and answer.[26] *Conversations* went through several editions and predated, by four years, James Mill's work also aimed at new students. Marcet's work drew very much on the work of Adam Smith, but also included Ricardian ideas before the publication of Ricardo's *Principles*. Martineau first read it in 1827. Mrs Marcet's success with her warmly received material, together with other evidence Martineau had from various responses to her own writing that touched on economic themes, convinced her that there was a market for her work.[27] Martineau set about, determinedly, to establish her project. This involved both developing the idea and finding a publisher.

Martineau had spent time developing skills in translation. She had at school tackled passages from Cicero and Tacitus. A good working knowledge of French and some knowledge of Italian and much effort in translation had made her skilled at interpreting foreign texts. She also knew how to plunder travel and other books for descriptive material on areas of the world that she did not know, thus adding verisimilitude to her writing.[28] Martineau was skilled in setting a scene or a situation with economy and conviction. The question of gathering together and interpreting works, presumably by Smith, Ricardo, McCulloch, Senior, James Mill and Malthus,[29] presented, at least to her mind, no great difficulties of interpretation, especially since she had decided on a very clear educational strategy. Whatever her sources, she wished to avoid ensnaring readers in her books and then surprising them with principles of political economy in an uncalled for and unannounced way.

Harriet Martineau was rejecting what might be called the 'sugared-pill' approach to literature. Certainly she sugared the economics pill in the sense that she was not writing a principles text. But she has to distinguish her work from, say, that of the imitators of Daniel Defoe or from the works of Maria Edgeworth in which the reader reads a story and discovers a homily and it is in this sense that she rejects the sugared pill. Her educational motivation was overt, though the teaching was to be executed by way of the tale. It would not be too exaggerated to suggest that Martineau took a well-established eighteenth-century literary form, the instructive moral tale, and gave it a peculiar nineteenth-century twist. There was, given the social crisis and the movement towards significant reform, a popular demand for education as well as a specific desire to understand the nature of economic issues. The Society for the Diffusion of Useful Knowledge, which followed the style of the Society for the Promotion of Christian Knowledge, attempted to produce suitable educational literature.

When Martineau offered her idea to the Society, it was turned down. According to Knight the Society held a Utilitarian hostility to fiction.[30] The general feeling amongst those approached elsewhere was that the country was preoccupied by the issue of reform. But, as will be shown, it was the relationship between political economy, the need to be informed of the economic processes thought to be at work in society and reform that created the space for Martineau's work. By sharpening her educational purpose, and concentrating on ideas useful to the setting out of policy arguments. Martineau was to be able to assist in focusing popular discussion. Her ability to achieve this was to win her the support of John Stuart Mill and others.

What the Society failed to see was that the moral tale with an overt educational purpose matched where the popular readership of the day was, in terms of the vehicle for educational writing, with a content – Political Economy – that was ardently desired. Harriet Martineau took the moral tale, domesticated it and used it as the overt vehicle of instruction. This view implies that Martineau's appreciation of situation is of as great importance as character development to the success of her writing. The success of her move provides her with a distinctive place in a line running through English literature directly from John Bunyan (the teaching of biblical authority through situation and concrete example) via the later Enlightenment to the social novels later in the century.

Martineau's insatiable appetite for learning and for reading is remarked on by J. S. Mill in a letter to Carlyle in which he says that the 'best thing about her, being her indefatigable industry and a ravenous thirst for knowledge and acquirements of all kinds, at least intellectual kinds . . .'.[31] This, and her ability to translate ideas from one language to another, helped her with her audacious plan to translate from scholarly text to illustrative novel. We can be certain that she is likely to have read the main works of the Political Economists as then published but that she had also read Dr J. Priestley whom she much admired and who is built into one of her stories as the hero of *Briery Creek*.[32] Textual analysis is required to establish more precisely the sources that she used.

It is in no way disrespectful to Martineau's achievements to suggest that skills in translation came to her aid. Much later in life Harriet Martineau summarised and translated the work of August Comte from rambling French into concise and much reduced English, a task acknowledged by Comte himself as having been brilliantly realised.[33] After her death an obituary, written by Harriet herself, was published in the *Daily News* on 29 June 1876, in which she describes her talent with trenchant clarity:

> Her original power was nothing more than due to an intellectual clearness within a certain range. With small imaginative and suggestive powers, and therefore nothing approaching genius, she could see clearly what she did, and give a clear expression to what she had to say. In short she could popularize, whilst she could neither discover nor invent.

Martineau did not see herself as developing original ideas and, late in life, looking back at the extraordinary episode of the runaway success of the *Illustrations*, she is hard on herself and on her work of that time. Her ability to see clearly and give clear expression was the solid foundation of her journalism and her educational work. She aimed to write for the public of her time and was contented that she had done so with considerable success.

The problem was finding a publisher. After many difficulties she was taken up by Charles Fox, then struggling into business, but on the strict understanding that she help finance the work by subscription. Her family and contacts rallied round. Early persuasive success with Fox was undermined by James Mill who felt that the work could not possibly be executed. James Mill had attempted to produce a work, *Elements of Political Economy*, intended as a 'school book of Political Economy' which did not readily achieve its aim as it lacked popular appeal.[34] James Mill, after the success of the tales, apologised to Harriet Martineau for his scepticism.

By February 1832, Martineau was in print. After what seemed like an enormous delay she received a letter from Fox with a series of postscripts, each adding significantly to the previous estimate of the reprint required to keep pace with demand. Martineau went from provincial obscurity and straitened circumstances to fame and some fortune. Both the fame and the fortune came only with very hard work. She had undertaken to produce not a quarterly edition of tales, as she had originally intended, but tales on a monthly basis. From January 1832, for a period of almost two years, Martineau was to write regularly and long at the task she had carved out for herself. She had proved that she understood the needs of the British reading public better than James Mill, Fox and numerous Members of Parliament and this was recognised by those in authority who were quick in their attempts to attach her to political causes.

The painful efforts that she made in the writing of her *Illustrations* are set out in the *Autobiography*. Her method was highly disciplined and systematic. Major works were reviewed, principles isolated and summarised. The ideas were then clothed in situations and lastly the material divided into chapters and written up. She worked for many hours a day and produced some twelve pages on each writing day.

Martineau was not driven solely by the need to earn a living. She believed, as did many of her contemporaries, in the truth-value of economic propositions as well as in the value of education. In her *Autobiography* she sets out how the Preface to the *Illustrations* was written: sitting unusually late into the night and never revising what she had once written. The Preface is important because it sets out how she understood what she was about. How she envisaged her task must be the starting point of any evaluation of her significance in the intellectual history of economics.

Few of the subsequent tales have Prefaces but those that do reiterate her basic stand. Martineau makes it clear that in the competition amongst subjects and ideas, she is set to canvass 'in favour of a candidate whom we would fain see more popular than at present'. Her target audience is 'the mass of the people' where Political Economy is viewed as 'dull, abstract and disagreeable'. She next defines the subject and draws educational parallels between improvements in Domestic Economy (a subject to which she successfully returns later in her writing career) and its implications for households, and benefits to be obtained by corresponding changes in the state. The benefits cannot be achieved till 'the principles of a better economy are established. It is the duty of the people to do this.'

This reference to the people's duty may seem a surprising conclusion. Martineau, writing at the time of considerable political reform and social turmoil, had a Benthamite view of the notions of the value of education and of good government. If the affairs of national economy are to be put right, the people need to have knowledge of the common interests of their fellow countrymen and of 'a few grand principles, which, if generally understood, would gradually remove all the obstructions, and remedy the distresses, and equalize the lot of the population'. It was such grand principles, held to have the force of natural law, that Martineau set out to illustrate. And, in recognition of the 'common interests', the *Illustrations* as a whole encompass the social landscape of the England of its day.

The people, on their part, are pictured as complaining that all that they can pick up are scraps 'because the works which profess to teach it have been written for the learned, and can interest only the learned'. This is the case, according to Martineau, because the science is new:

> It is natural that the first eminent book on this new science should be very long, in some parts exceedingly difficult, and ... not so clear and precise in its arrangement as it might be. This is the case with Adam Smith's Wealth of Nations – a book whose excellence is marvellous when all the circumstances are considered, but which is not fitted nor designed to teach the science to the great mass of the people.

Later works will work over disputed points and that when agreement comes it will come in a 'cold, dry form ... bare of illustration and made as abstract and unattractive as possible'. This is an important and significant point. Martineau seems to be saying that the social process of picking over disputed points, necessary to the authority of science, makes the work emotionally unattractive to the uninitiated. In her domestic settings, she contrives to find situations that are emotionally attractive.

Martineau, then, wants the science 'in a familiar and practical form' suitable for helping those new to the discipline. Works already written 'give us its history; they give us its philosophy; but we want its *picture*. They give us truths, and leave us to look about us, and go hither and thither in search of illustrations of those truths.' Sanders makes the point that Harriet Martineau's earliest memories of childhood, as set out in her *Autobiography*, are, in contrast with some male reconstructions of childhood, 'sharply visual'.[35] In a letter to W. J. Fox composed in February 1832, Martineau, in a creative outburst of vivid images, describes her potential literary companions and locations, adding: 'But what a blessing it is to have the empty picture gallery all to myself and to have hundreds, perhaps thousands urging me to fill one panel after another . . .'.[36]

Martineau wants truths and applications to be drawn together with an exposition of economic principles brought together with 'pictures of what those principles are actually doing in communities'. Martineau knew that she was, as an educator, breaking new ground and, whatever she says about herself, in educational terms her idea can only be described as forcefully original. She held the view that, 'This method of teaching Political Economy has never yet been tried, except in the instance of a short story or separate passage here or there'.[37] Her object is, then, 'to teach Political Economy' in the conviction that the subject is worth teaching:

> If it concerns rulers that their measures should be wise, if it concerns the wealthy that their property should be secure, the middling classes that their industry should be rewarded, the poor that their hardships should be redressed, it concerns all that Political Economy should be understood.

As Schumpeter reminds us, we are not entitled to laugh at the educational statements made by Harriet Martineau nor at the motives that inspired them.[38] Any critical attempts at formulating a set of objectives for education in economics must face similar issues. If curriculum design is to be systematic, appeals can only be made to the subject, to the social and educational needs to be addressed, to how uninitiated learners might best learn and to the problems to be solved. Living in the world of the hearing impaired, Martineau had given considerable thought to educational issues. Images, albeit word images, clearly had educational significance for her and for others.

How was it that Martineau arrived at the notion of economic truths? In the post-Napoleonic war era, the debate between those who accepted Ricardian ideas and those who did not was not conducted in public but, as Checkland puts it, 'in camera' and the support of the general public was neither required nor looked for.[39] Neither the latter-day physiocrats nor the reviewers of the heady days in the post-war period distinguished amongst those that supported Ricardian notions and those underconsumptionists like Malthus who opposed them. By the time that Martineau was reading the works of the Political Economists, the private debate had been settled in Ricardo's favour and the public debate was led by James Mill and McCulloch, both propagators of the Ricardian system. McCulloch was once said to have pursued his mission with a strong belief in the 'literal assertions of Ricardian finality'.[40] More recent investigations of McCulloch's writing suggest the possibility of a kinder interpretation.

If Martineau had read widely, as her contemporaries supposed, then her view that she was dealing with truths can the more readily be explained. The mood of the period suggested that 'truths' were willingly sought after. Whately, for example, writing in 1831, suggested that:

> There are some very simple but important truths belonging to the science we are now engaged in, which might with the utmost facility be brought down to the capacity of a child, and which, it is not too

much to say, the Lower Orders cannot even safely be left ignorant of.[41]

The idea of informing the lower orders of economic ideas was one generally held. The *Quarterly Review*, which could be critical of economic ideas, had suggested as early as 1825 that it would be a 'real blessing' to acquaint the working classes with economic principles.[42] And Malthus, for example, had read both Jane Marcet's *John Hopkins's Notions* and Harriet Martineau's *Illustrations*. In January 1833, he wrote to Mrs Marcet expressing his interest: 'I have read John Hopkins's Notions on Political Economy with great interest and satisfaction, and I am decidedly of opinion that they are calculated to be very useful. They are in many respects better suited to the labouring classes than Miss Martineau's Tales which are justly so much admired . . .'. He goes on to say that he would be happy to purchase several copies on publication to give to cottagers in the neighbourhood.[43] This lends credence to Robinson's view that Martineau's *Illustrations* were also likely to have been bought by one class for reading by another.[44]

The question in 1830 was, how could this be achieved? McCulloch's textbook, *Principles of Political Economy*, held the field until the publication of John Stuart Mill's *Principles* in 1848. Webb argues that Martineau drew very largely on the principles text produced by James Mill, a text which Schumpeter describes as 'elementary but not easy'.[45] It was assumed in the *Monthly Review* that she was a 'disciple of Mill' who proposed to become an 'evangelist of his doctrines'.[46] Reading James Mill might account for her desire to locate principles in concrete experience; reading McCulloch might add weight to the notion that his writing paved the way for 'lower-level Ricardianism'.[47] Although Webb argues that her primary source for theory was James Mill, he does not provide detailed textual evidence for the view. Webb also holds that her primary source for practice was the world of the Unitarian manufacturer, a world that she makes specific reference to in the introduction to *Berkeley the Banker*. McCulloch attempted to write on *Wages* for a working audience and failed to sell enough to recover his costs. As Webb reminds us, Martineau addressed the question of both content and style.[48] How she did this is illustrated below.

LIFE IN THE WILDS AND OTHER EXAMPLES

Accounts of the tales can be found in many works on Martineau.[49] Shackleton's account of the *Illustrations* made no significant progress on earlier accounts except to highlight the economic content over the storyline.[50] A review of each one would be both tedious and unnecessary, the more so since the very thing that made them so popular with readers of the 1830s tends to prejudice modern readers against them. In an effort to understand the educational principles underlying her writing, this review of *Life in the Wilds* stresses the interaction between the educational moves in the dialogues and the economics subject-matter. The tale is designed to illustrate the nature of wealth, the nature of productive and unproductive labour in relation to the growth of that wealth and the ways in which a growing society can economise on labour through the threefold division of labour, the development of machinery and the removal of partiality and artificial restrictions on labour's natural liberty.

It is carefully constructed to achieve the ends set and alternates, largely on a chapter-by-chapter basis, between storyline and dialogue. A settler society in the interior of South Africa is attacked by Bushmen who carry off much of the material goods and the domestic animals. The settlers have to reorganise the productive basis of their society to secure their future and end up by establishing a meritocracy based on the utilitarian contribution of its members to present needs rather than on past statuses. The titles indicate the purposes. Chapter 1, 'What have we left?', sets the scene, economically in the space of three tightly written paragraphs, and then consists of an inventory of useful trades and devices, i.e., it surveys the resources available. Chapter 2, 'What is wealth?', is a reflective dialogue in which the community leaders think about their 'strange day'. They review and clarify the notion of wealth, distinguishing it from banknotes and gold, noting that there can be no wealth without the application of labour. Examples are drawn from the society under consideration and then applied or reapplied to the wider world, 'old England' and hence to everyday examples that the reader would know.

Chapter 3, 'Earn your bread before you eat it', deals with the need to work for present problems rather than to insist on past status that has become irrelevant by social change. The discussion by this stage has mentioned numerous trades and professions: the ploughman, herdsman, smith, tanner, carpenter, farrier, butcher and numerous others. In short, the social landscape of rural England transported to the South African bush. Chapter 4, 'Hand work and head work', is essentially a dialogue on productive and unproductive labour in the context of economic growth. Illustrations are drawn from the ongoing story of survival, with the wider world drawn in. Chapter 5, 'Heart work', deals with medical problems and death, and Chapter 6, 'Many hands make quick work', is essentially a dialogue on the division of labour and its impact on production.

Chapter 7, 'Getting up in the world', is devoted to considering the changes and their implications for social order. 'A bright sunset', Chapter 8, is a recapitulation of main themes given in the form of an explanation to someone who has returned to the community after going off to seek assistance in Cape Town, and Chapter 9 ushers in the meritocracy of labour, a meritocracy which does not unduly disturb prior social arrangements.

Examples of the economy of Martineau's writing abound. The tale opens with 'There are few climates in the world more delightful to live in than that of the south of Africa'. The directness of the language and the certainty of the assertion is convincing. Whilst the setting is no doubt now seen to be contrived, Martineau could easily have been taking up a suggestion of McCulloch's who mentions in his book that, even in a well-stocked garden, man must still make the effort of stretching forth his hand for fruit. Martineau needed a self-supporting garden other than the Garden of England in which to conduct her social experiment.

The tales generally open with such directness. The dialogues, in which different characters are permitted at different stages to take part, achieve their educational goals by concrete example first drawn from the story itself and then generalised (see the exchange between the captain and Mr Stone on pages 22–23) to instances within the readership's general experience. Even the humble plum-pudding is used to illustrate the benefits of the division of labour and the cost advantages that arise from roundaboutness in production. Illustrating the division of labour with respect to the basic ingredients of the pudding gives way to a discussion of the problems involved in 'providing the means of producing and conveying the things which make a plum-pudding'. This device, some-times used in primary schools to encourage divergent thinking, is used to make concrete the idea of roundaboutness in production. Such a discussion brings in a whole network of topics. Mr Perry's notions of structured writing and the systematic nature of the underlying political economy merged under Martineau's efforts to give *Life in the Wilds* a sound educational structure.

The educational approach is carefully considered in the tales overall with definitions, exemplification, recognisable economic contexts, dia-logue; with application, reapplication, summarisation and objections; and monologue, carrying the specific economic messages. In *Demerara*, the anti-slavery tale, the example of the disincentive effects of slavery is con-trasted, in one episode, with the payment system of wage labour within the context of the same labour force. This example is made at the level of groups of workers, an earlier chapter having already contrasted an individual worker's efforts on his master's fields as compared with the efforts made on his own plot: not one, but two case studies illustrating the same theme.

The list of principles at the end of each text sometimes understates the economic content which also includes references to thrift, to the importance of contract and the possibilities of general improvement in economic and social conditions. The reader is not sent out 'hither and thither' looking for exemplification. The vocabulary and technical terms that she uses and the list of topics covered by her *Illustrations* provide enough evidence to show that she uses sources other than James Mill. For example, in the Ricardian tales, her heroine Ella uses the term 'real rent'. This term is not used by Mill nor can I find it in Ricardo but it is used by Nassau Senior published in 1821. The list of topics covered in the series does not exactly match those covered in Mill's text.

If James Mill tended to simplify, in his textbook, by abstraction (a key feature of all economic theory building), Harriet Martineau simplified by concretisation (a key feature of any educational activity of an introductory nature). In the summaries at the end of each of her tales, however, Shackleton has identified Martineau's use of another aspect of simplification: categorical forms, without qualification. But, in her *Moral of Many Fables*, her simplifications often stand in neat contrast to James Mill, as in the following:

> Mill: When the share of the commodity which belongs to the labourer has been all received in the shape of wages, the commodity itself belongs to the capitalist, he having, in reality, bought the share of the labourer and paid for it in advance.
> Martineau: The capitalist pays in advance to the labourer's their share of the commodity, and thus becomes its sole owner.

THE *ILLUSTRATIONS* AS LITERATURE

In the contemporary Reviews, see below, the publications were treated as much as literature as political economy and found to be wanting. Mrs Fenwick Miller, writing in 1884, by which time taste had changed, stated that the *Illustrations* 'are plainly damaged as works of art, by the fact that they are written to convey definite lessons'.[51] But, in the 1830s, Martineau was often seen as comparing favourably with Scott as in the *Literary Examiner* where reference is made to *Demerara*[52] in which 'she exhibits powers of grand description, which rival the best performances of Scott . . .'.[53]

Contemporary search for literary merit is made in the usual areas: plot, characterisation, fine language and refined emotions. The problem with this approach is that those features that made the work educationally useful come out as negatives; Martineau is using a popular form, the moral tale, with the didactic purpose overtly stated. In the moral tale it is the emotive force as well as the concrete nature of the episodes that leads to insight and understanding. In the *Illustrations*, quickfire development and didactic material is essential and literary refinement takes second place. Carlyle, consistently critical, especially of mechanistic political economy, in responding to Mill's description of Martineau, states:[54]

her Tales are no Artist pictures, and cannot otherwise be, but good

Twopenny Book coloured Prints, whereby catachumens, if they like, may learn the Alphabet. I hope she will not stop there. . . . She and her Tales are surely a sign of this Country and Time. Her works will do great good; the acme of the Laissez-Faire system, a crisis which the sooner brings the cure.

In view of Martineau's desire to paint a picture in a way that the mass of the people could understand, 'good Twopenny Book coloured Prints' is not an inappropriate metaphor. The merit lay in the openly didactic nature of the text, in the situation in which the characters found themselves and with which the readership could identify and the economy with which Martineau established character and setting.

THE *ILLUSTRATIONS* AS POLITICAL ECONOMY

If the educational purpose is to the fore and the structure and plot subservient to the need to provide general principles in an attractive form, then the economics must be investigated. Are the summaries an accurate reflection of the literature that Martineau was trying to illustrate? Did she hold a mirror to the discipline as then understood so that her faults are its faults or did she, in making the simplification of principal ideas, distort? Did she, in any sense, despite her own assessment of aims, add in any way to the discipline?

The consensus of the time is that the material treated is an accurate condensation of the principles. It is possible to quibble, as J. S. Mill did with one or two, as did the reviewers (see below) but the general principles are usually taken to be correctly summarised. It could be argued, as Carlyle did, that the notion of *laissez-faire* is taken to an absurd conclusion. Pichanick suggests that, overall, Martineau reflects the notion of good government, with responsibility for public goods and public order, in line with Benthamite and Smithian notions.

Martineau did not come to the texts without interpretive skills and without a background of her own. It might be possible to argue that Adam Smith and Malthus were more to her philosophical point of view than, say, Ricardo or James Mill. She was a democratic reformer but held to the significance of social harmony and the long-run possibility of bettering the social condition through such reform that recognises the principles underlying the economic and social order. This is fundamental to her educational philosophy and the educational strategy of the tales was worked out within this view. She wanted to improve the working class but the members of that class had to learn to use the laws of political economy rather than oppose them. It could also be expected that Martineau put certain notions in a compact, simplified form, easily labelled for public consumption and a search for such useful terminology coined by Martineau is not unreasonable, though difficult to undertake. Her analysis of slavery and of impressment might be an area in which she was, from the economic point of view, slightly ahead of the field. A full analysis of the economic aspects of slavery was not undertaken in Political Economy until J. E. Cairnes published *The Slave Power* in 1862.[55]

CONTEMPORARY REACTIONS TO THE *ILLUSTRATIONS OF POLITICAL ECONOMY*

Once published, Harriet Martineau was sought out by society, beset with admirers, beleaguered by politicians and publishers and, as her works became better known, inundated with letters. The latter must have had their share of those critical, passionate or abusive for in a Preface to another of her tales she is forced to write the following:[56]

> I shall henceforward take in no unpaid letters, directed in an unknown handwriting, which have not the name of the writer subscribed. The tax on postage for anonymous flatter or abuse is one which I cannot be expected to submit.

Martineau goes on to state that she will respond to criticism and comments that appeal to her reason but to none other. It is reasonable to suppose that she received a certain amount of postal abuse. It is this strength of reaction that makes the *Illustrations* so significant for she had tapped into the mood of the times, a mood that the academic Political Economists had failed, with their disputes within the Political Economy Club, to capture or to inform.

The published reactions to Martineau's *Illustrations of Political Economy* are to be found in a number of sources: in the columns of the literary journals of the day – the *Edinburgh Review*,[57] the *Quarterly Review*,[58] the *Monthly Repository*[59] and *Fraser's Magazine*[60] – as well as in the newspapers.[61] There was also private discussion amongst intellectuals and this was conducted in private letters both to Harriet Martineau and among critics of society such as Thomas Carlyle and John Stuart Mill. I propose to discuss the *Monthly Repository* and *Examiner* articles and Mill's exchanges with Carlyle in a section headed Mill's Response.[62]

The *Edinburgh Review*: Empson sets the scene for the success of the *Illustrations*. Martineau rescues the science of Adam Smith:[63]

> from the cloud which some persons have thought was gathering over its conditions and its fate. There are practical men who delighted in spreading the rumour that it had died outright in the cavern of obscure abstractions; whilst firmer and more philosophical believers

in its vitality, were compelled to bitterly lament that its nature as a science of facts, as well as of reasoning, is often forgotten.

Empson also shows great understanding of the feat that Martineau achieved: the plan would have failed in other hands, the work is not 'a theatrical deception', but rather 'a summons to the manifestation of solemn truths'. She is writing in two worlds which the reviewer sees as 'pathetic anecdote' and 'almost technical discussions'. Allowances need to be made on both occasions. How is the reader to react?

> She merely stipulates that we allow Political Economy to be talked
> by people and under circumstances where it was never talked before.
> This improbability, whilst it is not a much more serious one, is far
> more reasonably chosen. It is a necessary condition of her attempt
> to combine scientific instruction with amusement . . .

The review is analytical with respect to the work as both literature and as Political Economy, the reviewer being very aware of the need to look at the tales in terms of both literature and lesson, 'the singular combination of general beauty with a positive object of great utility.' With respect to the literary nature of the tales, the poetry and development of character is stressed. Empson accepts, however, that any failing in characterisation hurt the story more as tale than as lesson.

Empson expresses with great clarity the strengths of Martineau's approach which is seen as to 'at once authenticate and popularize the supposed elements of science'. He finds her audacity at tackling questions of considerable magnitude needing to be reigned in. And, in the latter stories, the link between the tale and the illustration of principle as summarised at the end is judged to be poor, being formed less by actions than by words: 'A disputable lecture is substituted for the promised probative events'. The reviewer adds that if one or two incidental scenes can be called illustrations, then, 'Manzoni, the friend of the plague doctor and of the corn-dealer, is entitled to claim the merit of priority for his *Promessi Sposi*'.

Martineau did not need to respond to criticism; the success of her works with the public had been established by the issue of the thirteen tales but, of all the reviews in the journals, she paid most attention to the advice contained in the *Edinburgh*. It was the one which most fully accepted her strategy of rejecting the sugared pill. She herself recognised the difficulties of maintaining standards under pressure and of keeping the story to the necessary principle or concept. (If we think of the tales as a kind of case-study, as suggested for example by Shackleton,[64] then those who write case studies frequently find that they can develop a case to demonstrate the application of a principle of analysis but it is more difficult to develop a case to suggest the development of a concept.[65])

Quarterly Review: The review in the *Quarterly* was one that Martineau found particularly hurtful[66] and gave rise to her exchange with Malthus, whom she regarded as the 'best-abused man' in England. The exchange throws light both on Harriet Martineau and Robert Malthus as personalities:[67]

> I asked Mr Malthus one day whether he had suffered in spirits from the abuse lavished on him. 'Only just at first', he answered. – 'I wonder whether it ever kept you awake a minute.' – 'Never after the first fortnight,' was his reply.

The review is satirical in tone and attacks the tales in terms of the political economy that is being offered up and for the didactic nature of the writing. The review says of anyone managing to read the material that: 'his powers of deglutition and digestion are such than an ostrich might envy'. Two paragraphs later the reviewers concentrate on the first tale, *Life in the Wilds*, and argue that the theme that it develops was illustrated like 'Robinson Crusoe – a story which has the advantage of making our little people fully sensible of the value of civilization . . .'.[68]

Martineau's tale is not about the value of civilisation but about the explicit illustration of the theory of growth and of the notion of productive and unproductive labour in the context of capital accumulation. Nor did she think of her intended audience as 'our little people': Martineau consistently worked for the liberation of working people from the demands of 'brute labour' and from the consequences of lack of educational opportunity. This, she felt, was best assured by technological change and the expansion of education. Martineau had set out, in her own words, to make known the '*moral character* of the poor'.[69] The 'fantastical refinements' of the didactic passages in which the notion of productive and unproductive labour is discussed are, in my reading of the tales, the strength and not the weakness of the text. The reviewers hold the 'sugared-pill' approach that Martineau rejected.

The two Garveloch Tales (the first dealing with Ricardian rent theory and the second with the population question) are also singled out for ridicule.[70] The illustration of the 'indestructible powers of the soil' is subjected to detailed textual criticism and the conclusion is that, in the illustration, Ella is placed in a situation in which 'there is not a single particle' of the rent she at any time pays which can be said to arise from 'the original indestructible powers of the soil! . . . this is illustrating a definition in an odd fashion. But thus it is – when the axioms and definitions of the political economists are tested by an application to facts, they are found not to fit one in a hundred.' Here, the reviewers are attempting to have it both ways: the illustrations are not facts! How Harriet Martineau must have bristled on reading this: when engaged in writing the early numbers, she wrote to W. J. Fox expressing the view that 'The doctrine of Rent is so simple & precise, & so transcendently exemplifiable! I shall need few or no conversational comments'.[71]

The Malthusian tale is subject to ridicule both at the level of Martineau's text and with respect to the underlying political economy:

It has always appeared to us one of the strangest inconsistencies of which the anti-populationists are guilty, that they, of all economists, are ever the loudest in crying up the advantages of every increase of inanimate machinery – in spite of its immediate effect in throwing labourers out of employment – at the same time that they decry every increase of the human machine, as a cause of immitigable want and woe.

In looking at Martineau's account of the absentee landlord, it is McCulloch who draws the ire of the reviewers. The underlying political economy is said to be as much at fault as Martineau's writing.

The review contains an attack on Martineau as a 'lean Benthamite spinster' and dispenses the advice that she ought to 'abstain from writing any more till she has mastered a better set of principles' and recommending that she study the works of 'a lady who, with immeasurably greater abilities in every way, was her predecessor in the line she considers so wholly original – the illustrating by fiction the natural laws of social welfare': Martineau is referred to the works of Maria Edgeworth. If the *Edinburgh* preferred Mrs Marcet, the *Quarterly* preferred Miss Edgeworth. Both thought it necessary to compare her work with that of other women, none thought it necessary to compare it directly with the writings of those men acknowledged as political economists.

The review concludes with the differences in the two approaches: 'the moral of Miss Edgeworth's tales is naturally suggested to the reader by the course of events of which he pursues the narrative: that of Miss Martineau is embodied in elaborate dialogues or most unnatural incidents ... with which her stories are interlarded and interrupted, to the utter destruction of the interest of all but detached bits of them'. The sugared-pill evaluation wins the day. Whilst criticising the political economy the reviewers are concerned primarily with a literary judgement, based on plot and characterisation, and in so doing miss the educational force and impact of the tales.

Fraser's Magazine: Martineau was lampooned in *Fraser's*. Martineau, though not pleased with the piece, felt that she was treated only as poorly as Godwin had been. The article was critical of Martineau's Utilitarianism, her support for Malthusian notions and made a sneering attack on her looks and personality. The attack on her views on 'preventative' check and 'moral' check implies that she ought not to be writing in an area best left in decent society to abstractions. The picture of Martineau shows her sitting by the fireside: 'Here is Miss Harriet in the full enjoyment of economical philosophy: her tea things, her ink bottle, her skillet, her scuttle, her chair, are all of the Utilitarian model . . .'. In short a radical spinster who might be better sticking to her kitchen. The author did not flatter Political Economists in general. Martineau sits by the fire, 'doomed to wither in the cold approbation of political economists . . .'.[72]

John Stuart Mill's response: Martineau's audience was not solely the popular reading public. She was welcomed to salons and in turn organised a limited salon of her own. Mill also read Martineau's work, as did the social reformer Francis Place. Any suggestion that they were read largely by governesses is a gross misrepresentation. With sales estimated at roughly 10,000 copies a month, the actual readership, given the existence of Mechanical Institutes, circulating libraries, extensive newspaper reviews that abridged the contents and the habit of reading aloud in a family circle, must have been several times greater than this number.

Mill, as early as 1833, was critical of Martineau's personality and shortly after ceased to be 'on terms' with her. However, he doubted neither her capacity for work nor her persuasive abilities. He acknowledges to Carlyle that her work deserves support. When faced with Carlyle's reaction to the absurd lengths to which Martineau pushes the concept of *laissez-faire*, Mill replied in the following terms:[73]

> Your criticism of Miss Martineau is, I think, just; she reduces the *laissez-faire* system to absurdity as far as the principle goes, by merely carrying it out to all its consequences. In the meantime that principle like other negative ones has work to do yet, work, namely, of a destroying kind, and I am glad to think that it has strength left to finish that, after which it must soon expire: peace be with its ashes when it does, for I doubt much of it will reach the resurrection.

The missionary role was, in this judgement, still necessary to further the process of reform. Mill does not analyse Martineau's 'absurdity', he merely reuses Carlyle's phrase. Mill generally gets credited with the observation (see for example the entry under Martineau in Vol. 3 of *The New Palgrave*). The quote usually does not include the second part.

It must be stressed that Martineau was wholeheartedly engaged in 'work of a destroying kind'. The targets in *The Moral of Many Fables* repeat those of the other tales. With respect to slavery, she illustrates the legislature's role in perpetuating the social and economic evil of slavery. For her, free trade, enemy of the slave-owner, of colonial monopoly and potential nourisher of the poor (by way of the abolition of the Corn Laws), was to be set against the 'partiality' of (unreformed) government, a partiality motivated by narrow and anti-progressive economic interests. Progress was more likely to be guaranteed by the market, freely operating, than by unenlightened government, and progress served the interests of the working people. It is in her fervent belief in progress and democracy and her attacks on monopoly interests that Martineau's radicalism is to be found.

But this is not to be taken to mean that there was no role for reformed government. Government expenditures were needed in the field of defence, public order and social improvement. Abuses, such as expenses on pomp and patronage, were not to be allowed but 'liberal measures for the advancement of national industry and intelligence' were to be permitted. Barracks, no longer required as a result of the peace in Europe, were to become the 'abodes of the sciences' as research and development centres, needed to sustain the development of technology that would liberate brute labour, and education, yielded up by the Church, would become a national concern. There was scope for policy and expenditure in appropriate contexts though not in the field of monetary policy. There was a positive dimension to Martineau's view of reformed government and we do her an injustice if this is not fully recognised.

Mill also reveals, in later correspondence with Carlyle, that he was the author of a lengthy piece in the *Examiner*, reviewing a *Tale of the Tyne* which he saw as an attack on the press gang.[74] Martineau correctly illustrates in the dialogue, with considerable irony and dramatic force, the disincentive effects and deep-seated resentment that forced labour brings in its train. Mill both recommends that the *Tale* be sent to government ministers for their enlightenment, strong evidence of the persuasive powers of Martineau's direct prose, and declared that the case is undoubtedly correctly analysed. He uses paragraph after paragraph of Martineau's prose to make points that he is very clearly associating himself with. Mill, whilst later holding that Martineau could over-sentimentalise on the subject of slavery full-blown, none the less was content in the case of impressment to argue against it in Martineau's words. As with the work still to be done by a more general understanding of *laissez-faire*, Mill was willing to give every encouragement to Martineau's efforts: he found her useful in the cause of reform.

With the completion of the last tale in which Harriet Martineau drew together and commented on the principles behind the tales, Mill took the opportunity of making a short, but telling review.[75] In it he argues that Martineau was not concerned with teaching the interconnectedness of speculative knowledge but, rather, with the illustration of such parts that lead 'directly to important practical results'. Mill argues that the *Moral of Many Fables* exhibits 'some semblance of an elementary treatise' and it is in this light that the *Moral* is reviewed.

Mill points out that more elaborate treatises share the problems that are to be found in Martineau. Such works also 'attempt to construct a permanent fabric out of transitory materials . . .' and take for granted 'the immutability of arrangements of society, many of which are in their nature fluctuating or progressive . . .' and present them to readers 'as if they were universal truths . . .'. The threefold division of English society – landlord, capitalist, labourer – Mill argues, is inapplicable in the West Indies where capitalists are landlords and where labour is property or in France where the labourer is the owner of capital. The methods of investigation are universal even if specific aspects (conclusions) are only locally true, but the analyst must make efforts to guard against taking arbitrary conditions to be laws of nature.[76] Such notions lead to taking the existing system as a standard of comparison and so to opposition to reform. He goes on to say that the English political economists:

> revolve in their eternal circle of landlords, capitalists, and labourers, until they seem to think of the distinction of society into those three classes, as if it were one of God's ordinances, not man's. . . . Scarcely any one of them seems to have proposed to himself as a subject of inquiry, what changes the relations of those classes to one another are likely to undergo in the progress of society; to what extent the distinction itself admits of being modified, and if it does not even, in a certain sense, tend to gradually disappear.

But, according to Mill, these are the faults of the political economists in general and 'Miss Martineau's little work' is less subject to this criticism than 'works of far greater pretension'. And he continues: 'as an exposition of the leading principles of what now constitutes the science, it possesses considerable merit'. With much reforming work still to be done, Mill's context for appreciating Harriet Martineau's works is the whole of the reform movement then under way. The textual analysis of *Moral of Many Fables* that then follows is carried out in four paragraphs with one major (concerning the principle of the poor laws) and several minor criticisms of notions in the text.

CONCLUSION

Harriet Martineau's *Illustrations of Political Economy* were a huge popular success, promoted by an author living in provincial obscurity and struggling against the 'better judgement' of those who ought to have been interested and better able to read the market. Martineau's purpose was to educate and to translate the generally held principles of Political Economy into a form that would help those unlikely to read the academic texts. Her aim was to explore situations that readers could easily picture and work within. She took the moral tale and recast it in an economics education mould. This in itself, whatever the detailed difficulties of execution, was an act of considerable educational insight. Domestication and concretisation made Political Economy a fit subject for popular discussion.

Contemporary reviewers took a stand on her work with respect to where they themselves were in a political spectrum. They grappled with the fact that the author was a woman as well as with the status of the writing as art, as education and as Political Economy. Under art went consideration of poetry and character and a criticism of improbability, thus overlooking the key feature of the texts which is not plot or character, though Martineau could write clearly and concisely, but easily imagined situation. And the situations that Martineau wrote about are those of every corner of society: capitalist, landlord and labourer in town and country, factory and farm, counting house and colliery, on hill, in dale, by the river's edge and on the seashore.

The response of those concerned with reform was welcoming even if the tales were ridiculed by others. The attacks in *Fraser's* and in the *Quarterly* concerning Martineau on population and the hint of a scandalous discussion of birth control, whilst it hindered Martineau reaching some readers, probably added to her reputation amongst reformers. James Mill apologised for his opposition. Robert Malthus warmed to her. John Stuart Mill supported the tales in so far as they furthered the movement towards reform, even using Martineau's own analysis of impressment to further his causes, and her summary as an occasion to reflect on English Political Economy. Mill was critical of aspects of the *Illustrations* when pushed by Carlyle. It is unlikely that Martineau added to the corpus of Classical Political Economy though she, at times, departed from it. Her belief in the possibility of social harmony is relevant to the content of the *Illustrations*.

If Martineau's longer-term impact was to fix notions of *laissez-faire*, as Keynes suggests, then that responsibility is not hers alone but is shared with both the wider society and others in the field. Martineau's views were informed by Bentham, Smith and others and her notion of what constitutes good government permitted much to be done. Her relationship with the economic ideas of her day is complex and her notion of economic truths was one widely held. The idea that Martineau was basically engaged in propaganda, rather than (say) practical reform underestimates the sources of her social and educational thinking, unless education itself is also propaganda.

What wider questions does Martineau's success pose for the relationship between the status of economics and economics education? The first one might be 'where were the economists' and why did they fail to capture the popular demand? The second concerns the nature of the professionalisation process of economics. The political economists of the post-Napoleonic war era might, with respect to their private disputes, be seen as a case of 'premature professionalization', talking to each other as fellow experts but eventually absent from the scene when the wider society, eager for reform and guidance, was starting to aspire to a share in their enlightenment.

Martineau's work comes half-way between James Mill's comparative lack of success in reaching an introductory readership and John Stuart Mill's success with his *Principles of Political Economy* published in 1847. J. S. Mill paid considerable attention to unifying, to being authoritative and to writing with a style that the reader found attractive, though his success was not as great as that of Martineau. However, his writing stood the test of time and he set the standard of clarity that Marshall, but not Edgeworth, was to insist on later in the century. In due course, Martineau's popular readership and those that frequented the world of Mechanical Institutes became either socialists or (and?) the participants in university extension work, and, hence, for a time, students of Marshall. Is it too fanciful to suggest that Martineau's popular success suggested the necessity to think clearly about the need to make an audience for economics? And is the question of the relationship between the professionals and the public, given the high degree of professionalisation, not one that should concern us, also living through tremendous social and political changes and at a time when the popular notion of economics is not always flattering? Economic thought does have social consequences and, in the post-Thatcher society, perhaps we have to reflect more seriously on the relationship between professional discussion and intended and unintended social consequences.

NOTES

1 J. R. Shackleton, 'Why don't women feature in the history of economics?', *Economics*, Autumn 1988, pp. 123–6.

2 Harriet Martineau, *Illustrations of Political Economy*, 9 vols, London, Charles Fox Paternoster Row, 1834. All references in this work will be to the collected edition.

3 J. R. Shackleton, 'Jane Marcet and Harriet Martineau: pioneers of economics education', *History of Education*, 1990, vol. 19, pp. 283–97.

4 Harriet Martineau, *Autobiography*, Vols 1 & 2, London, Virago, 1983. (Facsimile of original version published in 1877.)

5 The series ends on page 144 of the *Moral of Many Fables* with a grand Benthamite vision set out in capital letters.

6 Sidney Fine, *Laissez-faire and the General-welfare State*, Ann Arbor, University of Michigan Press, 1956.

7 See S. Leon Levy, *Nassau W. Senior 1790–1864*, David and Charles, Newton Abbot, 1970, p. 105 and note 218 on p. 311. His visits are mentioned in Martineau's *Autobiography*.

8 See F. A. Hayek, *John Stuart Mill and Harriet Taylor: Their Friendship and Subsequent Marriage*, Routledge and Kegan Paul, 1951.

9 Mark Blaug, *Ricardian Economics: A Historical Study*, Yale University Press, Newhaven, 1958, pp. 138–9.

10 Thomas Sowell, *Classical Economics Reconsidered*, Princeton, 1974, pp. 6, 20.

11 Guy Routh, *The Origins of Economic Ideas*, Macmillan, 1975. (Deals with Harriet Martineau in Ch. 3 'From propaganda to dogma', in a subsection entitled 'The popularisers'.)

12 J. M. Keynes, *Essays in Biography*, pp. 93, 103, *Lives of the Economists*, p. 222 and in *Essays in Persuasion*, pp. 276–7 as in *The Collected Works of John Maynard Keynes*, Macmillan for the Royal Economic Society, 1972.

13 A. Marshall, 'The old generation of economists and the new', *Quarterly Journal of Economics*, 1896, vol. XI, pp. 15–35.

14 Joseph Schumpeter, *History of Economic Analysis*, Allen and Unwin, 1954, and *Economic Doctrine and Method*, George Allen and Unwin, 1954, pp. 78–9.

15 See Robinson's review of J. C. Nevill's biography, *Harriet Martineau* in the *Economic Journal*, 1944, p. 116.

16 Martineau, *Berkeley the Banker*, no. XIV, *Illustrations of Political Economy*, op. cit., Vol. V, Preface.

17 See S. G. Checkland, 'The Birmingham economists 1815–1850', *Economic History Review*, second series, vol. 1, no. 1, 1948, pp. 1–19.

18 Mitzi Myers, *Women's Autobiography: Essays in Criticism* (ed. E. C. Gelinek), Indiana University Press, Bloomington, 1980. 'Harriet Martineau's Autobiography: The Making of a Female Philosopher', Ch. 4.

19 Valerie Sanders, *Reason over Passion: Harriet Martineau and the Victorian Novel*, Harvester Press, Sussex, 1986. *Private Lives of Victorian Women*, Harvester Wheatsheaf, 1989. *Harriet Martineau: Selected Letters*, Oxford, Clarendon, 1990.

20 Martineau, op. cit., pp. 63–4.

21 See Elizabeth Jay and Richard Jay, *Critics of Capitalism: Victorian Reactions to 'Political Economy'*, Cambridge, 1986.

22 Valerie Sanders, *Harriet Martineau: Selected Letters*, Clarendon Press, Oxford, 1990; Letter to W. J. Fox Friday night, Feb. 1832, p. 30.

23 For McCulloch's lectures, see D. P. O'Brien, *J. R. McCulloch: A Study in Classical Economics*, George Allen and Unwin, 1970, p. 50.

24 Martineau, op. cit., p. 71.

25 See W. O. Aydelotte, 'The England of Marx and Mill as reflected in literature', *Journal of Economic History*, 1948, vol. 8, pp. 42–58.

26 Jane Marcet also published *Conversations on Chemistry intended more especially for the female sex* (1806) and *Conversations on Vegetable Physiology* (1829). She is credited with introducing Faraday to science. See Greg Myers, 'Science for Women and Children' in J. Christie and S. Shuttleworth (eds), *Nature Transfigured: Science and Literature 1700–1900*, Manchester University Press, 1989.

27 Mrs Marcet published in 1833 *John Hopkins's Notions of Political Economy*, London, a work that was well received in the *Edinburgh Review* of April 1833 in the same article that dealt with *Illustrations of Political Economy*. Schumpeter is also specially warm about Mrs Marcet's writing, warning his readers that it is 'quite out of place to sneer'. See J. Schumpeter, *History of Economic Analysis*, George Allen and Unwin, 1954, fn. 12, p. 477.

28 For example, in the short preface to Ella of Garveloch she acknowledges her debt to 'Dr Macculloch's Description of the Western Islands of Scotland'. This is a reference to John McCulloch (1773–1835) and his work, published in 1819, on the geology of the Western Islands.

29 The *Quarterly Review* review article of 1833 opens with 'Here we have a monthly series of novels on Political Economy – Malthus, McCulloch, Senior, and Mill, dramatised by a clever female hand'.

30 Charles Knight, *Passages in a Working Life*, quoted in Bratlinger, op. cit., p. 24.

31 Letter from J. S. Mill to Thomas Carlyle, 2 February 1833, *Collected Works of J. S. Mill*, xii, *The Earlier Letters 1812–1848*, University of Toronto Press, Routledge and Kegan Paul, 1967, p. 141.
32 Martineau, op. cit., p. 254.
33 *The Positive Philosophy of A. Comte, freely translated and condensed by Harriet Martineau*, London, 1853.
34 Checkland, 'The Propagation of Ricardian Economics in England', *Economica*, 1948, p. 46.
35 Valerie Sanders, *The Private Lives of Victorian Women*, Harvester Wheatsheaf, 1989, p. 53.
36 Valerie Sanders, *Harriet Martineau: Selected Letters*, op. cit., Letter to W. J. Fox Friday, Feb. 1832, p. 30.
37 Political Economy had, of course, been ridiculed in literature. William Cobbett in *Cobbett's Two Penny Rubbish* had in 1831 published a comedy on population with Squire Grindum of Grindum Hall and an anti-populationist, Squire Thimble, as two of the characters living in the village of Nestbed in the County of Grindum.
38 Joseph Schumpeter, *Economic Doctrine and Method*, op. cit., pp. 78–9.
39 S. G. Checkland, 'The Propagation of Ricardian Economics in England', *Economica*, 1949, n.s. 16, pp. 40–52.
40 Checkland, op. cit., p. 48.
41 Whately is extensively quoted in Webb, op. cit., p. 107. The quote is taken from *Introductory Lectures on Political Economy*, published in 1831.
42 R. K. Webb, *Harriet Martineau: A Radical Victorian*, Heinemann, 1960, p. 105 referring to *Quarterly Review*, xxxii, October 1825, pp. 420–1.
43 B. A. Polkinghorn, 'An unpublished letter from Malthus to Jane Marcet, January 22, 1833', *American Economic Review*, 1986, vol. 76, no. 4, pp. 845–7.
44 Robinson, op. cit., p. 118.
45 Schumpeter, op. cit., fn. to p. 477.
46 *Monthly Review*, February 1832, n.s. VI, p. 136.
47 Schumpeter, op. cit., p. 477.
48 Webb, op. cit., p. 108.
49 Vera Wheatley, *The Life and Work of Harriet Martineau*, Secker and Warburg, 1957. Ch. 5 gives a descriptive account of the content of most of the tales. Ch. 4 of R. K. Webb, *Harriet Martineau: A Radical Victorian*, Heinemann, 1960, is an excellent source of ideas and insights. V. K. Pichanick, *Harriet Martineau: The Woman and Her Work 1802–1876*, in Ch. 3, attempts an analysis of Martineau's philosophical outlook as suggested by the tales. 'A sign of this country and time' is attributed by Pichanick to Mill; the reference is to a letter from Mill to Carlyle of 22 November 1833 but it is probably Carlyle's phrase. Carlyle uses it in a letter to Mill dated 22 February 1833: 'She [Martineau] and her Tales are surely a sign of this Country and Time'. His comment has a strong ironic force, and it is a pity that Pichanick is unaware of the irony. It is a play on Carlyle's essay, 'Signs of the Times' published in 1829. See Sanders and Fielding, *The Collected Letters of Thomas and Jane Welsh Carlyle*, Vol. 6, *Oct. 1831–Sept. 1833*, Duke University, 1977, p. 305.
50 Shackleton, op. cit., pp. 293–4.
51 Mrs Fenwick Miller, *Harriet Martineau* (Eminent Women Series) W. H. Allen, London, 1884, pp. 81–2 contains a sound analysis of the underlying conceptual problems faced in attempting to do what Martineau did and its implications for story telling and plot.

52 Martineau, *Demerara*, no. IV, *Illustrations of Political Economy*, Vol. II, op. cit., pp. 4–143.
53 See, for example, the review of *Cousin Marshall*, *The Literary Examiner*, 16 September 1832.
54 Carlyle to J. S. Mill, op. cit. Carlyle remained critical of Martineau. Thus, with the passing of the New Poor Law which Martineau supported by further tales he writes in 1837 to his brother in the following terms: 'On the one hand, Miss Martineau and Secretary Chadwick celebrating their New Poor Law Bill as the miracle of recent Legislation; on the other, the poor Nottingham Peasant hanging all his four children and giving himself up to be hanged that they may not go to … the Parish-Workhouse'. Alexander Carlyle (ed.) *New Letters*, London, John Lane, 1869 quoted in P. Brantlinger, *The Spirit of Reform*, op. cit., p. 20.
55 See Sowell, op. cit., pp. 13–14.
56 In the Preface to *The Loam and the Lugger*, Part Two.
57 'Mrs Marcet – Miss Martineau', *The Edinburgh Review*, no. CXV, April 1833, pp. 1–39.
58 Art. VII – *Illustrations of Political Economy*, Nos. 1–12, by Harriet Martineau, London, 1832–3, *Quarterly Review*, XLIX, April–July 1833, pp. 136–52.
59 'On Miss Martineau's Summary of Political Economy', *Monthly Repository*, VIII, May 1834, pp. 318–22.
60 'Gallery of Literary Characters No. XLII. Miss Harriet Martineau.' *Fraser's Magazine*, VIII, November 1833, pp. 576–7. The article has been attributed to William Maginn.
61 The *Examiner*, the *Spectator*, the *Tatler*, and the *Scots Times* all carried laudatory reviews of the *Illustrations*.
62 'Martineau's Tale of the Tyne', *Examiner*, October 1833, vol. 27, pp. 677–8.
63 'Illustrations of Political Economy, Mrs Marcet – Miss Martineau', *The Edinburgh Review*, April 1833, pp. 1–39. These comments were made at a time when political economy was not in the hands of a formal, professional group and when it would not have been unreasonable to expect wider discussion.
64 Shackleton, op. cit., p. 123.
65 See W. Henderson and E. Rado, 'Case study and the teaching of development studies', *IDS Bulletin Special Issue on Teaching Development of Graduate Level* (Inst. of Development Studies, Sussex), July 1980, vol. 11, no. 3.
66 There was an interesting reaction to the male attacks on women intellectuals. *The London and Westminster Review*, 1839, no. 32, pp. 459–75 contained an article by John Robertson entitled 'Criticism on Women' which was both a defence of women in general and of particular women writers including Maria Edgeworth and Harriet Martineau against the attacks of what Robertson called 'Crokerism'. The article in the *Quarterly* is now attributed to G. Paulett Scrope. J. S. Mill complained to Robertson of the unsuitability of the *Review* being involved in the publication of the article in a letter dated April (?) 1839.
67 Harriet Martineau, *Autobiography*, op. cit., p. 211.
68 Martineau, *Life in the Wilds*, No. I, *Illustrations of Political Economy*, Vol. I, op. cit.
69 Valerie Sanders, op. cit. Letter to William Tate, 10 November 1832, p. 38.
70 Martineau, *Ella of Garveloch*, no. V. *Illustrations of Political Economy*, op. cit., and *Weal and Woe in Garveloch*, no. VI, op. cit.
71 Valerie Sanders, *Harriet Martineau: Selected Letters*, Clarendon Press, Oxford, 1990. Letter to W. J. Fox Friday night, February 1832, pp. 28–9.
72 Carlyle had, of course, introduced the phrase 'the dreary professors of a dismal science'. Checkland, op. cit., p. 4, quotes Attwood as writing 'Political

economy ... a horrid work ... if you are to judge by the studies of those book-worms and theorists who have drawn all their knowledge from the mystifications of an abstruse and unintelligible philosophy' (*Birmingham Journal*, 30 June 1832).

73 J. S. Mill to Thomas Carlyle, 11 and 12 April 1833. *Collected Works of J. S. Mill*, op. cit., p. 152.

74 Martineau, *A Tale of the Tyne*, no. XXI, *Illustrations of Political Economy*, vol. VII, op. cit.

75 'On Miss Martineau's Summary of Political Economy', *Monthly Repository*, 1834, pp. 318–22.

76 Mill was to develop this argument more fully in the *Principles* which did not come to be published until the end of 1847. It was started in the autumn of 1845 and, by the time of its publication, many reforms, including the Repeal of the Corn Laws, had been enacted in legislation.

5

Thomas De Quincey reads
David Ricardo

Very little significant attention has been given by histories of economic thought directly to the economics writing of Thomas De Quincey (1785–1859). Where De Quincey is discussed, he has been discussed in the context of Ricardianism rather than in his own right. In the field of literary criticism, sustained, and growing, attention has been given to consideration of his economics writings.[1] *The New Palgrave* carries an entry on De Quincey by F. Y. Edgeworth, reprinted from the first edition (Edgeworth, 1987: 812–813). That Edgeworth, follower of the grand style of intellectual Victorian writing, wrote about De Quincey ought to come as no surprise. De Quincey's erudition, his familiarity with the classics and with classical rhetoric, mirrored Edgeworth's own sense of style. The political economy appealed because it contained three elements that Edgeworth also found attractive: a tendency (understated and under-achieved) towards geometry; an awareness of rhetorical argumentative forms; and the direct and easily pictured exemplification. It would be trivial, but not unreasonable, to be interested in De Quincey because Edgeworth (and few others) had been interested in De Quincey. It would also not be unreasonable to be interested in De Quincey's economics because he set out, initially at any rate, to 'simplify' Ricardo. He wrote, like Jane Marcet, a set of dialogues on Political Economy, exploring and developing Ricardian ideas. To propose adding him to the list of economics educators of the nineteenth century, rarely read today, but who had an impact on the economics understanding of Victorian society, would not be out of place. Edgeworth found his illustrations 'perfect' and 'shining' (Edgeworth, 1987: 812). Some of them were incorporated into John Stuart Mill's *Principles of Political Economy* (1848).

This, then, is the context in which I first approached De Quincey, but I soon discovered that his 'simplifications' generated critical comment, rather than a huge following and that they were, in educational terms, both richer and poorer than I had initially imagined. Unlike Marcet and Martineau, De Quincey is not motivated by an educational theory or by any sustained desire to educate the people at large, despite the fact that

91

he was 'in many ways an admirable expounder of the economic theories of his day' (Sackville West, 1936: 314). His exemplifications were, unlike those of Marcet and Martineau, intended to develop, as much as to illustrate, theory. His dialogues lack the sense of educational purpose and theory of Marcet, other than that suggested by the 'art of arranging and conveying ideas' for although he denies it, De Quincey is out to impress as well as instruct. Where both Marcet and Martineau avoid controversy, for the sake of teaching, De Quincey embraces it. Where Marcet and Martineau try to be comprehensive, both in the reading of political economy and in the setting out of the curriculum, De Quincey is concerned with the grounding of political economy in Ricardo's theory of value. Where they are arguing for reform, in conformance to the laws of political economy, De Quincey is more interested in conservative approaches to society. This is, of course, a modification of his alleged unbridled Ricardianism. De Quincey's political economy is primarily interesting because of his reading of David Ricardo. And his reading of Ricardo, which found that abstract economic thinking was not 'harsh and crabbed as dull fools suppose' (Edgeworth paraphrasing Milton), was based upon his understanding of rhetoric.

De Quincey's economics is derived, then, from Ricardo. This makes him of interest in the sense that 'lower-level Ricardianism' is interesting, as a socio-economic and literary phenomenon. His brief essays, the dialogues and the short textbook have more to offer than this degradation suggests, although the general (and misguided) view is that his work is unoriginal (Sackville West, 1936: 314; Stephen, 1871: 320). De Quincey, though thoroughly drenched in opium, was a fine writer (in McCulloch's words, an 'acute author') and had a clear, though unsteady and ill-disciplined intellect (McCulloch, 1825: 220n).[2] My interest in him is to be found in his reading of Ricardo.

By this I do not intend simply that he had read Ricardo. Many literary figures of the early nineteenth century had read Ricardo. De Quincey developed most of his economics in terms of his particular reading, and left, both explicitly and implicitly, that reading embodied in the text. This paper is concerned with an exploration of De Quincey's reading of Ricardo. This reading is marked by two considerations, first it is creative and, second, it is analytical. His desire to 'simplify' Ricardo is there and this, to some extent, dictates the genres that he uses, but his work, though conceived of as a commentary, is not best understood as a simplification. It is a reading of Ricardo by an author well-versed in classical rhetoric, in argumentative forms and in the communicative arts. It is not primarily as a (potential) educator that De Quincey reads Ricardo, but as a rhetorician and logician. This is both De Quincey's strength and his weakness. And it is this aspect of his reading that this chapter explores.

Thomas De Quincey

BIOGRAPHICAL BACKGROUND

It is not usual to provide biographical background in explorations of the history of economic thought. This convention puts emphasis on the thought itself rather than on individual experience, social context and circumstance. It is not a convention to be recommended since personality and circumstance have a part to play in the development of most people's thinking. Of course it would be tedious if every paper on Ricardo or Smith were to provide biographical material, for in the discourse community these authors are (too) frequently written about. In the case of De Quincey, some material is required given the unconventional nature of his life, the lack of knowledge about De Quincey amongst economists and the dramatic encounter that De Quincey first had with Ricardo's political economy.

But the more significant reason must be that a reading is undertaken in the context of individual experience. De Quincey's life consisted of a series of encounters with and retreats from everyday middle-class experience, with either erratic wanderings in the country, or, through London at night, with opium, which he first took in 1804, or the Lake District, providing the means of escape. It is ironic that De Quincey often had to escape from those to whom he owed money and that his flight often added to his debt (McDonagh, 1994: 44). Personal experience forced upon him an understanding of the links between money, debt and power over labour, relationships that he explores with literary skill in his writings.[3] However, despite his temperamental inability to face the world, and a personality rooted in Romanticism, he did possess a keen sense of intellectual curiosity and a delight in learning. It is as an analyst rather than as a Romanticist that he writes upon political economy.

De Quincey's self-education at Oxford (intermittently through the years 1804–1808) was sustained by a detailed study of the classics, of philosophy, of English and European literature. De Quincey (like Edgeworth) uses Latin and Greek with ease and natural ability, together with economic examples from classical texts. He seems to have developed a special skill in Aristotelian logic, attested to by his contemporary Richard Woodhouse, and embodied in the *Logic of Political Economy* (Sackville West, 1936: 75). Stephen is wary of De Quincey's logical ability and finds him, on inspection, to be 'a kind of rhetorical Euclid' who 'makes such a flourish with his apparatus of axioms and definitions that you do not suspect any lurking fallacy' (Stephen, 1871: 318). He also developed a knowledge of rhetoric and style which he further developed in the years 1828 and 1840. The essays on rhetoric were later gathered together and published under the title *Rhetoric, Style and Language* (1859). With De Quincey, the force of Romanticism is tempered by a highly self-aware critical facility.

De Quincey was an opium addict, 'happy, for a day, with a particular joint of mutton, cut according to a certain mathematical formula, and an ounce of laudanum'. Stephen also adds an elegant account of his strange life style. Under the effects of the opiates, he slumbered by day and 'it was only about two or three in the morning that he gave unequivocal symptoms of vitality, and suddenly gushed forth in streams of wondrous eloquence to the supper parties detained for the purposes of witnessing the display' (Stephen, 1871: 310). The title of Sackville West's biography on De Quincey, *A Flame in Sunlight*, vividly suggests the problems of his life style and character – burning intellectual passions, flickering inconsistencies, sudden enthusiasms, insubstantiality and drug addiction – as it has come to be understood by his interpreters and as propagated by himself. By De Quincey's own account, it was whilst sunk in an opium-induced state of imbecility, of some two years' standing, that he turned for 'his amusement' to political economy. A friend encouraged him by sending a copy, in 1818, of Ricardo's *Principles of Political Economy and Taxation.* De Quincey was instantly convinced that Ricardo was the 'transcendent legislator' that political economy required. De Quincey's account of the arousal from his drugged confusion is dramatic: Before he had finished the first chapter he exclaimed, 'Thou art the man'. In De Quincey's exaggerated account, Ricardo is no ordinary hero but a personal intellectual Messiah! Stephen's general judgement (general because little in the way of specific evidence is supplied) is that De Quincey's skills could only flourish when he had 'a safe guide' (Stephen, 1871: 318). In casting Ricardo as hero, in the *Confessions* (1823), De Quincey may have understood that himself. But his explanation of the outburst reveals the methodological delight that he experienced as well as his tendency towards exaggeration:

> Previous writers had been crushed and overlaid by the enormous weights of facts, details and exceptions; Mr. Ricardo had deduced, *a priori*, from the understanding itself, laws which first shot arrowy light into the dark chaos of materials, and had thus constructed what hitherto was but a collection of tentative discussions into a science of regular proportions, now first standing on an eternal basis.
>
> (De Quincey, 1936: 231)

De Quincey is, once again, demonstrating his command of English literature. Reference to the 'dark chaos of materials' draws upon Pope's view of Milton as well as on Milton's account of the creation in Book VII of *Paradise Lost.*

Earlier in the passage De Quincey describes how he saw political economy as an organic science, 'no part, that is to say, but what acts on the whole, as the whole again reacts on and through each part' (De Quincey, 1936: 230). Those interested in the hermeneutical turn in economics ought to take note! Yet, and this is also a guide to his subsequent efforts as an economics writer, 'still the several parts may be detached and contemplated singly' (De Quincey, 1936: 230, 231). His works detach the Doctrine of Value from the rest of Ricardo's text and deal with it singly though his treatment integrates value with the rest of the relevant polemical economics.[4]

'RICARDO' IN DE QUINCEY'S READING OF RICARDO

De Quincey's (formal) economics works are few in number and were first published in *Blackwood's Magazine* or in the *London Magazine*. Volume IX of *De Quincey's Works*, edited by Masson (1897) contains (almost) the entire corpus. There are, however, interesting snatches in other pieces. He was not the only writer interested in political economy. De Quincey makes an assessment of Coleridge's level of economics understanding: 'Political economy was not Coleridge's forte' (De Quincy, 1897f: 189).[5] The unstated assumption is that it is De Quincey's. He suspected Coleridge's attempts to broaden the frame of reference of economics and insisted upon concentrating upon key essential notions. In the process of the assessment, De Quincey attacks Malthus. His admiration for Ricardian rigour led him to a strict criticism of Malthus.[6] In the context of discussing the Socratic dialogue, in terms of style rather than logic, for the handling of 'polemic truth' on an item-by-item basis, De Quincey argues that the method is inappropriate for handling political economy. Systems of economic thought are all polemic in that they have 'moulded themselves in hostility to other systems' (1897c: 185). However the validity of economic systems cannot be assessed on an item-by-item basis for you must:

> keep fast hold on certain principles until you have time to catch
> hold of certain others – seven or eight, suppose; and then from the
> whole taken in continuation, but not from any one as an insulated
> principle, you come into the power of adjudicating upon the preten-
> sions of the whole theory.
>
> (De Quincey, 1897c: 185)

This is very close to Keynes's notion that for the study of economics, the reader must exhibit a certain amount of 'goodwill', going along with an idea until the reader understands where it is going. This notion of wholeness carries with it the notion of 'organicism', an essential idea of the Romantic movement. Personal experience formed the basis of some of his educational ideas, particularly with respect to the development of a reading strategy for an effective study of Ricardian economics. Using the example of the 'Doctrine of Value', De Quincey continues:

The Doctrine of Value, for example, could you understand that taken apart? could you value it apart? As a Socratic logician, could you say of it either *affirmateur* or *negateur,* until you see it coming around and revolving in the doctrines of rent, profits, machinery, &c, which are so many functions of value; and which doctrines first react with a weight of verification upon the other?

(De Quincey, 1897c: 185)

However unlikely, De Quincey's interest in and reading of economics had a large methodological component. His methodological understanding was founded upon an understanding of logic and of rhetoric. The language used in this passage is derived metaphorically from cosmology. However, he had already written *Dialogues of Three Templars on Political Economy* (1824). The dialogues are conducted amongst three characters, Phaedrus, interested, but not expert, in political economy, Philebus, who inclines towards the ideas of Thomas Malthus, and X. Y. Z., an enthusiastic Ricardian. X. Y. Z. was the name under which De Quincey normally published in magazines and the work was first published as a series of articles. As with Marcet's *Conversations on Political Economy,* Phaedrus and Philebus are permitted, like Caroline, to ask questions and pose objections. X. Y. Z.'s role is to demonstrate the truth, and here he shares much with Marcet and Martineau who, in common with many of their contemporaries, held that political economy consisted of useful truths. Truth, for De Quincey, is uniquely located in Ricardo's *Principles of Political Economy and Taxation.* A trio of discussants allows for greater textual variety than is achieved in Marcet's *Conversations,* where there are but two participants. It is perhaps a matter of taste and judgement whether or not the diversity, which includes a degree of friendly banter amongst the protagonists, adds to its educational value. Marcet's *Conversations* are less ornate and, to modern tastes, even less remote than De Quincey's. His other long work, *Logic of Political Economy,* did not appear until 1844, and it must be considered as a more mature expression of De Quincey's Ricardian critique, or in Edgeworth's terms his 'latest and greatest' (Edgeworth, 1987: 812). Though addressed to those new to the discipline, it is very much concerned with progressing the state of economic argument.

How, then, is Ricardo viewed in the two works? In the *Dialogues,* described by Hodgson as 'purely literary, not scientific', he is consistently viewed as far superior to all other contemporary and past political economists (Hodgson, 1881: 69).[7] Malthus is ridiculed as lax, lacking in logic, operating out of jealousy – a proposition put forward by Phaedrus and modified by X. Y. Z., but the damage is done as De Quincey well knew (De Quincey, 1897a: 46). Ricardo is ranked with the philosophers Kant and Leibnitz and his motives are of the purest that there can be:

Are my doctrines true, are they demonstrable? is the question for

Thomas De Quincey

him; if not, let them be overthrown; if that is beyond any man's power, what matters to him that the slumbering intellect of the multitude regards them as strange?

(De Quincey, 1897a: 48)

Putting elements of direct speech into the dialogue admits more than Ricardo, for the purposes of the orator are also admitted. De Quincey's understanding of rhetoric and of the needs of the dialogue as a form of exposition no doubt led him to cast the differences between Malthus and Ricardo in sharp terms. In *Rhetoric* he puts it thus:

Rhetoric is the art of aggrandizing and bringing out into strong relief, by means of various and striking thought, some aspects of truth which of itself is supported by no spontaneous feelings, and therefore rests upon artificial aids.

(De Quincey, 1897b: 92)

Whilst De Quincey recognised the systematic basis of economics knowledge, the dialogue is a genre in which, by giving participants different views, it is relatively easy to set up oppositions and so achieve the objective of 'strong relief'.[8] He was, however, predisposed to attack Thomas Malthus, even working him into an essay on *Greece under the Romans*. According to Sackville West, Malthus's views offended De Quincey's Christian beliefs (Sackville West, 1936: 305). Malthus, of course, doubted the staying power of the main part of Ricardo's doctrines, arguing that: 'the main part of the structure would not stand' (Ingram, 1893: 123).

As Malthus's faults are mean, so Ricardo's are heroic. De Quincey admits that the *Principles of Political Economy* requires a 'learned reader' and that much previous knowledge is assumed but defends Ricardo from the charge of paradoxical and obscure writing. This is accomplished in two ways: he allows two categories of paradox and two categories of obscurity. With respect to paradox, the categories are descriptive. These are 'the common and improper sense' of a paradox as that which looks true but is in fact false and the 'true' (and literal, in Greek) sense as 'that which contradicts the popular opinion'. Ricardo is paradoxical in the proper sense (De Quincey, 1897a: 48).[9] The treatment of 'obscurity' is the more interesting. That which arises out of a writer's own perplexity, he refers to as 'vicious obscurity', and that which arises from the suppression of 'links in a long chain of thought' he calls 'elliptical obscurity'. Malthus, of course, suffers from 'vicious obscurity'.[10] The contrast of 'elliptical' with 'vicious' implies a noble fault arising from the strength of the intellect rather than from any weakness. De Quincey is quick to spell this out in detail:

these [links] are often involuntary suppressed by profound thinkers, from the disgust which they naturally feel at overlaying a subject

97

Thomas De Quincey

with superfluous explanations. So far from seeing too dimly, as in
the case of perplexed obscurity, their defect is the very reverse; they
see too clearly; and fancy that others see as clearly as themselves.

(De Quincey, 1897a: 49)

De Quincey then enters a paradox of his own, for Ricardo to X. Y. Z. is:

a model of perspicuity. But I believe that the very ground of his
perspicuity to me is the ground of his apparent obscurity to some
others, and that is – his inexorable consistency in the use of words.

(De Quincey, 1897a: 49)

This concern for words which De Quincey detects in Ricardo matches
De Quincey's own concerns. It allows De Quincey, who saw himself as
skilled in words, privileged access to the text and provides a basis from
which he can comment.[11] Had Ricardo been perfect in all things, De
Quincey's facility with words and with logic would have been, of course,
redundant skills. Something of De Quincey's concern with words had an
impact on J. S. Mill. In discussing Adam Smith's use of the term
'exchangeable value', Mill adds, 'a phrase which no amount of authority
that can be quoted for it can make it other than bad English'. He prefers
to use De Quincey's 'exchange value' (Mill, 1929: 437). Contemporary
criticism, such as that of Bailey, and Senior, written as a result of reading
the *Dialogues*, detected an inconsistency in Ricardo's use of words.

Ricardo, though flawed, continues to be depicted as an intellectual
hero in his *Logic* and in minor works preparatory to it, though there is
both a greater critical tendency as well as a desire to further economic
analysis, in the *Logic* as compared to the *Dialogues*. Thus, in the *Logic*,
Ricardo is criticised for not consciously observing the 'exact coincidence
of riches . . . with "value in use" ' (De Quincey, 1897e: 127) but excused
on the grounds that: 'this was an accident likely enough to arise under
the absence of any positive occasion for directing the eye to that fact. It
was, no doubt, a pure case of inadvertence' (ibid.). Similarly on p. 179,
he depicts Ricardo's views, with respect to the early stages of value theory
as 'unsound as those of any man', but the final sentence of the paragraph
assures the reader that, 'Henceforward the powerful hand of Ricardo will
be felt in every turn and movement of economy'. His efforts to 'revol-
utionise' political economy remain 'the first and last effort that ever can
be made' and his brevity is still not the 'parent of obscurity'. If later
commentators, such as, according to Groenewegen, Hollander, overlook
areas in which De Quincey disagreed with Ricardo, or moved beyond
him, they are misled, to some extent, by De Quincey's own equivocations
(Groenewegen, 1982: 51).

The obscurity, where any exists in Ricardo, is rather permitted than
caused by his style of exposition: in part it adheres to the subject,

and in part it grows out of the lax colloquial application which most men have allowed to the words value, labour, and rent; so that, when they find these words used with stern fidelity to one sole definition, they are confounded.

(De Quincey, 1897d: 115)

De Quincey is often accused of inconsistency as an essayist, but with respect to his attitude towards and interpretation of Ricardo, and indeed of Malthus, there is a degree of stability in his views over the twenty years that separate the *Dialogues* from the *Logic*. His defence of Ricardo against charges of 'obscurity', 'paradox', 'over-refinement' and 'false subtlety' are energetic, Sackville West goes as far as to refer to 'the quaint violence of some of the judgements' found in both of his main economics works (Sackville West, 1936: 316). Even if they have something of the nature of special pleading about them, the *Dialogues* attracted attention. Bailey claimed in the preface to *Critical Dissertation* to have decided to attack Ricardian value theory as a result of reading De Quincey's account (Sackville West, 1936: 316).[12] Ricardo, even where flawed, is read as an enduring hero, Malthus as an illogical muddle-head.[13] De Quincey, in his ability to tidy and explain, shares some of these heroic qualities by association. Even when making a significant point about the nature of argument when cast in dialogue, there is a whiff of intellectual vanity:

Not that it is myself to whom I give the victory, but that he to whom I give the victory (let me call him by what name I will) is of necessity myself; since I cannot be supposed to have put triumphant arguments into any speaker's mouth unless they have previously convinced my own understanding.

(De Quincey, 1897a: 44)

Ricardo is a hero because he is a rigorous thinker, austere, abstract, concerned with truth and pure reason, and directing his mind to a critical inquiry of 'first beginnings'. His work is in the identification and analysis of error and confusion. The rhetorical and logical analysis that De Quincey makes is also concerned with sorting out error and confusion, either on the part of the reader or on the part of Ricardo himself. The sub-text is that if Ricardo was not faulty, there would be no need for a De Quincey. That his own reading, in general, was critical and exacting can be seen from the image of the careless 'flying reader' and the typical author set out in the *Logic*:

Verbal inaccuracies might indeed be cited from all; for in the age of hasty reading, and of contempt for the whole machinery of scholastic distinctions, it cannot be expected that authors will spend much energy upon qualities which have ceased to be meritorious, upon nicety of distinctions which perishes to the flying reader,

Thomas De Quincey

or upon a jealous maintenance of consistency which, unless it were
appreciated by severe study, could not benefit the writer.

(De Quincey, 1897e: 130)

This is essentially a rhetorical understanding of the relationship between
author and reader, though it may also be a socio-economic understanding
as well. De Quincey's concern abut the effects of quick and careless
reading were shared by others at the time. He understood that nice
definitions and detailed analysis of the meaning of terms would not
appeal to most readers. However, De Quincey saw his contribution as
assisting the development of a precise understanding and was sensitive
to the potential criticism on the grounds of over-scholasticism, or what
he refers to as 'scholastic trifling' (1897e: 157). As a result, in the *Logic* he
attempts to balance precision, which could be off-putting to potential
readers, with rhetorical flourishes, intended to sustain interest. His foren-
sic skills with language, directed against Ricardo, are to the fore in
Chapter 2 'On Market Value' when his unhedged disagreement with
Ricardo's lack of clarity with respect to 'price in a market' and 'market
price' (p. 203), take De Quincey towards the notion of equilibrium price
and short-term disturbances to equilibrium values. Even here, he
describes Ricardo as 'the great *malleus hereticorum*', and the fault 'scandalous' but, by implication, noble.[14] His admiration for Ricardo's achievements are maintained in the *Logic* whilst, at the same time, he reaches
beyond Ricardo towards a distinction between short- and long-term price
equilibrium and a subjectivist element in the determination of value.

There are other instances in which De Quincey's attempt at modesty
carries a hint of conceit: 'What a Ricardo has found difficult cannot be
adequately discussed in few words; but, if the reader will once thoroughly
master this part of the science, all the rest will cost him hardly any effort
at all' (1897a: 44). Here too, De Quincey generates a consistent reading,
value theory is the core of the system. De Quincey is also clear about the
nature of Ricardo's purpose and implied readership. Ricardo's principles
are misunderstood, because they are misjudged, Ricardo's aims were not
those of Adam Smith. Smith developed a system, Ricardo sifts through it
for error. Smith wrote for a wide audience, Ricardo wrote for 'the *clerus*,
not the *populus*'. In the opening chapter of *Logic*, De Quincey constructs
his target audience as 'the young student' (p. 129) and later as 'novices'
(p. 157). The view that De Quincey's reading of 'Ricardo' and his construction of him, is informed by rhetorical considerations (as McCloskey
would understand them) is confirmed by the evidence.

100

Thomas De Quincey

'POLITICAL ECONOMY' IN DE QUINCEY'S
READING OF RICARDO

De Quincey regarded political economy as a polemical science but a systematic one in which ideas about (say) value could be detached and considered within the surrounding and supporting ideas of rent, wages and capital. Despite the evidence of his superb examples, which will be discussed, but not admitted, later, his concerns were not essentially with the concrete experience of economic progress, nor with the state of society. There is little in either the *Dialogues* or *Logic* which suggests an interest in the details of economic life: indeed he was very specific that he was interested in Ricardo because Ricardo shut these out. De Quincey was attracted by the abstract nature of Ricardo's theory of value. Value theory represented the intellectual basis for economics: 'for he who has fully mastered the doctrine of Value, is already a good political economist' (1897a: 44). Of all the chapters in the *Principles*, De Quincey was interested in but twelve and these revolve around the doctrine of value, the 'all in all' of Political Economy. De Quincey's reading, as embodied in the *Dialogues*, dispensed with taxation on the grounds that the 'general doctrines have no sort of reciprocal dependency upon what concerns Taxation' (1897a: 52). He saw them as dependent upon the rest of the doctrines and advised students to read them 'separate' and 'after' the sections devoted to value. Further distinctions between 'affirmative' chapters and 'negative' chapters, reduced the core of Ricardo to Chapters 1, 4 and 30 (on value); Chapters 2 and 3 (on rent), Chapter 5 (on wages), Chapter 6 (on profits), Chapter 7 (on foreign trade), Chapter 19 (on sudden changes in trade), Chapter 21 (on accumulation), Chapter 25 (on colonial trade), Chapter 27 (on currency and banks), and Chapter 31 (on machinery) (De Quincey, 1897a: 52–53). This is the core economics curriculum according to De Quincey and its identification justifies his inclusion in the list of economics educators of the nineteenth century. Ricardo's writings were seen, by contemporaries, to be connected in a very loose way even although key ideas were used and re-used throughout the book. De Quincey's list has the potential for assisting those who found Ricardo difficult, for it sets out, and hence justifies, the view that there is a significant analytical core to Ricardo. In *Logic*, he also takes the point of view of the novice and sees that it is a great source of difficulty 'that the most metaphysical part comes first' (1897e: 148). Metaphysical problems arise wherever political economy makes statements for which there is no simple, definite sense. Thus statements about 'quantities of labour' or about 'equal value' are taken as metaphysical by De Quincey. The centrality of value theory made it difficult to start a study of political economy at any other point: 'Make a beginning at any other point, and the first explanation you attempt will be found to presuppose

101

and involve all that you are attempting to evade' (1897e: 149). Political economy is value theory.

Mill may have had De Quincey in mind (the gap from *Logic* to *Principles* is but four years) when, on introducing value theory, he mentions that 'in the apprehensions of some thinkers its boundaries confound themselves with those of the science itself'. In Mill's view, such an opinion is 'too confined' since it is concerned more with distribution than it is with production (Mill, 1929: 434). Mill was however happy, in 1848, that value theory was 'complete'. Mill also conforms to De Quincey's notion that, whilst the topic is difficult, a sound knowledge of value theory 'will enable [the student] to fathom most of the remaining questions of political economy' (Mill, 1929: 436).

De Quincey's educational insights are scattered throughout the text, and rarely as concentrated as in the passage in the *Dialogues* that presents the reading scheme for tackling Ricardo. There is no equivalent of Martineau's prefaces setting out and justifying an educational strategy. The skills used in the identification of the core are those of rhetoric and logic. It is characteristic that he never completed the treatment of the Ricardian core and, indeed, covers no more than six out of the twelve topics. In a postscript to the 1854 edition of the *Dialogues*, De Quincey, with a degree of defensiveness, states that, 'although fragmentary in relation to the entire system of Ricardo, and that previous system which he opposed, it is no fragment in relation to the radical *principle* concerned in those systems' (De Quincey, 1897a: 111). Value and distribution were the core (rent, profit and wages were an inter-acting 'triad' of ideas), all other things were secondary. The fundamental nature of value in the Ricardian system is re-stated, and evaluated, with a degree of sophistication, in the *Logic*:

> the collapse of this doctrine concerning wealth collapses the entire doctrine of Ricardo concerning value; and, if that basis should ever be seriously shaken, all the rest of Ricardo's system, being purely in the nature of a superstructure, must fall into ruins.
>
> (De Quincey, 1897e: 128)

Once again, De Quincey appreciates the method and the relationships implied by a methodological understanding of Ricardo's argument. His reading of Ricardo is based on an understanding of forms of argument.

But what about the examples, some of which were borrowed by Mill and drew admiration from Edgeworth; do they link De Quincey's notion of political economy with the worldly objects of economic speculation? Edgeworth mentions the longer exemplifications: 'the rhinoceros', 'the Boccaccio', 'the Popish reliques', 'the pearl market', and 'the slave market' (Edgeworth, 1987: 812). He does not mention 'the coal cellar' which is very effectively used to illustrate a problem in the theory of rent, nor does he mention the short, but no less vivid, examples, barely longer than one or two sentences, such as the 'wild strawberries' which may be 'gathered by shiploads' deep 'in the vast forests of Canada', which are also a feature of the text.[15]

In most of the passages listed, De Quincey is illustrating problems in the theory of value, and is unexpectedly close ('unexpectedly' in the context of the wider work) to Maria Edgeworth or Harriet Martineau in that it is his ability to write a tale, rather than his command of logic and rhetorical forms, that are to the fore. Edgeworth hints at this: 'Sometimes, however, the doubt occurs whether the writer was as competent to point a moral as to adorn a tale' (Edgeworth, 1987: 812).[16] The examples, which are of a high literary standard, are mainly fictional or historical, the products of imagination rather than episodes from contemporary society. They are constructed to suggest theoretical reasoning rather than as exemplification of an established principle and so are cases from which ideas are to be derived, rather than situations illustrating the application of existing knowledge. If Smith's examples are linked with social life as he knew it, De Quincey's are essentially creations of the imagination, dealing with value under extreme conditions. They are of greater contextual and literary worth, and more firmly based upon some genuine historical understanding, than are the relationships between Ricardo's 'trade-minded savages'. However, political economy remains bound to value theory and to abstract principles: De Quincey remained close to his definition of the core of the Ricardian system and his critique in *Logic* is constructed as a critique of that core. De Quincey's interest in and conception of political economy was primarily that of a rhetor than of a potential social analyst, luxury rather than grim details of production attract his attention. He delights in political economy because of the metaphysical problem presented by value theory as he understood it from Ricardo. His faults are also, then, the faults of his hero.

Social implications and contexts are not entirely ignored. De Quincey appreciated the possible turbulent social implications of Ricardian theory and attempted to soften their radical potential. Potential links between political economy and social reform, so strong in other economic educators, however, hold but little interest for De Quincey.[17] He does however recognise, and does his best to soften, the radical implications of distribution theory as presented by Ricardo. The clash, noted by McDonagh (McDonagh, 1994: 45)[18] between his admiration for Ricardo and the 'High Tory' political values that he himself holds, and which he refers to in an article on Ricardo published shortly after Ricardo's death, is found close to the surface in the treatment of the social consequences of rent (De Quincey, 1897a: 38). He recognises that 'either we must destroy rent ... or rent will destroy *us*' (De Quincey, 1897e: 249) (the 'us' is interesting since for most of his life he was a debtor) but rescues landed property, and the social class supported by it, from the 'dreadful class' of 'systematic enemies', depicted not as industrial workers but as *sans-culottes*, by discussing 'the just exposures' and 'the unjust concealments of Ricardo'. The specific context is the social unrest and activities of the Chartists and 'Jacobins'. De Quincey, sensitive here as elsewhere to the savings in production that technical change brings about, stresses an 'eternal counter-movement', the 'skill, capital and energy of freemen' (1897e: 248), which must off-set the tendency for rent to consume all.[19] De Quincey is pointing to the role of technical change but he clothes technical change within the 'energy of freemen', i.e. self-motivating, rather than mechanistically determined, individuals. Whilst De Quincey's economic argument is not without economic justification, the accompanying rhetorical flourishes, carried out over several pages, highlight the political contradictions. Ricardo's 'triad' of rent, profits and wages is in this context an 'instrument of mischief the most incendiary' (De Quincey, 1897e: 250). De Quincey's reading of *Political Economy* is not naïve as might be suggested by his Ricardian enthusiasms. He likes the spare, hard argument and the clarity of the theory of rent, but works against its antagonistic conclusions because it offends his sense of individualism (a challenge to the mechanistic notion of agency) and conservative cultural values. And because he likes picking over bones he finds fault with parts of Ricardo's theoretical apparatus. Such are the political contradictions of the text.

'VALUE' IN DE QUINCEY'S READING OF RICARDO

Sustained critical treatment of Ricardian value theory is to be found in the *Logic*, the work in which his analysis is more acutely based upon Aristotelian logic, though rhetoric is still an important feature. The pro-Ricardo rhetoric tends to obscure the originality of De Quincey's *Logic*. Value and rent constitute 'the well-heads' of Ricardian economy. De Quincey divides value into two elements, value in use and value in exchange, the former being a regulative idea (like pure geometry) and the later constitutive (the terms are derived from Kant, De Quincey's philosopher hero). Value in use he assimilates to wealth. Value in exchange, the key, is founded upon the object's capacity to meet a 'natural desire' and on 'difficulty of attainment' which is intended to imply costs of production. The two elements are illustrated within the context of a story involving a steamboat on Lake Superior and the reader ('you') moving to settle in a region '800 miles ahead of civilisation'. A fellow passenger has a 'powerful musical snuff-box' and 'you' receive the final chance of purchasing this item. The point of the tale is that 'D', defined as negative value, which is to be thought of as the cost of producing the item, is no longer relevant in any sense other that 'an unlimited D' and so 'U rushes up to its highest and ultimate gradation'. 'U' is to be seen as affirmative value or utility understood in a psychological sense. The moral is that 'D' and 'U' 'must concur to raise any motive for purchasing; but one separately it is which rules the price' (De Quincey, 1897e: 140). De Quincey then generalises his results using geometry, considering 'U' and 'D', 'only in so far as they are liable to the affectation of more or less' (ibid.). De Quincey then argues that affirmative value, the power in an object which attracts a consumer, is 'the intrinsic service-ableness of the article towards some purpose of his own' (p. 149), is associated with affirmative price. Utility is the key. De Quincey is clear that although use rests on this intrinsic power, it is simply that of 'ministering to a purpose, though that purpose were the most absurd, wicked, or destructive to the user that could be imagined' (p. 179). Opium, of course, fits the bill nicely!

The treatment of value theory is broadly based on scholastic analysis. Terms from classical argumentation are frequently used: '*conditio sine qua non*' (De Quincey, 1897e: 131); *principium cognoscendi*; *principium essendi* p. 153); affirmative and negative (many instances); *genera* and *species* (p. 187); teleological value (p. 190 and other instances) and teleological price (p. 191); *nominal* and *real* definitions (p. 228); *evidentia* and *discursus* (p. 237).[20] Aristotle is mentioned at least twice and classical incidents and language incorporated into the text. That the approach is based on scholastic considerations is predicted from the preface. Lack of progress since Ricardo is to be found, 'in the laxity of some amongst the distinctions which are elementary to the science' (p. 118). In the *Dialogues* De Quincey has returned to his 'exquisite science of distinctions' on which 'all minds . . . alike depend in many cases of perplexity' (De Quincey, 1897a: 41). The consequences of a *precarious* use of axioms in geometry is explored, the subject which holds 'acquaintance with the stars' would become as useful as 'stairs of sand'. Political economy is, in De Quincey's reading, in just such a position, 'for anarchy, even as to the earliest principles, is predominant'. Value, yet again, needs a thorough re-examination.[21] The summary highlights what is to be expected: an analysis of terms, starting with Adam Smith who, by 'total misapprehension', confused 'use' with 'useful' and going on to explore 'market value as a fact' and 'market value as a law'.

The use of scholastic distinctions and logical analysis is best illustrated in the *Logic* in section VI, of Chapter 1 'On Value'. Paradoxes, as has been shown, attract De Quincey, and he is essentially dealing with the paradox of value (see De Quincey, 1897e: 136, fn1). First he provides a verbal summary of the possible relations between value in use and value in exchange: sometimes divided against each other as 'collateral *genera* of value', sometimes with value in use subordinate to value in exchange. The distinctions are made clearer in a logical diagram which, based upon

105

the concept of *genera* and *species*, provides an elementary taxonomy of value. De Quincey committed himself in the *Dialogues* to the search for a ground of value, the last line of his diagram subdivides value in exchange into 'value in use (as a possible ground of price)' and 'value in cost (as the ordinary ground of price)' (De Quincey, 1897e: 187). Value in use only interests 'the economist' when it 'coincides' or 'has itself become value in exchange' (p. 188).

De Quincey then becomes vague, for 'often enough the use value becomes for a time the sole basis of the exchange value'. And here is one of the problems with his solution: how are we to recognise that this is the case in any particular economic circumstance? His interests tended to be rooted in scholasticism, in pure thought and not in any direct exploration of economic circumstances. He recognises the need for a measure or 'weight' in comparing diamonds and water but continues to think in absolute terms and exits from the paradox by contemplating the term 'use'. Here he concentrates upon the notion of teleological purpose, from *telos* meaning purpose or final cause. Teleological value is value which derives from 'the purpose which the *article* contemplates' (De Quincey, 1897e: 190, my emphasis) De Quincey recognises that political economy offers 'little . . . for distinguishing between the truly useful and the spuriously useful' (p. 191) (a point taken up by Ruskin who demands that a true political economy ought to be able to do just that).[22] De Quincey perceived something significant in his analysis of value in use, for everything he says about it suggests the possibility of subjectivism, and, indeed, according to Sherburne, Ruskin, who had read De Quincey and who later worked with a subjectivist notion, gave the sort of attention to utility that De Quincey strains towards (Sherburne, 1972: 138). But, despite the carefully constructed psychological elements (see below) in the musical 'snuff-box' story, and the many interesting things that he says about use, the language of teleology keeps him in the objectivist camp. Such are the analytical ambiguities in the text.

De Quincey is certain that his distinctions are useful, and, despite the geometric method designed to deal with more or less, his notion of 'U' (which corresponds to utility) is based upon an absolute quantity rather than upon any notion of the margin. It is characteristic of De Quincey's economics that, when a story is to be told or an example given, to suggest a point, it is set out and developed with economy and directness:

> You are on Lake Superior in a steamboat, making your way to an unsettled region 800 miles ahead of civilisation, and consciously with no chance at all of purchasing any luxury what so ever, little luxury or big luxury, for a space of years to come.
>
> (De Quincey, 1897e: 137–139)

Here, any reader is pulled straight into the author's imaginary world, the 'you' is forceful. The second person singular is used throughout the story and its economic explication. It personalises and individualises the act of consumption: the market is introduced into the discourse as the imaginative product of an individual psychology. The verbs are in the present tense, which, together with the time constraints surrounding the opportunity for making a purchase, add to the sense of immediacy. The final hyperbolic flourish is effective: 'you pay sixty rather than lose it when the last knell of the clock has sounded which summons you to buy now or forfeit for ever' (1897e: 139). There is nothing of this level of literary sophistication or psychological insight in Ricardo. Substitute the stronger narcotic, opium, for the musical snuff-box and its contents, and a telling basis for De Quincey's understanding of consumer psychology is revealed. De Quincey models economic subjectivities on his experience of drug addiction. Opium, rather than Bailey, is the significant influence (see also McDonagh, 1994).

The episode is striking and the story, and its subsequent analysis, is blended perfectly into the text. Mill, who had an eye for effective writing, quotes the whole passage, including the explication, in his *Principles* (Mill, 1929: 442). However, where a logical analysis of ideas in the theory of value is being developed, the flourishes, rhetorical questions and self-conscious cleverness of the writing can give it a complexity greater than the contents merit. Take, as an example, the introduction to the (innovative) geometrical analysis of 'D' and 'U'. Notice the stiff formality of the approach, especially when compared with the boldness of the snuff-box passage: 'Let not the reader quarrel beforehand with illustrations by geometrical symbols: the use which will be made of them is not of a kind to justify any jealousies of a surreptitious logic' (De Quincey, 1897e: 140). As the passage progresses, it becomes lexically and grammatically more complex, making it difficult to follow precisely what it is that De Quincey intends. His text, perhaps as his mind, is very busy with all sorts of points and prolixities. Opium is a basis for his clarity of his conceptualisation of consumer psychology but logic and rhetoric and traditional value theory, the basis for his argumentative structures. Such are the educational and personal contradictions of the text.[23]

Similarly with the interesting, and progressive, ideas associated with the notion of 'U', which, like De Quincey's educational insights, have to be extracted from significant sentences lodged in wordy paragraphs over the space of some twenty pages. We pick them out as significant because of our Sherlock Holmesian prior knowledge concerning what happened to value theory in the course of the rest of the century. Had De Quincey concentrated what he had to say about 'affirmative value', where he challenges the ambiguity found in Adam Smith's notion of 'use', he may have been able to move from the 'power of objects' to a thorough-going subjectivist position on the nature of value. Hodgson is clear that in undertaking the analysis based upon affirmative and negative values, De Quincey is developing an original idea, not something extracted from Ricardo, and argues that De Quincey's approach is, in fact, superior to Mill's (Hodgson, 1881: 88). A more forceful subjectivism in turn could have led to a critical reading of Bailey (mentioned, and rejected, in the preface to *Logic* though yielding some material for De Quincey's use) and, perhaps, the anticipation of Jevons.[24] He was blocked by his methods and by his very explicit rejection of supply and demand: 'A crazy maxim has got possession of the whole world: viz. that price is, or can be determined by the relation between supply and demand' (1897e: 206). De Quincey rejects the idea of market price as anything other than secondary because there must exist 'a *modificabile*, (i.e. an antecedent price, arising from some other cause)' (1897e: 121). This other price is 'natural price'. This view, heavily criticised by Mill, prevents De Quincey reaping the full benefits of his insight into the nature of utility. Hodgson, however, rightly stresses De Quincey's understanding of 'the desires of men' and 'the play of certain motives, certain volitions, in human conduct' and opposes this to the mechanical approach to supply and demand outlined by Mill (Hodgson, 1881: 94). In terms of a transition from Ricardian to subjectivist notions of value, De Quincey may indeed be more interesting than Mill. Mill's initial judgement of *Logic*, that it was a good introduction to Ricardo, underestimates its progress made towards non-Ricardian ideas of value (Mill, 1929: 122). Edgeworth, though aware of De Quincey's views with respect to supply and demand, certainly thought that the geometric analysis of 'D' and 'U' held out the possibility of greater progress: 'had he worked with dU instead of "U", he might have anticipated Jevons' (Edgeworth, 1987: 813) was not, and could not be the case. Although 'U' and the theory of rent are dealt with geometrically, the sustained intellectual tool, in *Logic*, is De Quincey's application of Aristotelian logic, an application which is incompatible with the emotional insights on consumerism generated by opium addiction.

Scholastic analytical methods could help De Quincey reveal problems with Ricardian value theory. It is difficult to see how they could help shift the basic premises. De Quincey struggled to free himself of Ricardian analysis, and his literary passages, and to some extent his geometric passages, contrived his escape. There is an ambiguity in his attitude towards Ricardo and his own logical methods finally prevented his freedom. Any system of logic is largely concerned with the validity of argument rather than *directly* concerned with the validity of the initial premise. In criticising Ricardian argument, De Quincey tends to work within Ricardian structures, in contemplating his own consumer psychology, he encounters 'insatiability' and attempts to relate it to the framework of Ricardian scarcity. Edgeworth's hope misreads De Quincey's ability to

Thomas De Quincey

operate on a sustained basis outside structures generated by Ricardo's 'powerful hand'.

NOTES

1 For a literary analysis of his economics writings see Maniquis (1976) and references in Heinzelman (1980). Literary approaches to De Quincey's economics attempt to integrate the development of his economics with his main works including his autobiography.

2 According to R. M. Rauner (1961), the note in which this observation is contained, made in the context of De Quincey's contribution to the clarification of Ricardian value theory, remained unchanged in the three editions of the *Principles*. McCulloch preferred the *Dialogues* to *Logic* and so, according to Groenewegen, prejudiced later economists against the *Logic*. See Groenewegen (1982: 51–58).

3 For an account of De Quincey's flight from those who had lent him money see 'Debt and Desire: the Psychology of Political Economy', Chapter 2 in J. McDonagh (1994). In *Logic*, De Quincey explores the question of 'tick' in the context of a story of Argyrippus, and Coelereta (a *lena*). Ruskin took up, and developed, De Quincey's notion of money as debt and as command over labour.

4 *Confessions* gives the impression in such passages that De Quincey's conversion to economics was sudden. It must be remembered that De Quincey was a great dabbler and, given the intellectual climate in the early part of the nineteenth century, he had made some excursions into the subject. See Maniquis (1976: 115).

5 This was a judgement with which J. S. Mill agreed. He refers to Coleridge's writings on economics as the writings of 'an arrant driveller' (Mill, 1929: 155).

6 Adam Smith also suffers in any comparison with Ricardo. Smith's ambiguities with respect to the meaning to be attached to the notion of 'quantity of labour' is pounced upon by De Quincey.

7 Hodgson is making a distinction between what he sees as the literary form and merit of the *Dialogues* and the scientific merit of the *Logic*. He protects De Quincey's *Logic* from the attack, by Mill, on De Quincey's notion of market value.

8 In the preface to *Logic*, De Quincey tells us that the purpose of the *Dialogues* 'was to draw into much stronger relief than Ricardo himself had done that one radical doctrine as to value by which he had given a new birth to Political Economy'.

9 It is probably true to say that, given his understanding of rhetoric, De Quincey was attracted to paradox. In this sense the paradox of value is a significant example of his love of paradox in general.

10 De Quincey is attracted to the two-category division of ideas, in the same passage he talks about 'subjective' and 'objective' obscurity. Later in the text he talks about the 'doctrinal or *affirmative* part, and the polemic or *negative* part' of Ricardo's work. He uses two-fold classifications from established systems of rhetoric and legal argument. He takes very readily to various two-fold classifications in economics such as 'market' and 'natural'.

11 'De Quincey implicitly puts forward a claim which has been accepted by many competent critics. They declare, and he tacitly assumes, that he is master of the English language. He claims a sort of infallibility in deciding upon the

precise use of words and the merits of various styles' (Stephen, 1871: 311). Certainly numerous footnotes in his works in economics are concerned with precise usage.

12 For an account of Bailey's work see R. M. Rauner (1961).

13 By the end of the century, De Quincey's view of Ricardo was subject to polite ridicule: 'De Quincey's presentation of him as a great revealer of truth is now seen to be an extravagance' (Ingram, 1893: 136). Such views ignore the potential irony of De Quincey's hedged comments upon Ricardo and ignore the unhedged comments. De Quincey does directly criticise Ricardo, i.e. without hedging, e.g. 'LAND is another illustration, and of the first rank. Ricardo ought not to have overlooked a case so broad as this' (De Quincey, 1897e: 177) and 'A VERY short chapter, and a very bad one (the worst in the whole series) has been introduced by Ricardo upon market value, quite out of its natural place' (1897e: 200).

14 Ricardo is at greater fault than Adam Smith because Ricardo founded his theory 'upon a much severer logic' (De Quincy, 1897e: 207).

15 Mill (1929: 443) borrowed the 'strawberries' too.

16 Here is another aspect of style which Edgeworth shares with De Quincey: the use of phrases from the established canons of English literature. 'To point a moral as to adorn a tale' is borrowed by Edgeworth from Samuel Johnson's *Vanity of Human Wishes*. I am indebted to Tony Davies for this point.

17 Even his work on Malthus's population theory is focused upon the proportionality analogy, land is to food as food is to people, rather than on a direct concern for social conditions. Where he does mention Poor Relief it is to criticise Malthus and justify Christian charity. See *Greece Under the Romans*.

18 McDonagh cites De Quincey's anti-free trade stance and his opposition to the abolition of slavery as examples of political contrasts between Ricardo and De Quincey (McDonagh, 1994: 52).

19 See his comments on the beaver hat (De Quincey, 1897e: 185) and on Ricardo's 'neglect of the antagonistic principle, which is eternally at work to compensate the declensions of land by countervailing improvements of endless kinds' (1897e: 223).

20 Mill comments on De Quincey's use of teleological value as the 'extreme limit of its exchange value' (Mill, 1929: 442).

21 Once again the tendency towards exaggeration with respect to the justification of De Quincey's judgement.

22 John Ruskin, *Munera Pulveris, The Works of John Ruskin*, Vol. II, George Allen: Orpington, Kent, 1880, Chapter 1.

23 This example is one of many that can be pointed out in the *Logic*. According to Emile Legouis and Louis Cazamian, it is a problem found more generally in De Quincey: 'we find traces of an affected language, which impair an otherwise genuine gift of expression' (Legouis and Cazamian, 1957: 1080). Maniquis talks of passages 'always moving towards a hyperbolic flourish' (Maniquis, 1976: 112).

24 But see Groenewegen (1982: 54 fn3) where a comparison of Chapter I of *Logic* is suggested with Chapter XI of Bailey. Bailey is also mentioned by De Quincey on pp. 269 and 270.

Thomas De Quincey

REFERENCES

De Quincey, T. (1897a) [1824] 'Dialogues of Three Templars on Political Economy' in Masson, D. (ed.) *De Quincey's Works: Political Economy and Politics*, Vol. IX, pp. 37–112.

De Quincey, T. (1897b) [1828] 'Rhetoric' in Masson, D. (ed.) *De Quincey's Works: Literary Theory and Criticism*, Vol. X, London: A & C Black.

De Quincey, T. (1897c) [1840–1841] 'Style' in Masson, D. (ed.) *De Quincey's Works: Literary Theory and Criticism*, Vol. X, London: A & C Black.

De Quincey, T. (1897d) [1842] 'Ricardo and Adam Smith' in Masson, D. (ed.) *De Quincey's Works: Political Economy and Politics*, Vol. IX, London: A & C Black.

De Quincey, T., (1897e) [1844] 'Logic of Political Economy' in Masson, D. (ed.) *De Quincey's Works: Political Economy and Politics*, Vol. IX, London: A & C Black.

De Quincey, T. (1897f) [1845] 'Coleridge and Opium-Eating' in Masson, D. (ed.) *De Quincey's Works: Biographies*, Vol. V, London: A & C Black.

De Quincey, T. (1936) [1823] *De Quincey's Confessions of an English Opium Eater*, London: J. M. Dent and Sons.

Edgeworth, F. Y. (1987) 'De Quincey, Thomas (1785–1859)' in Eatwell, J., Milgate, M. and Newman, P. (eds) *The New Palgrave: A Dictionary of Economics*, London: Macmillan, 812–813, Reprinted from *Palgrave's Dictionary of Political Economy*.

Groenewegen, P. L. (1982) 'Thomas De Quincey: "Faithful Disciple of Ricardo?" ', *Contributions to Political Economy*, I, 51–58.

Heinzelman, K. (1980) *The Economics of the Imagination*, Amherst, Mass.: University of Massachusetts Press.

Hodgson, S. H. (1881) 'De Quincey as Political Economist' in *Outcast Essays and Verse Translations*, London: Longmans, Green and Co.

Ingram, J. K. (1893) *A History of Political Economy*, Edinburgh: A & C Black.

Legouis, E. and Cazamian, L. (1957) *A History of English Literature*, London: J. M. Dent and Sons.

McCulloch, J. R. (1825), *Principles of Political Economy*, London.

McDonagh, J. (1994) *De Quincey's Disciplines*, Oxford: Oxford University Press.

Maniquis, R. (1976) 'Lonely Empires: Personal and Public Visions of Thomas De Quincey', *Literary Monographs* 8, Madison: University of Wisconsin Press, 111–127.

Mill, J. S. (1929) [1848] *Principles of Political Economy* (ed. W. J. Ashley), London: Longmans, Green and Co.

Rauner, R. M. (1961) *Samuel Bailey and the Classical Theory of Value*, London: G. Bell and Sons.

De Quincey, T. (1936) [1823] *De Quincey's Confessions of an English Opium Eater*, London: J. M. Dent and Sons.

Ruskin, J. (1880) *Munera Pulveris: The Works of John Ruskin*, Vol. II, Orpington: George Allen.

Sackville West, E. (1936) *A Flame in Sunlight: Thomas De Quincey*, London: Cassell.

Sherburne, J. C. (1972) *John Ruskin or the Ambiguities of Abundance: A Study in Social Criticism*, Cambridge, Mass.: Harvard University Press.

Stephen, L. (1871) 'De Quincey', *Fortnightly Review* 9, January–June, 310–329.

6

John Ruskin or the political economy of 'soul'

John Ruskin, rarely mentioned in the lengthy histories of economic thought, is popularly known as a critic of art and architecture who taught the mid-Victorians how to 'see' art with new eyes. Though he is credited with influencing the contrasting economic concerns of Marshall and Veblen, the number of essays written on his economics, by economists, are few in number, the contributions by Hobson and Lee being notable exceptions. It is to James C. Sherburne that we have to turn in order to find a thorough-going study of the influences on, and background to, his social and economic thinking.[1] Yet, in the gap between the modified classicism of John Stuart Mill and the marginal revolution inspired by Jevons, Ruskin stands out as the last of the literary Romantics, lashing against the mechanist rigidity of what he saw as an over-developed, over-narrowed, classical political economy. Ruskin wrote no formal economics in the style of De Quincey, or even of Coleridge.[2] He wrote no free-standing economics stories, long or short, in the style of either Edgeworth or Martineau. He read Smith and John Stuart Mill's *Principles*, though the general view is that his study was 'superficial'. By the end of the century he was being read as a great socio-economic reformer and forward-looking thinker (Hobson, 1898; 1919).

This chapter will analyse Ruskin's literary economics in terms of key words and parables, in order to show the consistency and force of his deconstruction of political economy. The method of analysis, based upon ideas derived from the recent 'rhetorical turn' in economics, and on Kurt Heinzelman's interesting exploration of 'the economics of the imagination', will itself also illustrate what is required for the development of an economics understanding of a literary economics that is poetically, rather than canonically, structured (Geddes, 1883: 21; Heinzelman, 1980: x).

John Ruskin

BIOGRAPHICAL INTRODUCTION

Ruskin's biography is relevant to his economics writings in a number of ways. A religious education under his parent's guidance brought him into daily contact with the authorised version of the Bible, a close study of which undoubtedly helped form his love of, and extraordinary skill with, language. The biblical knowledge was used to great effect in *Unto this Last* (1985 [1862]) to attack the economic values of his contemporaries. The use of the parable, a favourite device in his economics writings, also has its origins in bible study. By thrift and hard work, his parents had risen in society but lived, according to Ruskin, without much social refinement or sense of taste, in an atmosphere of near puritan piety and social isolation. John Ruskin respected thrift and came to see it as one of the sources of a justifiable and natural inequality (*Munera Pulveris*, 1880b: 18–19).

Ruskin's familiarity with Carlyle furthered his interest in the nature of words and in etymology as a powerful rhetorical device with which to rebuke his peers. An understanding of words, derived from Carlyle and the Bible, empowered his analysis of economics (Lee, 1981: 74). His study of art and architecture entailed an understanding of artistic production as well as building processes and involved him in the observation of a variety of decorative industries. Forays into workshops and masons' yards, gave him direct contact with aspects of economic life, a contact which Adam Smith (before) and Alfred Marshall (later) also prized. Ruskin stressed the value of this experience. In making any evaluation of the relevance of such knowledge, Bagehot's economics paradox ought to be kept in mind: 'those who are conversant with its abstractions are usually without a true contact as to its facts; those who are in contact with its facts have usually little sympathy with and little cognizance of its abstractions' (Bagehot, 1885: 10). Bagehot is pointing out a bifurcation between theory and practice, between the conflicting evaluations of one form of knowledge and another. Ruskin was to be a victim of the concept of a hierarchy of knowledge in which 'science' is superior to 'literature' and 'masculine' reason superior to 'feminine' emotions. His observations on the development and uses of art and architecture stimulated his interest in the concept of value, of values, of price and of the nature of demand. It is a short step from concern about public taste in art to taste in general and from there to an understanding of the need for consumer education. It is by virtue of biography that his first sustained exercise in economics was *The Political Economy of Art.*

His major works of an overtly economic nature, products of the late 1850s and early 1860s, developed organically from work upon art and architecture and cannot be considered as constituting a radical intellectual break, as he himself tended to present it, with earlier concerns.[3] The works that most directly tackle economic issues are *The Political Economy of Art* (n.d. [1857]), *Unto this Last* (1985 [1862]), *Munera Pulveris* (1880b [1863]), and to a lesser extent *The Crown of Wild Olive* (1882 [1866]), *Time and Tide* (1880c [1867]) and *Fors Clavigera* (1871). These works, though far from standard political economy, certainly fall within the scope of economics education as developed by the earlier writers such as Marcet, Martineau and De Quincey.[4] However, his sense of mission was fundamentally different from theirs. Whereas they propagated classical economics, Ruskin offers a scathing critique. Where they saw 'truths', he saw 'lies'. Where De Quincey narrows, Ruskin stretches. Where Marcet and Martineau saw political economy as a pattern for reform, he saw political economy as a pattern to be reformed. Where Martineau saw economics as a source of ethics, he saw ethics as the source of 'true' economics.

ANALYSING RUSKIN'S ECONOMIC WRITINGS

Ruskin's economics writings are both a source of profound inspiration (Gandhi read and rejoiced in, *Unto this Last*) and of intellectual puzzlement (Wilmer, 1985: 30). Several distinct attempts to convince his contemporaries of his vision of a 'true' economics stirred up little but alarm and resentment.[5] By the end of the century, however, he was being acclaimed by radical liberal reformers as the great prophet of socio-economic change.[6] Even today the richness of his insights have not yet been fully exhausted for he can be seen, without too much forcing, as the first environmental economist, the first human resource manager, the first ethical consumer. Ruskin, then, can be read with a mixture of awe and excitement both for the glory of his most exaggerated and absolute passages and for what commentators tend to see as almost random shafts of light with which he illuminates the various issues relevant to the study of economic abundance.

The main economics writings can be considered either chronologically or thematically. Sherburne initially settled upon the chronology as the simplest. Such an approach carries with it the disadvantage of repetition for Ruskin's insights are layered as his work progresses. The thematic approach, adopted here, can lead to clarity and economy but also to some confusion, as it can obscure some of the problems. Where he knew and understood his audience, Ruskin could speak directly to his society with energetic effect; when there was a mismatch, as must surely be the case with *Munera Pulveris*, he seems not only to lose the reader but also himself. Where his economic ideas are developed primarily as lectures, the rhetorical arts directly informed their structure and style. In treating his audience as society itself and making all questions concerning moral action direct and active, the effect of, say, *The Crown of Wild Olives* must

John Ruskin

have been astounding. Imagine the effect, in a public lecture, of Ruskin's 'What do you mean by doing this?'

WORDS AND IMAGES IN RUSKIN'S 'POLITICAL ECONOMY'

Ruskin is noted for the painterly brilliance of his language. This was used as part of the case against him, by friend as well as foe. As J. W. MacKail puts it, he was dismissed

> as an eccentric and irresponsible man of genius, a writer with a wonderful gift of eloquence who generally talked nonsense, and a champion of absurd paradoxes. It was his bitterest and best-ground complaint, that people read for his style and paid no attention to his meaning.
>
> (McKail, 1919: 10)

Lee quotes Stephen's view that Ruskin was 'a brilliant partisan in a random guerrilla warfare' as a means of buttressing his, that Ruskin's mind worked 'primarily in terms of visual perception, not verbal analysis'. 'Style', the 'added ingredient', rather than the economic content accounts for Ruskin's appeal (Lee, 1981: 74). Whilst there is much in Lee's view, it is based upon a misunderstanding of the relationship between visual perception and verbal analysis, especially when it comes to the written expression of Ruskin's thinking. Lee looks for logic, Ruskin tends to supply literary or poetic analysis which can obscure his underlying analytical content. Lee's view underestimates the power of the imaginative approach to economics as well as the coherent exploration of economic agency to be found in Ruskin's work. Ruskin requires a different kind of reading.

Key words

Ruskin is concerned with words and meanings, the stuff of much literary economics.[7] In justifying a poetic investigation of the words used by economists, Heinzelman calls upon Macfie's notion that in rationalising, economics 'creates the experience with which it deals' (Heinzelman, 1980: x). If political economy created the economic experiences of the nineteenth century, Ruskin is creating an alternative economic experience. Key words, as used here, are taken to be concept words, so important to shaping the discourse and common to both the discipline of political economy and to Ruskin. He returns, throughout his writings on economics, to these essential words. It is not easy to separate them from the rhetorical contexts within which they are developed. In a sense the meanings are cumulative and organically part of his writings. There are

115

at least two things to be gained by attempting a systematic separation: it helps order the various writings and helps point up the consistency.

We can start from Hobson's assumption that after Smith, political economy experienced 'a narrowing and degrading process' which led to it becoming not a critique of society but 'the bond slave of the rising manufacturing and trading classes' (Hobson, 1919: 83). This view need not be swallowed whole for Hobson rewrites Ruskin in his own image. Mill and others argued for the neutrality of political economy. However, from at least 1832, and earlier, and thanks to Martineau and others, there was a recurrent notion that political economy was a set of truths. This notion was contested. It was also recurrent. If this is the context, then, Ruskin engages in a process of helping society 'see' a wider and more humanising possibility for political economy. In the face of social truths, Ruskin stresses the reality of moral choice. Visual pictures are important, and their role is analysed below, but, if they are to be taken seriously, need to have some intellectual substance. For Ruskin, words such as 'value' and 'economy' as used by economists illustrated a particular form of the narrowing process. In Ricardo's economics, also noted by De Quincey, 'value depends not upon abundance, but on the difficulty or facility of production'. In economics usage, 'value' loses the sense both of 'values' (ethics) and of 'valuable', for in the discourse of the economist, inferior coloured etchings are also 'valuable' (Ruskin, 1880b: vi).

'Economy' too gradually loses its associations with 'the household' and the sense of moral order that a well-run household exhibits. Ruskin pushes the ideas back to their origins in order to frame economic life on an organic rather than a compartmentalised or mechanistic basis. The domestic origins are explored within a set of domestic images that together constitute a parable. The parable is analysed as a set of images in the section headed 'Words and pictures'. For Ruskin, political economy is not some abstract, mechanistic and self-referencing system, justified by 'arithmetic', but a set of ideas focused upon the problem of economic behaviour and justice within given social settings. However, care is required. Ruskin uses the term 'political economy' to refer to the theories of conventional political economy, and to the values that such theories engendered, sometimes referred to as 'mercantile economy' in which the chief value is individual greed. He uses it also to point to the 'true' political economy, analogously constructed upon domestic economy, to which Ruskin himself adheres. Such confusions give rise to the 'unfair to political economy' argument often used against Ruskin. Popular criticism and even scientific criticism of political economy continued into the 1870s and 1880s and in 1876 an attempt was made to remove the Economic Section from the British Association. In 1878 Ingram delivered a strong criticism of the methods of political economy judged by at least one contemporary as to be 'exceeding anything of that kind ever

John Ruskin

attempted by Mr. Ruskin' (Geddes, 1883: 8). The 'true' political economy sometimes consists in the application of ideas to specific kinds of problems such as the modification of demand by ethically informed expenditures and sometimes to individual moral agency. 'True' value requires economic morality, hence honest workers, engaged in 'wise work' (work which is 'honest, useful and cheerful') are all 'political economists in the true and final sense' (Ruskin, 1882: 52). Ruskin does not always signal the usage.

The concern for the meaning of words gives him a bond with De Quincey and with the other Romantics and a direct line to late postmodernism. Although Mill too, and Ricardo and De Quincey, were concerned with meanings, Lee's consciousness of the 'peculiarity' of Ruskin is partly derived from expectations engendered by how words are used in canonical writings. It is Ruskin's key words; 'economy', 'values', 'riches', 'wealth' and 'illth' and a family of words associated with his critique of the narrowing and distorting notion of 'economic man', and his treatment of them, that constitute the basis for any systematic element in his economics thinking. De Quincey and Mill share this concern for words with Ruskin. The nineteenth century gave rise to a whole new set of words or meaning, part of the set 'industry, democracy, class, art and culture', which had their origins in the need to construct as well as describe the new manufacturing society (Williams, 1960: xv, xvii). Economics as a science attempted to pin down meanings of words associated with changes in economic life, words relating to value, to production, competition and work. Ruskin attempted to open them up. The list of key words derived from Ruskin given here is not exhaustive. Ruskin's own list would have contained the word 'co-operation' by which he meant aspects of behaviour which were the opposite of 'competition' (Ruskin, 1880c: 6).

The nineteenth-century economists, in the interests of science and of professionalism, developed a specialist vocabulary which attempted to separate key terms from associations established in social discourse (Heinzelman, 1980: 70–109). Ruskin attempts to restore the wider usage to discussion about economic life. He is deconstructing the existing system and showing the possibilities of a new system, though, even in (or especially in) *Munera Pulveris*, he is unable to construct it on a coherent and sustained basis. The force of his writing is therefore analytical as well as educational, it focuses on altering perceptions and in the achievement of change, he resorts to whatever works. Through his analysis of meanings, however, Ruskin achieves a measure of theoretical insight from which policy conclusions can be derived.

John Ruskin

Value and values

The question of value is a recurrent theme in Ruskin's polemical economics. It is so central that the themes are best suggested through the examination of his other notions of 'work' and 'labour' and of 'wealth' and 'illth'. Value is located in the absolute power of anything to support and sustain life in the fullest sense. From a consideration of the classical origins of the notion of value, Ruskin holds in *Unto this Last* that, 'to be "valuable" is to "avail towards life" ' (Ruskin, 1985: 209). Ruskin keeps his eyes firmly fixed on the capacity towards life. But this is not enough, for economic action is not lodged in inanimate things but in the responses of human beings: the right things in the right hands (Ruskin, 1985: 211). Moral action is inescapable in the contemplation of value and in other areas of political economy. And moral action is based upon the reality of human choice rather than upon any 'laws' of economics (Ruskin, 1880b: xxiv). He also insists, in a way which would appeal to modern notions of literary criticism, that terms in a thoughtless political economy are capable of implying their opposite, of operating through their own negations. Thus 'wealth' implies 'illth', 'riches' implies 'poverty' and 'getting on' implies impeding the progress of others. Ruskin is able to give these insights analytical substance in his consideration of the nature of economic welfare.

Work and labour

Ruskin's concerns include the disassociation of 'labour' from 'work' and from that of the person working and the removal of the emotions from any direct contact with the formal discourse. The objection to the notion of 'economic man' is his most general critique of the political economist's notion of human agency, his concern about 'labour' and 'work', the more specific. His views on economic man are carried, in *Unto this Last*, by a brilliant aphorism. Ruskin is as 'uninterested' in the conclusions of a science based upon the human being as a 'covetous machine' as he would be 'in those of a science of gymnastics which assumed that men have no skeletons' (Ruskin, 1985: 168).[8] However, Ruskin continues by making an imaginative illustration of the inappropriate assumption of selfishness by presenting the problem of distributing an 'only crust of bread' in a starving household. Ruskin shows that the outcome will not necessarily be antagonistically determined. This type of context is precisely what contemporary economists, critical of neo-classical approaches to the allocation problem, use to illustrate the role of reciprocity and justice.[9] He then generalises:

> And the variety of circumstances which influence these reciprocal interests are so endless, that all endeavour to deduce rules of action

from the balance of expediency is in vain. And it is meant to be in vain. For no human actions were intended by the Maker of men to be guided by balances of expediency, but by balances of justice.[10]

(Ruskin, 1985: 169)

Justice is intended to include possibilities of social sympathy, reciprocity and self-realisation. The motivating power of the economic agent is neither 'steam, magnetism, gravitation, or any agent of calculable force' but 'Soul'. 'Soul' is to be taken to mean individual personality and capacity for 'moral energy' and to stand in contradiction to depersonalised 'labour'. For 'brave and rightly-trained men; their work is first, their fee second' (Ruskin, n.d.: 46). This insight leads to an understanding, shared by modern human resource management theory, that:

The largest quantity of work will not be done by this curious engine for pay, or under pressure, or by help of any kind which may be supplied by the chaldron. It will be done only when the motive force, that is to say, the will or the spirit of the creature, is brought to its greatest strength by its own proper fuel: namely, by the affections.

(Mill, 1844: 47)

Ruskin's poetics achieves a conclusion which has implications for both scientific argument and humanitarian sentiment (Hobson, 1919: 87; Geddes, 1883: 37–38). Money gives power over fellow human beings but people 'themselves are the wealth', the 'true veins of wealth are purple – and not in Rock, but in Flesh' (Ruskin, 1985: 189). These are not cheap jibes at conventional thinking, though they can be construed as such, but interesting insights. Ruskin knows that it is not enough to point out the paradoxes and contrasts. *Munera Pulveris*, in ironic mimicry of the political economy textbook, sets out to offer a re-construction but fails.

A concern for 'work' rather than depersonalised 'labour' informs his vision of the degradation which flows from the division of labour: 'It is not, truly speaking, the labour that is divided, but the men; Divided into mere segments' (Ruskin, 1880a: 196). Ruskin argues for variety and self-expression and gives, in *The Political Economy of Art*, a convincing concrete example (the carving of capitals) of how variation may reduce cost through the stimulation of effort. Sherburne argues that in making the analysis, Ruskin is not original but part of longer-term criticism of the negative consequences of the division of labour (Sherburne, 1972: 49). However, there are two areas in which Ruskin's analysis is original. In *Unto this Last*, there is a richer and (to bourgeois sentiment) more disturbing idea found in his notion of the exchange of labour. If payment is demanded then 'equity demands time for time, strength for strength, skill for skill' (Ruskin, 1985: 195). Life is finite; time spent working cannot bc redeemed, labour is 'the spending of life' and a true measure of cost is the 'distress' involved (Ruskin, 1880b: 52).

The finite nature of human life and the understanding that enhanced human beings constitute the 'true' wealth of nations leads to the idea that the management of people is a central aspect of economic management both at the level of the household and of the state. The individual consumer, whose money gives power over the allocation of labour time, should avoid items produced by degrading working people and purchase only the products of 'healthy and ennobling labour'. In *Unto this Last* Ruskin makes the rules of ethical consumption, as understood today by Oxfam and others, clear:

> In buying, consider, first, what condition of existence you cause in the producers of what you buy; secondly, whether the sum you have paid is just to the producer, and in due proportion, lodged in his hands; thirdly, to how much clear use, for food, knowledge, or joy, this that you have bought can be put; and fourthly, to whom and in what way it can be most speedily and serviceably distributed.
>
> (Ruskin, 1985: 227)

The consumer is not a mechanistic dummy but a sentient being capable of reflecting upon the ends being pursued and the costs of pursuing them. The problem of agency is again faced: the market, in which the demand for commodities is a demand for labour, is not so much rejected in this view as modified by the educated consumer.

Wealth and illth

In attempting an analysis of wealth, Ruskin in *Unto this Last*, in contradistinction to Mill, seeks for 'metaphysical nicety of definition'.[11] He insists upon riches as a 'relative word' which implies its opposite: 'riches are a power like electricity, acting only through inequalities or negations of itself'. Ruskin depicts the road to riches as 'the art of establishing the maximum inequality in our own favour' (Ruskin, 1985: 182). Whether such inequalities are advantageous or disadvantageous depends on whether or not wealth was justly or unjustly established. Justly established inequalities 'benefit the nation in the course of their establishment; and, nobly used, aid it yet more by their existence'. Ruskin sustains the image of a healthy economic morality through the analogy of the circulation of wealth with that of the circulation of the blood, a further development of the notion of 'The Veins of Wealth'.

He follows up the description with an illustration, heralded by the word that was to become the trademark of economic story telling: 'suppose'! The passage tells the story of two cast-away sailors and the society that they create. The story carries two interacting ideas, that of money as the product of debt and that of how a 'mercantile economy' leads to decreases in total wealth. The sailors agree to divide their land and to cultivate separately. One falls ill and remains so for several seasons. The sick sailor pledges, in the form of written promises, his labour in the future against present provisioning by the healthy man. When he returns to health and work, he must pay off the debt. One would then be commercially rich and with no need to work, purchasing the labour of the other with the written promises, and the other commercially poor. But the 'mercantile wealth which consists in a claim upon labour, signifies a political diminution of the real wealth which consists in substantial possessions' (Ruskin, 1985: 185–186). The inequalities have been unjustly arrived at and the result is neither harmonious nor noble.

Ruskin restates these points, more formally, in *Munera Pulveris*. In looking at the quantity of a nation's wealth, we need to be also concerned with its distribution and 'we have to inquire, with respect to any given state of riches, precisely in what manner the correlative poverty was produced: that is to say, whether by being surpassed only, or being depressed also' (Ruskin, 1880b: 20). The real value of national wealth 'depends on the moral sign attached to it, just as sternly as that of a mathematical quantity depends on the algebraical sign attached to it' (Ruskin, 1985: 187). Here is the modern notion that the size of the national product is not a measure of welfare, and that further questions, about aspects such as the distribution of income, the composition of output and the quality of life, need to be asked. Elsewhere, Ruskin had made it clear that the hidden poverty of the seamstress and the gaudy clothes of the followers of fashion are only made possible by an unjust distribution of income. His use of the parable of the vineyard suggests that Ruskin was vividly aware of the notion of the poverty-trap and was searching for a moral vocabulary and set of personal actions which would help to avoid it. The epilogue to the 'Veins of Wealth', rich in visions of Byzantine gold in the eyes of the barbarians, makes further moves that complete his extended metaphor: he identifies 'wealth' with living souls. Wealth in the tale consists in 'power over men'. It is but a short step from there to the notion that 'persons *are* the wealth' and hence to the notion that 'whether, among national manufacturers, that of Souls of good quality may not at last turn out a quite leadingly lucrative one?' (Ruskin, 1985: 189).

Life is wealth and 'Intrinsic value is the absolute power of anything to support life'. Sherburne has encapsulated Ruskin's views on wealth and value as 'the drive towards life'. The maturing Ruskin felt that 'all the peace and power and joy' that can ever be won can only ever be won in life (Ruskin, 1882: 18). Production is for supporting and enhancing life in all its possibilities. Anything in production that is not producing 'wealth' in this respect is producing 'illth', its natural opposite. It is the business, according to Ruskin, of a 'true' political economy to be able to distinguish between the two categories, to support *laissez-faire* is to abandon ethical responsibility. In poor societies, the problem scarcely arises because such economies are in the grip of scarcity. Ruskin was one of the first, according to Sherburne to contemplate the problems of economic organisation in a context in which abundance was quickly becoming the economic basis within which society operated. Abundance implies an ability to choose and Ruskin raises the question 'what to choose'? Conventional economics tends to talk only in terms of 'goods' even when the 'goods' are recognisable 'bads'. It is not hard to distinguish items which could be considered as 'illth'. Ruskin includes degrading working conditions: spoiled countryside, described as 'the slow stealing of aspects of reckless, indolent, animal neglect' (Ruskin, 1882: 2), spoiled cities, the manufacture of guns and the capitalist-inspired international trade in them, iron railings and much more. Under a subjective notion of value and a market system of allocation, it is difficult to find a non-authoritarian basis for agreement as to what ought and what ought not to be included in the list. Ethical consumers would help, of course, to reduce 'illth' as would governments motivated by a concern for people. Ruskin is aware that by concentrating on the necessary constraints upon liberty, he is making an argument from a different stand-point from that of Mill in *On Liberty* (1977 [1859]).

RUSKIN'S STYLE

Words and pictures

What had helped change perceptions in his art and architecture writings were elaborate word-pictures and vivid images. This technique is applied to developing a picture of political economy and the verbal analysis and poetic pictures come together. In this sense, he is very close to Martineau. Ruskin's pictures are more vivid and more concentrated. Their role, unlike pictures in Martineau, is to provide a striking symbol in whose terms his economic parable can be told or an alternative moral image understood. Ruskin's pictures consist in parables, biblical quotations and aphorisms. His favourite device is to use wholesome images, to contrast with mechanistic greed, and simple contexts: the image of the perfect housewife balancing utility with the decorative arts; of the farmer's wife concerned with the productive employment of the domestic servants; the almost literal picture of the ethical requirements of good government derived from a painting in Sienna; the moral nature of government and its domestic responsibilities for the just regulation of economic life.

The Sienna fresco is brilliantly analysed as a symbol of good civic government and glowingly conveyed to the reader. The key concepts are

John Ruskin

Faith, Hope and Charity together with the dependent virtues of 'fortitude, temperance and truth' (Ruskin, n.d.: 47). His notion of the economic responsibility of government suggests a role in the maintenance of economic stability and full employment. The domestic basis of the economy is stressed, its integration into life as it is lived. Although working towards a wider notion of political economy, Ruskin is not pursuing the social science method of empiricism, nor the literary device of social realism: his farmyards and economic storehouses are neither the product of field studies nor of fiction seeking to imitate fact. They are, rather, products of his imagination, perhaps having more in common with biblical notions of rural estates than contemporary ones. He insists that the economic world and its 'true' regulation can only be created by imaginative force.

Three parables can provide illustration of his method. The first is the use that is made of the parable of the talents, drawn straight from the Gospel according to Matthew, in the New Testament (Matthew 25:14–30). Ruskin challenges the standard interpretations by insisting that it is to be taken literally. The subject is 'money', another of Ruskin's key words. The problem that the parable deals with, according to Ruskin, is the use to which wealth is to be put in the proactive promotion of human economic activity essential to support and sustain others. The burying of a talent of money can bring nothing but distress to the wider community, as Keynesian demand analysis makes clear. Hoarding is not useful. A talent, in biblical times, was a huge amount of money: Goulder estimates that Matthew's householder 'entrusts nothing less than a talent to his servants, ten, twenty and fifty thousand *denarii*, a man's wage for 30, 60, 150 years' (Goulder, 1968: 54). If this is the case then the force both of the economic concept and the moral concept is powerful: a lifetime of consumerism or of hoarding is to be accounted for. Here Matthew's parable is given direct economic force by a literal interpretation (it does not work so well with Luke's, for he moved in a much stingier world). Those with wealth must understand their moral obligations. Money is command over the work of others; it is better used than not used. Wise use is life promoting and non-use, life defeating. Ruskin is preoccupied with the notion of economic agency and agency is a general phenomenon because it is embodied in people and not in abstractions. The contrast between his notion and that created by the withering image of economic man is huge. Agency in this parable is that of the ethical investor.

The second example is the parable of the farmyard, in which the good farmer's wife regulates the productive employment of the domestics rather than have them stand idle. The word 'economy' is derived from *oikonomia*, a Greek word suggesting the management of a household (Heinzelman, 1980: ix). Ruskin is not alone in making reference to the domestic origins of the term economics. Such usage is to be found in

123

writers of classical economics such as McCulloch and, indeed, these origins allowed Martineau to envisage domestic scenes within which the problem of agency in political economy can find illustration. Margaret Thatcher, during the 1980s, used very similar images to argue for the radical extension of market forces within society. By taking the original meaning at face value, Ruskin is able to develop and sustain an analogy between the household and society as a basis for an alternative political economy and source of authority. Although the farmyard provides a strong link with nature, Ruskin, as with the parables of Matthew, is concerned not with nature but with human action and values. Whilst the Greek derivation of economy points to the classical origins of Ruskin's economic thinking, Matthew's parables and their association with work and with rural estates, underscore much of Ruskin's sense of justice. Ruskin challenges the notion of economy which makes it co-extensive with the idea of 'sparing' and 'saving' and provides his first fully fledged definition of economy:

> It means the administration of a house; its stewardship; spending or saving, that is whether money or time, or anything else, to the best possible advantage. In the simplest and clearest definition of it, economy, whether public or private, means the wise management of labour.
>
> (Ruskin, n.d.: 16)

This notion of stewardship is also consistent with the parables of Matthew.

In *The Political Economy of Art*, the move from the administration of a house to the housewife is accomplished very quickly and the image of 'the perfect economist' introduced: the mistress of a household who balances 'division of her care between the two great objects of utility and splendour' (Ruskin, n.d.: 17). The sexual economy is clear, for the farmer's wife is not the farmer, but the precise role of the farmer is unclear. Ruskin stresses the notion of balance as a means of avoiding the passion for property and reinforces this with images of domesticity, the 'wise cottager's garden' where produce is balanced between vegetables and flowers, produce which satisfy the body and the soul, and 'the good housewife' balancing resources. Where the balance is lost, the economy is wanting. For all the natural elements, balance is the responsibility of the people concerned. At the same time, the passage also makes clear that the husbanding of labour is an important aspect of household economy.

The economical management of labour consists in rational application, the preservation of its 'produce' and 'distributing its produce seasonally'. Here the language implies the garden or farm: work leading to a harvest to be stored and distributed over time. Ruskin is drawn to an analysis based upon stocks, rather than upon flows, of commodities. The origin of this is 'farm domestic' but also stems from the contemplation of accumulated stocks of paintings from the past which need to be protected from decay and mistreatment (illustrated in the next parable below). The agent is concerned with household economy but the wise allocation of labour is an essential feature of such economy. Leaving workers standing idle is a waste of their productive time, for there is a direct fulfilment to be found in work that is not to be found in idle gossip, and leads to a loss of alternative production that follows on from lack of direction.

The paternalism is clear, the point of view is not primarily that of the workers themselves. The lesson is that government as economic agent stands in an analogous relationship to the population in terms of the regulation of the 'national store'. The analysis of 'household economy' is developed in order to contrast it with 'mercantile economy', the contrived picture of both formal political economy and the set of economic values which it was popularly deemed to support. Ruskin embodies agency in human action rather than in abstract market forces and attempts to derive from the actualisation of agency, rules for the regulation of economic life that go beyond an uncritical reading of the market. Ruskin is consistent in his criticism of political economy as a subject 'based on the idea that an advantageous code of social action may be determined irrespectively of social affection' (Ruskin, 1985: 167).

The third parable providing an illustration of Ruskin's method is the 'Tintoret' episode taken from the introduction to *Munera Pulveris*. The passage is another lesson reflecting on the nature, rather than the uses, of wealth. Three paintings by the artist are hanging in tatters on 'the roof of the School of St. Roch' as a result of 'Austrian heavy shot'. Their neglect is contrasted with the demand, in Paris, for tinted lithographs depicting 'the modern dances of delight', including 'the cancan'. Ruskin contrasts the 'false riches' of the coloured lithographs with the 'absolute and inestimable wealth' of the sorry fragments in Venice (1880b: vii–ix). This contrastive approach is again reminiscent of Matthew's (and Luke's) parables in which contrasts have an important part to play (Goulder, 1968: 56). Ruskin challenges the notion of an unquestioning acceptance of a market evaluation by using the notion of intrinsic value. He generalises his results from the arts to 'beasts of burden' and supplies further evidence, from the relief of the siege of Paris, of the necessity for maintaining a standard other than the market for regulating economic life. Here, the problem is not so much one of illustrating agency but of illustrating the consequences of an uncritical reading of the market as understood by his contemporaries. The lesson becomes a richer one when it is understood, as he makes clear in *Munera Pulveris*, that whilst there is intrinsic value, it is of little consequence unless consumers have the capacity to make use of the value that is potentially on offer to them: 'A horse is no wealth to us if we cannot ride, nor a picture if we cannot see, *nor any noble thing except to a noble person*' (1880b: 11). Nobility can be the product of education and experience, for it is a matter of moral quality rather than of birthright. To achieve a critical reading of the market, consumer education becomes essential.

Order and authority in Ruskin are not derived from the abstract notion of the market but from the integration of moral values and action within the context of established social institutions. This is what justifies Ruskin's self-styled Tory label. He is not, however, complacent about institutions. In considering the attributes of 'expectant' government he states: 'if it ceases to be hopeful of better things, it ceases to be a wise guardian of present things; that it ought never, as long as the world lasts, to be wholly content with any existing state of institution or possession' (Ruskin, n.d.: 47). But it is by reason and 'peaceful strength' that any institutional reform is to take place (Ruskin, 1880c: 17). Ruskin is deeply suspicious of any notion of 'economy' or 'market' cut off from what he sees as an ethical base. He does not totally reject the market but wishes to see it regulated by good government and by a well-informed consumer who thinks before spending money. Good government is economically active, wise and compassionate and capable of keeping faith, promoting work on a steady basis, in spite of adverse economic conditions (Ruskin, n.d.: 47). This can be interpreted as a concern for economic stability. For a good consumer thought is essential for what money gives is not command over commodities but over the time of the worker. Time spent by finite human beings is lost from life for ever. He also wishes to see all young, and not just artistic, talent brought to the best fitting 'occupations' by some system, other than 'by malicious collision and competition' (Ruskin, 1880c: 8). The allocation of life opportunities is considered too important to be left to the market alone.

What are the elements of this style which caused so many different reactions? Is it possible, in Ruskin, to distinguish style from substance? Was he the victim of his own rhetorical strategies? Parables and homely analogies, rather than worked out logical interrelations, constitute the educational core of his work. Unlike the gospel parables, which, according at least to Matthew, were delivered not to instruct and enlighten but so that many could hear and *not* understand (in other words there is an intended allegorical element in some parables), Ruskin's parables, created within a rich web of brilliant language, and sometimes first encountered by his public as spoken, rather than written, discourse, are to be felt, experienced and so imaginatively understood. Whilst Ruskin drew strength from the domestic origins of Greek thinking on economy, his parables have many New Testament elements. Biblical quotations, set within the context of such wordy subject matter, were selected to shock the first generation of readers but could also be used to draw the listener or reader into the discourse as with the story of Jacob's dream set in 'the moorland hollow' of Wharnside (Ruskin, 1882: 75).

John Ruskin

Ruskin's characteristic style is, in a manner, that which F. Y. Edgeworth was later also to use, piling image upon image, clause after clause, and so building to a climax: 'the vice of jealousy, which brings competition into your commerce, treachery into your councils, and dishonour into your wars' (Ruskin, 1882: 69). Parallelisms of this nature, either at the level of the sentence or extended over a whole paragraph, are sustained by a poetic use of a large and impressive vocabulary and are designed to be heard as it is read, make each point count. As each individual brings a personal framework for the interpretation of a text, an emotionally strong text is very likely to have unpredictable impacts. This was the case with the public reaction to *Unto this Last*. The fact that Ruskin operates upon the emotions, both in the images that he paints and in the language that he uses, tends to obscure the more measured analysis, an analysis which he insists, paradoxically, is not there to be evangelically propagated!

The emotional nature of Ruskin's writing was despised by his critics, leading to judgements about the hysterical and feminine nature of his writing. The intention was to shock his listeners and readers out of complacency and help them imagine better possibilities for production, consumption and distribution. He also analysed them and was disheartened when his analyses were overlooked. Such analyses are carried by his evaluation of the meanings of key words though these meanings, as in *Unto this Last*, need to be gathered from various points in the text. *Munera Pulveris*, because it is ironically constructed in the form of a political economy textbook, is more systematic. None the less, by carefully recording the insights, the methodological challenge to mechanistic thought and its market and social implications, constructed upon a sustained critique of the notion of economic man and of a self-referenced economic system, provides the means for reading beyond existing views of economic life.

CONCLUSION

John Ruskin's poetic construction of a 'true' political economy does not represent a fully developed set of ideas of the same logical order as those embodied in the canonical writings of David Ricardo or John Stuart Mill. Equally, they are not to be considered simply as a jumbled set of imaginatively constructed, but none the less naïve, images and insights. Some of his ideas are, of course, naïve. The re-establishment of guilds or his notions of price could certainly be considered as such. But the set of ideas, taken as a whole, cannot be simply considered in this way. Ruskin's analytical strengths are to be located, contrary to Lee's assessment, both in his parables and in his challenging verbal analyses. The works, when explored in terms of key words as well as key images, can be seen as a series of constructive reflections upon the nature of economic agency in the context of potential social abundance. In this context they then exhibit a consistency of purpose and image, capable of carrying ethical, policy and scientific implications. Ruskin's work is not, strictly speaking, an evaluation of canonical writings but an alternative to them, though a complete assessment requires them both to be considered together. Ruskin challenges the scientific coldness of economics which he feels distances the reader from social realities. Nevertheless his alternatives to the market economy, the household, based on the sexual division of labour and paternalistic government, remain unattractive.

In his ethical economics, life is the initiation, and death the negation, of economy. The objectives are not narrowly fixed upon a depersonalised consumer, but on human agency operating in every social context (including government) relevant to production, distribution and consumption. He asked his contemporaries to look beyond a mechanistic interpretation of the market and to work towards an imaginative understanding of economic problems within the framework of human, rather than mechanistic, agency *and* of abundance. Ruskin targets a set of values founded upon a narrowed classical economics as well as classical economics as such. His work speaks as directly to present day British society, attempting to come to terms with the legacy of Thatcherite economics, as it did to Britain at the end of the nineteenth century. Thatcherite economics is, none the less, in terms of its location in household economy and domestic management, rhetorically indebted (paradoxically) to Ruskin.

Ruskin rarely gives critical attention to any particular text, though John Stuart Mill is consistently criticised in the context of *Unto this Last,* and the term 'political economy' is used in a number of different senses. Mill's *Principles* text today is, possibly, not much more than an interesting, and finely written, historical document carrying little of the continued intellectual interest of his essay *On Liberty.* Ruskin's critique of the social and ethical basis of 'economy', of value and values, of wealth and of 'illth' and of the mechanistic and atomistic construction of economic life retain an interest and freshness in much the same way as Mill's essay. This is particularly true of *Unto this Last,* less so of *The Political Economy of Art* and perhaps not at all so of *Munera Pulveris.* The ethical messages that they carry still have contemporary significance. Economic agency, the nature and measurement of economic welfare, the ethics of the market place, the limitations of the market economy, ethical consumerism and other issues exercised Ruskin and speak directly to us. To gain access to them we need to shed expectations generated by canonical writings and be prepared to explore Ruskin as an interconnected series of poetic and imaginative impulses designed to help us read beyond the logical structure of economic thinking. In terms of literary economics and economics education, Ruskin, heir to Carlyle, both carries on, and also negates, the literary traditions established by the women writers at the start of the century. If they taught society how to read economics, Ruskin taught how to go beyond that reading to undertake an imaginative re-reading, both of text and of society itself, and hence undertake a liberating deconstruction of the results.

NOTES

1 See Hobson (1898), (1919); Lee (1981); Sherburne (1972).
2 Coleridge, although he too wished to see a broader economics, had at least read individual texts and responds to them directly. Ruskin criticises a general, perhaps even popular, version of the ideas to which he is opposed.
3 In his autobiography, *Praeterita*. See Ruskin (1978).
4 *Unto this Last*, when published in book form, did not achieve any popular success until nearer the end of the century (Lee, 1981: 83).
5 Patrick Geddes gives a generalised account, which he later contests, of popular reaction:

> Our would-be economist is but an artist born out of his proper mediaeval time; his mournful jeremiads, nay, whole books of lamentations, with their wailing retrospects of the good old times, and their bitterly pessimistic prophecies, far out-Carlyling Carlyle, are perhaps natural for him but clearly useless for us.
>
> (Geddes, 1883)

6 Ruskin was content 'to wait the public's time' though he announced himself frustrated at his inability to convince that the real value of work 'depends on the final intrinsic worth of the thing that you make' (Ruskin, 1882: 9).
7 His statement in 'The Veins of Wealth' ought not mislead: 'I would not contend in this matter (and rarely in any matter) for the acceptance of terms' for it is immediately followed by a 'But' (Ruskin, 1985: 181).
8 It is customary to spring to the defence of political economy at this point. Mill, for example, was aware of the need to be careful of the way in which human agents were viewed. Mill said of Bentham that he never recognised that 'Man' was 'a being capable of pursuing spiritual perfection as an end'. Mill, 'On Bentham and Coleridge', p. 66.
9 See, by way of illustration, Mehta, 1993: 85.
10 Ruskin's writing is the product of art not simply of inspiration. Specific examples are often followed by generalisation:

> honesty, or generosity, – or what used to be called 'virtue' – may be calculated upon as a human motive of action, people always answer me, saying, 'You must not calculate on that: that is not in human nature: you must not assume anything to be common to men but acquisitiveness and jealousy; no other feeling ever has influence on them, except accidentally, and in matters out of the way of business.'

11 Ruskin tends to attack Mill by taking his ideas out of context. It is clear from Mill (1929: 47) that Mill accepted that new usages were required and that the skill of the worker constitutes part of wealth. Agreements or disagreements with Mill are interesting but not essential for the development of an understanding of Ruskin.

John Ruskin

REFERENCES

Bagehot, W. (1885) *The Postulates of English Political Economy*, London: Longmans, Green and Co. (student edition).

Geddes, P. (1883) *John Ruskin, Economist*, Round Table Series III, Edinburgh: William Brown.

Goulder, M. D. (1968) 'Characteristics of the Parables in the Several Gospels', *Journal of Theological Studies*, N.S. xix, 51–69.

Heinzelman, K. (1980) *The Economics of the Imagination*, Amherst: University of Massachusetts Press.

Hobson, J. A. (1898) *John Ruskin Social Reformer*, London: James Nisbett.

Hobson, J. A. (1919) 'Ruskin as Political Economist' in Whitehouse, J. Howard (ed.) *Ruskin the Prophet and other Centenary Studies*, London: George Allen and Unwin.

Lee, A. (1981) 'Ruskin and Political Economy: *Unto this Last*' in Hewison, R. (ed.) *New Approaches to Ruskin*, London: Routledge and Kegan Paul.

McKail, J. W. (1919) in Whitehouse, J. H. (ed.) *Ruskin Centenary Address 1919*, Oxford: Oxford University Press.

Mehta, J. (1993) 'Meaning in the Context of Bargaining Games – Narratives in Opposition' in Henderson, W., Dudley-Evans, T., and Backhouse, R. (eds) *Economics and Language*, London: Routledge.

Mill, J. S. (1929 [1848]) *Principles of Political Economy* (ed. W. J. Ashley), London: Longmans, Green and Co.

Mill, J. S. (1977 [1859]) *On Liberty* in *Collected Works of John Stuart Mill* (ed. J. M. Robinson), Toronto.

Ruskin, J. (n.d. [1857]) *The Political Economy of Art*, in *Sesame and Lilies etc.* London and Glasgow: Collins Clear-type.

Ruskin, J. (1888a [1853]) *The Stones of Venice* in *The Works of John Ruskin*, vol. I, Orpington: George Allen.

Ruskin, J. (1880b [1863]) *Munera Pulveris* in *The Works of John Ruskin*, vol. II, Orpington: George Allen.

Ruskin, J. (1880c [1867]) *Time and Tide* in *The Works of John Ruskin*, vol. V, Orpington: George Allen.

Ruskin, J. (1882 [1866]) *The Crown of Wild Olive* in *The Works of John Ruskin*, vol. VI, Orpington: George Allen.

Ruskin, J. (1978 [1889]) *Praeteria, the Autobiography of John Ruskin* (ed. K. Clarke), Oxford: Oxford University Press.

Ruskin, J. (1985 [1862]) *Unto this Last and other Writings* (ed. C. Wilmer), London: Penguin Books Wilmer, C. (1985) 'Introduction' in *Unto this Last and Other Writings*, London: Penguin Books.

Ruskin, J. (1886 [1871]) *Fors Clavigera* in *The Works of John Ruskin*, vol. VII, Orpington: George Allen.

Sherburne, J. C. (1972) *John Ruskin or the Ambiguities of Abundance: A Study in Social and Economic Criticism*, Harvard: Harvard University Press.

Williams, R. (1960) *Culture and Society 1780–1950*, London: Chatto and Windus.

Wilmer, C. (1985) 'Introduction' in *Unto this Last and Other Writings*, London: Penguin Books.

7

The problem of
Edgeworth's style

Comments on the significance of Edgeworth in the history of economic thought normally make references to Edgeworth's style. Keynes, for example, in his splendidly wicked *Essays in Biography*, commented on Edgeworth's style in the following way:

> Edgeworth's peculiarities of style, his brilliance in phrasing, his obscurity of connection, his inconclusiveness of aim, his restlessness of direction, his courtesy, his caution, his shrewdness, his wit, his subtlety, his learning, his reserve – all are there fully grown. Quotations from the Greek tread on the heels of the differential calculus, and the philistine reader can scarcely tell whether it is a line from Homer or a mathematical abstraction which is in course of integration.
>
> (Keynes, 1972: 257)

This assessment is quoted, with approval, by Creedy who holds that the description can be applied to Edgeworth's other two books (Creedy, 1986: 27).

Keynes had other things to say. Fearing criticism, Edgeworth, in his later works, endeavoured:

> to draw a veil of practical concealment over his native style, which only served however, to enhance the obscurity and allusiveness and half-apologetic air with which he served up his intellectual dishes.
>
> (Keynes, 1972: 258)

Creedy, in a brief examination of Edgeworth's character, reports Butler on the family convention of 'rather formal good manners and conversation' (Butler, 1972: 136) and Graves on Edgeworth's avoidance of 'conversational English' and his persistent use of 'words and phrases that one expects to meet only in books' (Graves, 1960: 136).

Questions of character and personal style are interwoven by others interested in Edgeworth and his writings. Newman has a lengthy section headed 'Character and style' (Newman, 1987: 87). In the field of written

The problem of Edgeworth's style

work Creedy suggests that Edgeworth's easy access to publication meant that he was not 'really forced to "polish" his work thus intensifying his problem of communication' (Creedy, 1986: 20). In this, he is echoing Marshall who wished that Edgeworth, when writing *Mathematical Psychics*, 'had kept his work by him a little longer till he had worked it out more fully, and obtained that simplicity which comes only through long labour' (Marshall, 1881: 457).[1] Marshall, whose concern for lengthy polishing is notorious, wanted Edgeworth to be more like Marshall!

Jevons, in a review that concentrated upon the 'problems of hedonic science,' found *Mathematical Psychics* hard reading and likely to be found by some to be 'an uncouth and even clumsy piece of literary work' but one of 'unquestionable power and originality' (Jevons, 1881: 583). He also found episodes in the work 'showing much command of language and no slight elegance and picturesqueness of style'.

Jevons himself has not escaped judgement on questions of style. Blaug says of his *Theory of Political Economy*: 'its originality, and perhaps the haste with which it was written, produced an uneven quality in which many arguments are left incomplete' (Blaug, 1986: 101). Mill, against whose authoritative position, established earlier by his *Principles of Political Economy* (Mill, 1965), Jevons struggled, is seen to have derived his position from the synthesis achieved and the elegant style of his writing. Style and to some extent audience, with respect to the seminal nineteenth-century works of Mill, Jevons, Sidgwick and Marshall, are issues both for contemporary critics and for modern interpreters.

However, Keynes, though he was certain of the 'peculiarities', also acknowledged Edgeworth's 'brilliance of style'. Galton, who had read Jevons's review of *Mathematical Psychics*, expressed an opinion to Edgeworth himself that the topics had been dealt with 'with great lucidity and vivacity'.[2] Stigler, who is, according to Newman, the most observant of those who have commented on Edgeworth's style, notices that his metaphors were intended to help the reader 'grasp ideas whose depths and originality required the hardest response of all, a wrenching of the mind from its old familiar routines' (Stigler, 1978: 290).

All, it seems, are in agreement that Edgeworth's style was peculiar, but not all are in agreement as to the reasons or the consequences. To some, the difficulty of style is because of the obscurity of subject matter, while to others there is a suggestion that the obscurity of the style made the subject matter harder to understand. There does not seem to exist, then, a simple categorisation of Edgeworth's style. Keynes gives a list of attributes, without matching the attributes to evidence. These come in a biographical text of some literary claim where Keynes himself was anxious to display his own rhetorical skills. As McCloskey has attempted to make style, in general, an issue for modern economics writing, an attempt to look systematically at Edgeworth's style might serve to illustrate problems that have to be faced in making informed judgement on such matters (McCloskey, 1991). The problem of Edgeworth's style might then be cast in the following terms: how can we describe and analyse Edgeworth's style and how does his style relate to his purpose?

STYLE AND DISCOURSE

Style of speech or writing can be characterised as the way in which an individual communicates in sustained prose, poetry or speech. Crystal and Davy point to the multiplicity of definitions of the word style, ranging from the language habits of one person, confused and identified with that person (hence, perhaps the lumping together of Edgeworth's style of writing with his personality) or, more narrowly, to the selection of idiosyncratic language (hence, perhaps Keynes's concern with the 'peculiarities' of Edgeworth's style) (Crystal and Davy, 1969: 9–11). Of course, opinions differ. Buffon holds that 'le style est l'homme même' (Buffon, 1753) and Barthes states that:

> Imagery, delivery, vocabulary spring from the body and the past of the writer and gradually become the very reflexes of his art. Thus under the name of style a self-sufficient language is evolved which has its roots only in the depths of the author's personal and secret mythology.
>
> (Barthes, 1967: 16)

Crystal and Davy point out that the evaluative use of the term style rarely makes reference to the formal analysis of the language used. Barthes' insight is useful for an understanding of Edgeworth, Crystal and Davy's for a way of proceeding with the analysis. They contrast these uses of the term style with 'stylistics' which is concerned with the pattern of language use in a discourse community, for example in late nineteenth-century economics. In the classical tradition of rhetorical analysis, style has the force of *elocutio*, the selection of appropriate language within which to clothe thought. This is of particular relevance to a study of Edgeworth's style. While there has been much concern as to how and where Edgeworth obtained his training in mathematics very little attention has been paid to the implications of his training and excellence in the classics.[3]

But what of the analysis of style, especially when dealing with works of analytical or scientific rather than of fictional intent? Rhetoric, old and new, provides us with guidance. Corbett points us in the direction of diction or lexis, length, kind and variety of sentence and sentence patterns, coherence devices, uses of figures of speech and length, development and transitional devices in paragraphs (Corbett, 1971: 439–50).

In technical or scientific writing, some consideration also needs to be given to the ways in which the text relates or refers to other texts through references, footnotes and the treatment of 'authorities' (Price, 1926: 371–7). This is particularly the case when examining Edgeworth since his treatment of authorities is both deferential and casual. At the same time, punctuation is also worthy of examination.[4] This could be subsumed under grammatical complexity but it could also be investigated in its own right as could the use of italics, an emphatic device that Edgeworth uses on virtually every page in *Mathematical Psychics*. The inclusion of figures of speech, particularly metaphor, is of paramount importance since it links the generation of ideas with style.

Genre analysis is also relevant, with its stress on patterns in communication as is an analysis of the intended role of the reader (Swales, 1990). In the development of economic thought, Edgeworth is seen as writing for the few, Marshall for the many. It is worthwhile reflecting therefore on the way in which the reader is incorporated into the text.

The distinction that Crystal and Davy make between style in the above sense and stylistics is also relevant. Stylistics aims to identify from the mass of linguistic features those that are restricted to a certain kind of social context such as the research monograph (Crystal and Davy, 1969: 9–14). It is essential, in making any judgement on Edgeworth's style that we do not confuse features of late nineteenth-century academic writing in economics with Edgeworth's personal approach to writing. Any analysis of Edgeworth's 'peculiarities of style' requires a notion of what was or would have been taken to be, standard at the time. To do this thoroughly would require an analysis of Marshall, Jevons and of the scientific texts upon which Edgeworth himself drew. The only attempt at this made here will be a reference to a short comparative survey of some pages of Marshall's writing.

EDGEWORTH'S STYLE

Edgeworth's writing is extensive. A rough tally of his work includes four books, 172 articles, pamphlets and notes, 173 book reviews, and 132 entries in the original Palgrave (Newman, 1987). It would be unrealistic and unnecessary to contemplate a stylistic analysis of so many works. Samples of text can be used. Keynes held that Edgeworth's native style appears fully developed in his earliest sustained writing and is modified, as a result of peer-group reaction, in his later works. If Keynes is right about earlier and later style, study of the earlier pieces will provide a basis from which later style can be evaluated and any changes measured. The source material for this essay will be *Mathematical Psychics*. Some reference will be made to a three-part article published in the *Economic Journal* some twenty years later, dealing with taxation, and illustrating aspects of Edgeworth's style that were maintained over time. The sample relates only to Edgeworth's writing on economics.

The problem of Edgeworth's style

Lexical items

General comments have already been made on Edgeworth's fondness for formal expression and words derived from the classical languages. Polysyllabic Latinate language takes pride of place before words of Anglo-Saxon origin. Thus, on page 9 of *Mathematical Psychics* we have:

> *Atoms of pleasure* are not easy to distinguish and discern; more continuous than sand, more discrete than liquid; as it were nuclei of the just-perceivable, embedded in circumambient semi-consciousness.

Circumambient is the only full Latinism in the sentence.

Edgeworth's fondness for the classics leads him to use Latin (very rarely), Greek (more frequently than Latin) lexis at unpredictable moments in the text. This is particularly striking in *Mathematical Psychics* where Demosthenes is alluded to (p. 29) as a way of elaborating the meaning of 'deadlock, undecidable opposition of interests' (see below) with respect to the indeterminate contract curve. It is, however, important not to over-emphasise the use of classical lexis. It is a shock to the modern reader but is not necessarily a shock to Edgeworth's contemporaries. The number of words used in Greek is limited: in the main body of *Mathematical Psychics*, Greek words are used no more than twenty-nine times in eighty-two pages. In some of the usages it is easy to guess a meaning:[5]

> When the given conditions are not sufficient to determinate the problem – a case of great importance in Political Economy – the ἀγεωμέτρητος is less likely to suspect this deficiency, less competent to correct it by indicating what conditions are necessary and sufficient.

> (p. 3)

It is not too difficult, given the subject matter of the surrounding discourse, to guess 'mathematically ignorant' which, while not technically correct, approximates the meaning and does not alter the force of the sentence. This sentence would have been familiar to classically educated readers as a reference to the (supposed) inscription over the door of Plato's Academy. It was in general use at the time to refer to those who were not initiated in a given subject.

This is hardly the Greek 'treading on the heels of the differential calculus' that Keynes's deliberate and delightful hyperbole makes out. The philistine reader is not totally at a loss. In the later papers, Latin replaces Greek and the use of classical lexis diminishes but does not disappear (Edgeworth, 1900: 175).

Edgeworth's fondness for the classics is in evidence in *Mathematical Psychics* but while the extent of his use of classical lexis may be unusual, references to the classics by other economic writers at the time were not.

135

A study of the first volume of *The Economic Journal* reveals that the classical world is part of the frame of reference of several of the contributors. The use of Greek cannot be considered a major problem for them, neither can the sometimes stilted Latinised vocabulary.

The strength of his preference for a classical vocabulary and for obscure words diminishes but is never entirely removed: 'fructify', 'infraction', 'obviate' and 'redound', 'infelicitous' and 'modes of detriment, diminution of the total production and aggravation of unequal distribution' are all to be found in the articles on taxation, as is a reference to the 'Platonic dialogue' (Edgeworth, 1900: 175). In *Mathematical Psychics* Edgeworth does not restrict himself to words from the classics, for he uses French sentences and small snatches of Italian as well. Edgeworth was a man of letters who ranged widely in his reading and frequently adapted a fine or striking phrase to his own purposes.[6] Such items, no doubt, add to the problems that some readers have with the text but they cannot be considered major problems. Others will find them a source of pleasure.

An aspect of the lexis that may give rise to problems for modern readers, and may, or may not, have given rise to problems for Edgeworth's peers, is the preponderance of terms derived from science, used to sustain and develop the fundamental analogy Edgeworth draws between the use of mathematics in physics and its potential use in social analysis. The first fifteen pages of *Mathematical Psychics* are noted as much for their terms taken from mathematics and physics ('energy', 'motion', 'vortices', 'motion of rotation', 'dynamics', 'electricity', 'conductors', 'electro-magnetic force') than from words taken from the classics. Greek is used once in the first fifteen pages, and thirteen words of Latin in a sentence that adds little to the sense of what is already there. It is not until 'Economical Calculus' that an economics vocabulary comes into its own ('competition', 'contracts', 'auctioneer', 'settlement' and so on) some of which is new and defined by Edgeworth (see p. 20). The specialist vocabulary of the section devoted to the 'Utilitarian calculus' differs again. The vocabulary of that section is drawn from the language of ethics and of Utilitarianism. Perhaps the range of vocabulary in a work so short was, and is, a source of difficulty but no such claim can be confirmed until an investigation is made of the lexis of other works in the field at the time.

Sentence length and complexity

Edgeworth used a variety of sentence types ranging from the simple to the complex. Some of the examples provided here are taken from the 'Introductory description of contents', a section of *Mathematical Psychics* four pages in length containing twenty-three sentences organised in ten paragraphs. Others come from the main body of *Mathematical Psychics* and none are drawn from the appendices. Five of the paragraphs in the introduction are one-sentence paragraphs and four of the relevant five sentences are highly complex. The shortest sentence has five words, the longest has fifty-eight. The average length in the first part of the work, up to page 16, is thirty words to a sentence with the longest containing ninety-three words and the shortest five. This count is made on the basis of taking the sentence as from initial capital letter to full stop.

In the search for stylistic difficulties. Edgeworth's fondness for over-elaborated sentences would seem to be the area on which to concentrate. What follows is a classification of sentences with only moderate attention to the role that such sentences play in the wider discourse. Some difficult sentences are shown. A full analysis of difficulty requires the linking of the sentence to the paragraph and to the series of paragraphs both before and after it and cannot be fully treated at the level of the sentence alone. Keynes highlights the problem of coherence as 'his obscurity of connection'.

The simple sentence

The simple sentence in *Mathematical Psychics* is rare but it can be found. The examples of simple sentences given below are the only examples found in the four-page 'Introductory description of contents'. There are in addition a further three sentences that are simple but adorned by symbols, italics and page numbers. This section does not differ markedly from the rest of the work and may be taken as representative of it, in so far as sentence structure is concerned.

Mathematical Psychics may be divided into two parts – Theoretical and Applied.

Dissent has often been expressed. (p. viii)

This appears to be the shortest sentence in the whole work.

Edgeworth can complicate even the simplest of sentences, as in this wonderfully poetic anastrophe.[7] 'Of this inference what would be the consequence?' (p. 50). While the sentence has a poetic ring to it, the elements are arranged logically in the text, moving from what is already known or given (i.e. what has already been dealt with) to the new (i.e. what is to be next treated).

Slightly more complex sentences are made so by use of the semi-colon:

The Calculus of Pleasure (Part II) may be divided into two species – the Economical and the Utilitarian; the principle of division suggesting an addition to Mr. Sidgwick's 'ethical methods (p. 16)'.

(p. v)

The problem of Edgeworth's style

There are a further five sentences in the introduction making use of the semi-colon in this way. They tend to become more complex in each of the parts of the sentence as in the following example:

> Mathematical reasonings are employed partly to confirm Mr. Sidgwick's proof that Greatest Happiness is the end of right action; partly to deduce middle axioms, means conducive to that end.

> (p. vii)

The complex sentence

Another sentence form is based on elaboration. This form also occurs frequently in the main text and does need to be read with great care though the elements are normally correctly, or at least carefully, signalled by appropriate punctuation:

> For if sentients differ in Capacity for happiness – under similar circumstances some classes of sentients experiencing on an average more pleasure (e.g. of imagination and sympathy) and less pain (e.g. of fatigue) than others – there is no presumption that equality of circumstances is the most felicific arrangement; especially when account is taken of the interests of posterity.

> (p. vii)

The function of the inserts signalled by '–' and '()' is to exemplify, the dash carrying the general exemplification and the parentheses the specific example. This technique, if technique is the correct word, of elaboration is a recurring feature of Edgeworth's writing. Another splendid example, of possibly greater difficulty but which can be understood simply by removing the inserts, signalled by ',' and '–', is found on page 4:

> To illustrate the economical problem of exchange, the maze of many dealers contracting and competing with each other, it is possible to imagine a mechanism of many parts where the law of motion, which particular parts moves off with which, is not precisely given – with symbols, arbitrary functions, representing not merely *not numerical knowledge* but *ignorance* – where, though the mode of motion towards equilibrium is indeterminate, the position of equilibrium is mathematically determined.

It is possible to discern a pattern based upon the notion of generalisation–exemplification at each stage in the development of this sentence as it leads towards its conclusion. Once the pattern is recognised, the difficulty with the words and ideas can be resolved by removing the examples in order to grasp the generalisation and then restoring the examples in order to understand, in more concrete terms, the significance. The reader must work at the sentences to fully grasp the significance of the ideas.

The lengthy sentence remains in 'The incidence of urban rates' as an enduring feature of his writing as does his fondness for the semi-colon and the colon. Italicisation and dashes are, however, used less frequently. The complex, eighty-six-word sentence beginning 'In general...' to be found on page 191 of *The Economic Journal* is a fine example of Edgeworthian complexity.

The artistic or poetic sentence

There is one more style of sentence that ought to be considered though it is difficult to label. The term 'artistic' or 'poetic' sentence, while referring to the intended role of such sentences, best captures their main features. The two-paragraph introduction that appears before the section headed 'Part One' in *Mathematical Psychics* can be used to illustrate the type.

> The application of mathematics to *Belief*, the calculus of Probabilities, has been treated by many distinguished writers; the calculus of *Feeling*, of Pleasure and Pain, is the less familiar, but not in reality more paradoxical subject of this essay.
>
> The subject divides itself into two parts; concerned respectively with principle and practice, root and fruit, the applicability and the application of Mathematics to Sociology.
>
> (p. 1)

Both sentences exhibit most of the early Edgeworthian features: complexity, the use of the semi-colon, the use of inserts in a way that builds additional material on a single stem, the Latinised vocabulary, the contrastive language and instances (see below), the italics. It also contains the seemingly casual but carefully located descriptive metaphor, 'root and fruit'. This carries with it the idea of branches of learning and helps sustain the series of two-part classifications that is the principal structural feature of the second part of the sentence. 'Root and fruit' is not to be understood as a casual piece of textual decoration. On page 30, when dealing with the application of mathematics to the development of economic theory, Edgeworth returns to his metaphor:

> The mathematics of a perfect market have been worked out by several eminent writers, in particular Messrs. Jevons, Marshall, Walras: to whose varied cultivation of the mathematical science, *Catallactics*, the reader is referred who wishes to dig down to the root of first principles, to trace out all the branches of a complete

system, to gather fruits rare and only reached by a mathematical substructure.

It is difficult to accept that this splendidly extended metaphor, complete with a mathematical ladder and with Edgeworthian parallelism, is careless or clumsy writing. These two references are separated by twenty-nine pages of text. It is difficult to accept that the use of the earlier is, once we have discovered the later, anything other than deliberate. It is also, as are many other examples of Edgeworth, highly pictorial. There is evidence elsewhere in the text that Edgeworth was aware of his use of metaphor. On page 24, he reminds the reader of another instance of (a different) metaphor '... in the metaphorical language above employed ...'. The relationship between 'root and fruit' is how Edgeworth regarded first principles in relation to subsequent output. (See also the alternative matter of physics and the 'deep first principles' that are to be sought in the 'boundless ocean of perfect fluid', 'Hydrodynamics', on page 5.) Examples such as these no doubt convinced Keynes of Edgeworth's brilliant phrasing.

The problem comes in understanding the role in the discourse. The paragraph immediately following the passage just given is a less happy one, containing many features that Jevons might point to as clumsy.

The artistic sentence is not used in places where technical analyses or ideas are expounded. However, artistic sentences and paragraphs are to be found in numerous places in *Mathematical Psychics* for example:

> Imagine a material Cosmos, a mechanism as composite as possible, and perplexed with all manner of wheels, pistons, parts, connections, and whose mazy complexity might far transcend in its entanglement the webs of thought and wiles of passion;

(p. 9)

Later in the paragraph, at line 29, a quotation, identified by Creedy as from Pope's *Essay on Man*, 'a mighty maze but not without a plan' reinforces the idea of complexity. Earlier, on page 4, Edgeworth has already referred to the market in terms of the 'maze of many dealers contracting and competing with each other'. His allusions are not casual, spur-of-the-moment ideas but worked upon and consistent over a number of pages.

Elements of the poetic can be found in the two inspirational paragraphs on the '*Mécanique Sociale*' on pages 12 and 13:

> 'her every air Of gesture and least motion' a law of Force to governed systems – a fluent form, a Fairy Queen guiding a most complicated chariot, wheel within wheel, the 'speculative and active

instruments,' the motor nerves, the limbs and the environment on which they act.

(p. 15)

'Her every air' is a reference to Milton's *Paradise Lost* IX which describes Eve's effect on Satan. The most complicated chariot and the related mechanical images are intended to further the speculative and imaginative involvement of the reader.

Examples of the poetic sentence tend to be from 'Part I'. They are not there to provide light relief, but seem rather to be asking the reader to engage in the work using imagination (or pictures) as well as reason, to think about, and be excited by, the possibilities.

Part II yields fewer of the more fanciful sentences but has some that are robust. For a description of market strife, Edgeworth turns to the New Testament. 'The whole creation groans and yearns, desiderating a principle of arbitration, an end of strifes' (also p. 51). This is drawn from Romans 8:22: 'For we know that the whole creation groaneth and travaileth in pain together until now'. The New Testament (see p. 142) also suggested images and phrases for 'The incidence of urban rates'. All of the examples of the 'artistic' sentence seem to be designed to stress, imaginatively, particular points of Edgeworth's model, especially the problem of recontraction with or without consent and the problem of finding a principle of arbitration.

FIGURES OF SPEECH: THE SCHEMES

It is difficult, without an extensive analysis of other texts, to be certain that all examples provided below are examples of 'artful deviations' from the ordinary mode of writing. There is no doubt that Edgeworth in his early, and in some of his later writing, relished a fine phrase. Some of these fall into one or other category in the established schemes, as defined by Corbett. For example, the apt illustration, carried in a striking phrase, is a literary device that Edgeworth used in his later, and much drier, writings on taxation. The following, essentially pictorial, examples, can be found in the 'Incidence of urban rates':

> But would regard for production be an adequate inducement to exempt a minimum from income tax, or to spare the comforts of the masses? It is only the more intelligent 'shepherds of the people' who, in order the more frequently to shear, will take care never to flay, their flocks.
>
> (Edgeworth, 1900: 178)

The example illustrates not only metaphor, but also (perhaps) anastrophe

141

and in the repetition of the 'fl' sound in the latter part of the last clause, alliteration.

And:

> The cleansing of streets and sewers has the result that the occupiers of residences in the improved neighbourhood enjoy a commodity of higher market value: but the removal of a stain from the national flag is not an asset to the average citizen even approximately proportionate to his share of taxation.
>
> (Edgeworth, 1900: 181)

The synecdoche in the last clause is particularly appealing as is the parallelism of the concrete image 'cleansing of streets' and its realisable benefits, and the more abstract, but readily pictured, cleaning of the flag and less direct benefits.

In *Mathematical Psychics* he used a variety of devices, sometimes separately, sometimes together as in the example provided from a passage taken from pages 7 and 8. Sentences have been numbered for ease of reference.

> [1] Such comparisons can no longer be shirked, if there is to be any systematic morality at all. [2] It is postulated by distributive justice. [3] It is postulated by the population question; that horizon in which every moral prospect terminates; which is presented to the far-seeing at every turn, on the most sacred and the most trivial occasions. [4] You cannot spend sixpence utilitarianly, without having considered whether your action tends to increase the comfort of a limited number, or numbers with limited comfort; without having compared such alternative utilities.

In modern use the 'if' clause in [1] would probably be more likely to come first with the implication 'such comparisons can no longer be shirked', second. This may well be an alteration of the normal order and hence an example of the reversal of a grammatical structure in the clause. [2] and [3] involve the repetition of, 'It is postulated' and is an example of the use of anaphora. Anaphora is defined as the repetition of words or groups of words at the beginning of successive clauses (for definitions of all the relevant schemes see Corbett, 1971: 493–5). Edgeworth uses a version of this device later on the same page, in a much quoted, but linguistically un-analysed sentence: 'We cannot count the golden sands of life; we cannot number the "innumerable smile" of seas of love; . . .'. The last clause of [3] contains an example of antithesis (sacred and trivial), while [4] contains an example of antimetabole (the repetition of words) in successive clauses, in reverse grammatical order.

The problem of Edgeworth's style

Parallelism

This is defined by Corbett as similarity of structure in a pair or series of related words. Edgeworth is fond of the device which he makes use of to handle both contrast and emphasis. While recognising their overlapping nature, the use of parallelism is dealt with under contrastive parallelism and synonymous parallelism, below.

Contrastive parallelism

The series of contrasts, 'root and fruit', have already been considered. Sometimes, in *Mathematical Psychics*, it takes the form of a simple set of contrasts directly relevant to the purpose:

> Where there are data which, though *numerical* and *quantitive* – for example, that a quantity is greater or less than another, *increases* or *decreases*, is *positive* or *negative*, a *maximum* or a *minimum*, there mathematical reasoning is possible and may be indispensable.[8]
>
> (p. 2)

At other times, it is used playfully, for ironic or dramatic effect. In 'The incidence of urban rates', immediately following a passage that reviews support for Edgeworth's point of view, is to be found: 'The experts who are not quoted as gathering with the doctrine here propounded are not to be understood as scattering against it', a reference to a passage in the Synoptic Gospels (Matthew 12–30; Luke 11:23). The reference is reinforced later in the paragraph with a reference to 'synoptic economics' (Edgeworth, 1900: 186).[9] Or, returning to *Mathematical Psychics*, his comparison between what takes place where the contract is indeterminate with what takes place in an open market is linked by the sentence 'With this *clogged* and *underground* procedure is contrasted the *smooth* machinery of the *open* market' (page 30, emphasis added).

Synonymous parallelism

Another recurring feature of his writing, is a form or parallelism in which a forceful effect is created by the addition of synonymous, rather than of contrastive, elements.

> He that will not verify his conclusions as far as possible by mathematics, as it were bringing the ingots of common sense to be assayed and coined at the mint of the sovereign science, will hardly realize the full value of what he holds, will want a measure of what it will be worth in however slightly altered circumstances, a means of conveying and making it current.
>
> (p. 3)

Here the golden images are arranged in order of increasing significance in situations of wider importance. Other examples are easily found.

Edgeworth clearly relishes sending wave upon wave of related ideas crashing down upon the reader. Those who appreciate Edgeworth surely enjoy the energy of these waves. Edgeworth knew how to turn a fine phrase. Given his background in the classics, it is highly likely that the turning was accompanied by considerable self-awareness, for the devices used are well understood in the classical rhetorical canon. Edgeworth is drawing on what he knows best as his model for writing economics.

THE TROPES: METAPHOR AND ANALOGY

Since McCloskey's dramatic rediscovery of the use of tropes in economics writing, there has been some concern to cover the whole range. I am not interested in exploring the lesser known, but not necessarily lesser used, tropes. For most purposes, the theory of metaphor can be used as a means of thinking about some of the others as such a simile, synedoche and metonymy (Henderson, 1982: 147). Pride of place in terms of tropes must be given to metaphor and analogy. Analogy is sometimes considered under 'topic' since it is a form of argument by comparison, proceeding from the known to the unknown. But metaphor, too, is not restricted to comparison of knowns (e.g. the qualities of a 'lion' and the qualities of a 'warrior'), it can be used as a model for argument or for possible attributes stemming from some similarity of form. Linked with the idea of metaphor is the notion of exemplification.

There are difficulties to be faced in dealing with Edgeworth's use of metaphor and analogy in *Mathematical Psychics*. The biological metaphor, 'root and fruit', and the directional metaphor 'deep' and by implication shallow,[10] are, as has been shown, elegant images of how Edgeworth thought about the role of mathematics in the search for social knowledge. The instances are few. *Mathematical Psychics*, despite its important moments of poetic and of biological imagery, is developed and sustained by a consistent set of scientific analogies related to physics, the machine and to thermodynamics. Mirowski has correctly referred to Edgeworth's explicit references to physics and to Edgeworth's acceptance of the primacy of the physical metaphor over Benthamite notions (Mirowski, 1989: 220–1). Metaphor has two uses in Edgeworth rather than one. It is used as a way of stimulating ideas through imaginative and compelling images. Success in this respect cannot, of course, be assumed. Marshall blamed the 'frequent use of unexplained metaphor' for the difficulties of following some of the argument (Marshall, 1881). It is also a device for developing specific arguments. Often both aspects are developed at the same time.

The analogical force or tenor of the argument is at its most overt, in

The problem of Edgeworth's style

Part I where the concern is with the 'applicability of Mathematics to Sociology' (p. 1). Edgeworth is aware of the style of argument he intends to use and gently introduces the reader to it. The word analogy is first tied to the use of an apt example: the allocation of fuel so as to obtain the greatest energy among a given set of engines differing in efficiency. Introducing the problem, he says 'The following instance is less trivial, analogous to an important social problem'. The aim is to illustrate the application of mathematical reasoning. Edgeworth, some paragraphs later, (p. 4), then makes the explicit link between the allocation and social problem: the example illustrates the problem of utilitarian distribution. But there is no explicit backward reference to the example! To explore the economic problem, the exercise becomes one of imagining a mechanism of many parts where the law of motion is not precisely given, the path to equilibrium indeterminate but its position mathematically determined. No exact match between mathematical physics and the economics of exchange is proposed but the cause of reasoning without numerical data sustained.

Edgeworth then anticipates an objection to the specific example provided from the field of hydrodynamics. Hydrodynamics has some precise data – so too has economics. Edgeworth then points out the parallel conditions, *fullness* and *fluidity* of the market. These items are defined in ways that make the connections explicit. Edgeworth, however, recognises that to give a whole series of matched examples would be both tedious and superfluous and says so in a characteristic way: 'To attempt to select instances from each branch of mathematical inquiry would exceed the limits of this paper and the requirements of the argument' (pages 5–6). The calculus of variations will suffice.

Edgeworth then explores the notion of greater and less pleasure-units, integrating his poetic sense of the 'golden sands of life' and, on page 9, establishes his main link: 'The application of mathematics to the world of soul is countenanced by the hypothesis that Pleasure is the concomitant of Energy'. This important connection is then followed by an appeal to the imagination and to the development of another poetic image: that of the mechanism 'perplexed with all manner of wheels'. The imaginative act, leads to a narrower example, 'certain parts are less stiff than others' and to an implication: those less stiff parts take on more energy.

> This rough, indefinite, yet mathematical reasoning is analogous to the reasoning on a subsequent page, that in order to the greatest possible sum total of happiness, the more capable of pleasure shall take more means, more happiness.
> [p. 10 pointing onwards, as directed by the footnote, to page 64]

The illustration is then broadened in the next paragraph and an appeal is made to Lagrange and Hamilton, leading to the conclusion that many unknowns are reduced to one unknown and the one unknown is connected with the known. The next paragraph reinforces the linkages:

> Now this accumulation (or time-integral) of energy which thus becomes the principal object of the physical investigation is analogous to that accumulation of pleasure existing at each instant of time, the end of rational action whether self-interested or benevolent. The central conception of Dynamics and (in virtue of pervading analogies it may be said) in general of Mathematical Psychics is *other-sidedly identical* with the central conception of Ethics; and a solution practical and philosophical, although not numerical and precise, as it exists for the problem of the interaction of bodies, so is possible for the problem of the interaction of souls.

The passage quoted above is complete with additional Edgeworthian features such as the contrastive parallelism of the clause after the semicolon. Edgeworth's fondness of 'seemingly endless analogies and metaphors' found to be 'singularly instructive' is noted by Stigler (Stigler, 1978: 29).

The remainder of the section deals in both poetic and practical images in making further connections: 'The invisible energy of electricity is grasped by the marvellous methods of Lagrange; the invisible energy of pleasure may admit of a similar handling' (p. 13) and to the imaginative prospects of the possibilities of the (personified) *'Mécanique Sociale'*.

Interwoven, then, with the general and specific analogies, which set out the linkages, are a series of poetic or metaphorical passages that draw their inspiration from them and help, imaginatively, to sustain them. Most of these have been analysed in the context of the poetic sentence (above). The images here are drawn consistently from the machine and while not written as an allegory, are certainly maintained and consistent.[11] Here, the examples and images are carefully rather than haphazardly selected and enough provided to further the argument. The reader, sometimes being expected to further the argument on his or her own ('in virtue of pervading analogies'), Edgeworth supplying enough to demonstrate his argument.

There are, however, two other sustained metaphors which, though in evidence in Part I, do not come into prominence until the second part of *Mathematical Psychics*: electricity and the notion of the atom. I deal here only with the notion of the atom which, together with the theory of vortices shared the important role for formation of Edgeworth's thought.

Atoms are mentioned in passing on page 8 where 'atoms of pleasure' are, 'as it were nuclei of the just-perceivable, embedded in circumambient semi-consciousness'. The use here is not casual, but equally not part of an extended conceptualisation either. On page 31, Edgeworth introduces the catallactic molecule with respect to the case of perfect competition.

This catallactic molecule is compounded later in the page. By page 40, the poetic and extended notion of the atom is set out:

> But if our reasonings be correct, the one thing from an abstract point of view visible amidst the jumble of catallactic molecules, the jostle of competitive crowds, is that those who form themselves into compact bodies by combination do not tend to lose but tend to gain in the sense described, to gain in point of utility.

On page 48 there is a reference to 'neuter atoms' but it is not until page 50 that the reader is presented with the piece that draws the references together and which implicitly but not explicitly refers back to terminology first familiarised with respect to the analogy with hydrodynamics on page 5:

> But if it should appear that the field of competition is deficient in that *continuity of fluid*, that *multiety of atoms*, which constitute the foundations of uniformity in Physics, if competition is found wanting, not only regularity of law, but even the impartiality of choice – the throw of the die loaded with villainy – economics would be indeed a 'dismal science' and the reverence for competition would be no more.

At this point Edgeworth makes a reference in the footnotes to the foundations of uniformity in physics, the theory of vortices and the theory of atoms. Thereafter, the references to atoms are confined to incidental comments (see pages 76 and 80).

Argument by analogy remained a feature of Edgeworth's work. Drawn from 'Incidence', one small-scale analogy illustrates both his use of comparison and his wit: 'The economist has not to construct a special law of taxation for the taxing of houses, any more than the physicist has to construct a special law of gravitation for the tumbling of houses' (Edgeworth, 1900: 183). His visionary metaphors were, however, as far as 'Incidence' is concerned, tamed and reduced.

THE READER

What can we tell about Edgeworth's intended audience and his relationship with it, from a study of *Mathematical Psychics?* From the analysis so far, the intended audience is assumed to be highly literate, capable of understanding Greek, Latin, French and Italian; capable of reading the lengthy sentence and understanding the emphatic grace of the tropes and schemes employed. Edgeworth also makes assumptions as to the reader's intellectual background, Plato's notion of being and not-being is referred to without being referenced, as are Herbert Spencer and the author of the *Mécanique Céleste*. In addition there are particular phrases used that the reader is simply expected to know as part of the common currency of intellectual life, for example, the word 'felecific' to refer to authorities such as Bentham. The referencing is inconsistent; Lagrange is mentioned, once in the text and once in a complex footnote, four paragraphs before any specific reference is made to the application of Lagrange techniques to a scientific problem and details of source given.

Edgeworth can go to some length to avoid a direct, personal relationship with the reader. He refers to himself as the 'writer' (p. 43) and, with some justification for the use of the more general role, as 'the advocate of mathematical reasoning' (p. 3). The indirect and passive voice is often chosen as the way of addressing the reader as in 'the particular hypothesis adopted in these pages' (p. 9). At the same time, the reader is not shut out. Indeed, 'our' data is to be found on page 1, indicating a commonality of purpose. Questions also are intended to involve the reader in the discourse. Page 8: 'In virtue of what unit is such comparison possible? It is here submitted: . . .'. The answer is submitted to the reader and Edgeworth develops the thinking '. . . we find no peculiar difficulty' and so into 'We cannot count the golden sands of life.' Edgeworth and the reader are together as they are intended to be in other imaginative passages: 'Imagine a material Cosmos . . .'.

Edgeworth's relationship with the reader in Part II, while retaining elements of discomfort and of distancing, becomes closer as a result of the integration of the mathematics and English: 'Let us commence', 'consider', 'if we supposed', and in the mathematical section leading up to, on page 28, 'To gather up and fix our thoughts, let us imagine a simple case – Robinson Crusoe contracting with Friday.'

The reader is imagined as working along with Edgeworth, as being imaginatively and creatively involved in the work. If they do not have the tools, they are expected to develop them outside the text just as Edgeworth himself had done. Edgeworth restricts his instruction to the requirements of the argument and ignores the requirements of pedagogical techniques. Pervading analogies, exemplifications beyond that required for the benefit of the argument are ignored. The reader, skilled in thinking, mathematics and physics must fill them in for his or her self. And this constitutes the main rhetorical problem of *Mathematical Psychics*: the audience is not one audience but several. Those needing the first part cannot understand the second. Those who are capable of understanding the second, would have no need of the first. The work is, of course, an amalgam: the applicability of mathematics to social phenomenon having been published earlier in the journal *Mind*. Furthermore, his audience was used to the scientific or economics text with pedagogical intention (as in Mill, Jevons and Marx). *Mathematical Psychics*, is, though delightful in many ways, an unhappy amalgam of the inspirational and pedagogic text and the technical research paper within the context of discourse drawn from several domains (economics, ethics, physics, mathematics). An example of the confusion with respect to audience and with respect to expression can be found in the linguistically difficult and inelegant footnote on page 12 which is reproduced here:

> The mathematical reader does not require to be reminded that upon the principles of Lagrange the whole of (conservative) Dynamics may be represented as a Maximum-problem; if without gain, at any rate without loss. And the great principle of Thomson (Thomson and Tait, arts. Cf. *Theory of Vortices*, by Thomson, Royal Society, Edinburgh, 1865), with allied *maximum-principles*, dominating the theory of fluid motion, dominates Mathematical Physics with a more than nominal supremacy, and most indispensably efficacious power. Similarly, it may be conjectured, the ordinary moral rules are *equivalently* expressed by the Intuitivist in the (grammatically speaking) *positive* degree, by the Utilitarian in the *superlative*. But for the higher moral problems the conception of the *maximum* is indispensable.

STYLISTIC COMPARISON WITH MARSHALL[12]

In quantitative terms, Marshall's sentences proved to be of similar length and complexity to those of Edgeworth and, like Edgeworth's, the semicolon is much in evidence. Marshall restricts the use of italics to special or technical terms,[13] whereas Edgeworth tends to use italics as an emphatic device in a manner not dissimilar to the way in which Queen Victoria used them in her letters and journals.[14] Marshall used parenthesis as a gloss on what has come before. The parenthetical comment is retrospective, that is, it is placed immediately after a clause or noun phrase in the sample of text analysed. Ten pages of Marshall produced six sentences in which parentheses are used. Ten pages of Edgeworth from *Mathematical Psychics* produced thirty-seven instances of the use of parentheses. In ten of the sentences from Edgeworth, the parenthetical comment refers to a clause or completion of a clause or a noun phrase that *follows* the comment. In other words, the comment is *prospective*. This undoubtedly adds to the difficulties that the reader experiences in tackling Edgeworth's prose. Edgeworth thinks ahead! In addition, Edgeworth's parenthetical comment can be complex whereas Marshall's are usually straightforward glosses that follow the main idea.

A full comparison with Marshall would require consideration of the part played by metaphor and the nature of the intended audience. Marshall, of course, used metaphor in his economic writing but current thinking suggests that Marshall was much more concerned with popularisation and systematisation than theoretical innovation. He uses metaphors as a heuristic device and though impressed by the usefulness of biological analogies, which he does use, he accepts the significance of mechanical analogies for the development of theory (Maloney, 1985: 24; Mirowski, 1989: 262–3). A fuller stylistic analysis of Marshall is yet to be undertaken.

CONCLUSION

Edgeworth's style has been appraised by his contemporaries and by a number of subsequent commentators. Generally his style has been found wanting. Keynes, who admired much of the writing, characterised the style in a superb hyperbole, but, like the others did not analyse it systematically. This chapter analyses his style using a variety of techniques selected on a pragmatic basis. Generally it shows that an analysis of style, as opposed to an impressionistic understanding of style, requires close attention to text and textual detail, at the level of the sentence and beyond.

With respect to Edgeworth, it has shown that, though there are exceptions, his writing at the level of the sentence, though complex, is often far from clumsy. Much of the foreign lexis is recoverable with very little effort. Sustained analogy, imaginative metaphor and apt example are used with a high degree of skill. His long sentences sometimes lacked the polish of Marshall's. The reader sometimes needs to develop a strategy for analysing the sentences, especially those where the parenthetical comment is prospective or where 'inserted' material has had additional comment added within the original insertion. The work is rich in ideas and imagination but difficult in as much as the range of language, concepts and mathematical ideas that it calls upon is large. There is, certainly, a dissonance between the scientific intention and the poetic language which suggests an uncertainty concerning the most appropriate readership. Or was Edgeworth trying to persuade by referring to the classical rhetorical canon?

His use of classical rhetoric, readily suggested by his training, and his sustained use of metaphor, almost verging on allegory, together with other features of the writing, demand a highly literate audience. 'Language that is understood of the people' was not for Edgeworth (adapted from Marshall, 1881). It seems reasonable to accept a merger of style and personality that traditional approaches to Edgeworth's style take. His use of elements of classical rhetoric reflects his education, and his use of metaphor reflects the way in which his creative mind worked: imaginatively, metaphorically and hence pictorially and, above all, quickly. There can be little doubt that this writing has its roots 'in the depths of the author's personal and secret mythology'. If Edgeworth's mind did work in this way, his innovative nature would make the acts of polishing and re-polishing his prose in order to achieve a Marshallian simplicity, a terrible chore. The various forms of imagery and the anticipation of ideas, when coupled with the nature of the ideas being explored, provides *Mathematical Psychics* and the writer, paradoxically, with a reputation of being poor in expository skills.

Forward and backward referencing, so important for coherence of exposition beyond the individual paragraph is, for some of the ideas, weak. Cohesion over sequences of paragraphs can be implicit as illustrated here in the use of the atom as a metaphor. The implicit nature of linkages over longer stretches of text can give the impression of lack of integration. Weak cohesion beyond the level of the paragraph means that the reader must work hard to see the line of development. This problem is reinforced by the problem of integrating the mathematics and the English, a problem not studied in this analysis. But the reader who is prepared to do the work on the language, finds a reward. This is not a dry text, but work of some passion (indeed as a text it could be seen as part of the Romantic movement) in which classical rhetoric and scientific purpose merge to absorb the careful reader.

From an examination of the role of reader taken from throughout the main body of the work, Edgeworth did not have a clearly defined intended reader in mind and this does lead to a failure in exposition. His ideas were unfamiliar and he compensates for this by urging the non-mathematical reader to imaginative feats. However, when dealing with the application of mathematics to social phenomena, Edgeworth overlooks the needs of the non-mathematical reader.[15] It is in the strangeness of the ideas, the creative energy of the writing (in which so much is left implicit) and the difficulties of integrating the language and the mathematics and the lack of a consistently defined audience that the problems of communication are likely to arise. *Mathematical Psychics* is not the authoritative pedagogic text that Edgeworth's contemporaries may have expected. Edgeworth thought of it as an essay, and Marshall, with one eye on the wider public, rather unwillingly accepted it as such. It is a mixture of the instructive text, the research paper (a genre not then developed), in a context requiring ease in a number of differing kinds of discourses, and the individual act of creative thinking. In his early writing, Edgeworth perhaps chose, to paraphrase Barthes, loneliness of style in preference to the security of the established ideas on how economics ought to be written (Barthes, 1967: 18).

NOTES

1 In the same paragraph, Marshall admires the work's 'brilliancy, force, and originality' (Marshall, 1881).

2 Letter from Francis Galton to Edgeworth dated 28 October 1881 and reproduced in Stigler (1978).

3 Edgeworth studied Classics at Trinity College, Dublin and later at Balliol

The problem of Edgeworth's style

College, Oxford. He obtained a first in *Literae Humaniores* in 1869 and later did some teaching of Greek at Bedford College, London.

4 As it turns out the use of punctuation is very similar across texts with the semi-colon much in use.

5 But see the second sentence on page 61 in which three Greek terms are used and where it is unlikely that the reader will easily arrive at the meaning of the Greek.

6 Edgeworth was to review continental writing on economics topics for the *Economic Journal* and the earlier editions of the *Journal* had many articles and reviews of continental writing, particularly Italian and French.

7 Defined as inversion of the natural and usual word order.

8 See also the much quoted, but usually un-analysed sentence 'We cannot count the golden sands of life . . .' on page 9 which exhibits this form of parallelism.

9 Did Edgeworth also pioneer, among other things, the economics survey article?

10 See the 'deep first principles of physics' (Edgeworth, 1881: 5).

11 McCloskey sees allegory as the combination of metaphor and story and, in these terms, *Mathematical Psychics* is not an allegory. McCloskey goes on to categorise economics as a whole 'an allegory of self-interest' (McCloskey, 1990: 12) and this is what the hedonical calculus is about.

12 The method employed to make the comparison was to store ten pages of *Mathematical Psychics* and ten pages of Marshall's *Principles* on computer and using a program, developed by Tim Johns, to examine examples of sentence construction (e.g. the mutual use of parenthesis, the use of emphasis, and so on). This work is continuing in co-operation with Tim Johns and only the briefest of consideration is given to it here.

13 Scientific texts from the same period adopted a similar convention. See the italicised technical terms in Thomson and Tait (1890).

14 See her use of underlining and capitalisation in her letters and journals as quoted in Longford (1964).

15 Marshall noted this point in his review. He also noted the need for the writer who used mathematical reasoning to 'throw aside his mathematics and express what he has to say in language that is understanded of the people' (Marshall, 1881: 457).

REFERENCES

Barthes, R. (1967) *Writing Degree Zero*, London: Jonathan Cape.
Blaug, M. (1986) *Great Economists Before Keynes*, Brighton: Wheatsheaf Books.
Buffon, Comte de (1753) *Discours sur le Style*, Paris: Académie Français.
Butler, M. S. (1972) *Maria Edgeworth: A Literary Biography*, Oxford: Oxford University Press.
Corbett, E. P. J. (1971) *Classical Rhetoric for the Modern Student*, New York: Oxford University Press.
Creedy, J. (1986) *Edgeworth and the Development of Neoclassical Economics*, Oxford: Basil Blackwell.
Crystal, D. and Davy, D. (1969) *Investigating English Style*, London: Longman.
Edgeworth, F. Y. (1881) *Mathematical Psychics*, London: Kegan Paul.
—— (1900) 'The incidence of urban rates' *Economic Journal* 10: 172–93, 340–8, 487–517.
Graves, R. (1960) *Goodbye to All That* (2nd edition) London: Longman.
Henderson, W. (1982) 'Metaphor in economics', *Economics* Winter 1982. (Reprinted in M. Coulthard (ed.) (1986) *Talking about Text*, Discourse Analysis

Monograph No. 13, English Language Research, Birmingham: University of Birmingham, pp. 109–27.)

Jevons, W. S. (1881) 'Review of Mathematical Psychics' *Mind* 6: 581–3.

—— (1970) *The Theory of Political Economy*, Harmondsworth: Penguin.

Keynes, J. M. (1972) *Essays in Biography, The Collected Writings of John Maynard Keynes*, Vol. X, London: Macmillan for the Royal Economic Society (first edition 1933).

Longford, E. (1964) *Victoria R. I.*, London: Weidenfeld & Nicolson.

McCloskey, D. N. (1990) *If You're So Smart: The Narrative of Economic Expertise*, Chicago: University of Chicago Press.

—— (1991) 'Mere style in economic journals, 1920 to the present', *Economic Notes* 20(1): 135–58.

Maloney, J. (1985) *Marshall, Orthodoxy, and the Professionalization of Economics*, Cambridge: Cambridge University Press.

—— (1990) 'Gentlemen versus players, 1891–1914', in J. D. Hey and D. Winch (eds), *A Century of Economics: 100 Years of the Royal Economic Society and the Economic Journal*, Oxford: Blackwell.

Marshall, A. (1881) 'Review of *Mathematical Psychics*', *The Academy*, 457. (Reprinted in J. K. Whitaker (ed.) (1975) *The Early Economic Writings of Alfred Marshall*, London and Basingstoke, pp. 265–8.)

Mill, J. S. (1965) *Principles of Political Economy, with Some of their Applications to Philosophy*, textual editor J. M. Robson, Toronto: University of Toronto Press, London: Routledge and Kegan Paul.

Mirowski, P. (1989) *More Heat Than Light*, Cambridge: Cambridge University Press.

Newman, P. (1987) 'Edgeworth, Francis Ysidro' in J. Eatwell, M. Milgate and P. Newman (eds) *The New Palgrave: A Dictionary of Economics*, London: Macmillan, pp. 84–98.

Price, L. L. (1926) 'Francis Ysidro Edgeworth', *Journal of the Royal Statistical Society* 89: 371–7.

Quintilian, *Institutio Oratoria*, books VIII and IX, as published in the Loeb Classical Library, Harvard University Press, 1922, translated by H. E. Butler.

Stigler, S. M. (1978) 'Francis Ysidro Edgeworth, Statistician', *Journal of the Royal Statistical Society* A 141, part 3: 287–322.

Swales, J. M. (1990) *Genre Analysis: English in Academic and Research Settings*, Cambridge: Cambridge University Press.

Thomson, W., and Tait, P. G. (1890) *Treatise on Natural Philosophy Part One*, Cambridge: Cambridge University Press.

8

Style, persuasion and *The General Theory*

Keynes's *The General Theory of Employment, Interest and Money*, published in 1936, has been described as the last great economics book, written for professionals, to which an educated public could still gain access. Whilst there has been considerable disagreement since on its accessibility, and related concerns about its 'meaning', contemporary readers such as Robinson thought the work 'the most readable book for its weight ever' (Gerrard, 1991: 278; Hession, 1984: 282). Style has been an issue with respect to the status and meaning of the work, both with respect to contemporary and to current readers. For example, Mini sees it as incorporating an economic drama between the 'fickle' and 'feminine' forces of 'liquidity' and the 'robust' and 'masculine' forces of enterprise whose union brings forth production. Mini suggests that the dramatic element in Keynes's approach to life is also, then, incorporated into his text (Mini, 1991: 131). Similarly, the issue of the suitability of Keynes's chosen literary form (with the associated problems of ambiguity) for his analytical and scientific purpose has made 'style' an issue with respect to the problem of interpretation (Gerrard, 1991: 278). Mini's work points to the link between narrative, style and 'l'homme même' that is found in other analyses of style in economics writing. Gerrard's comments raise indirectly the question of suitability of format and purpose posed by 'literary economics' for scientific endeavour.

This chapter sets out to make a stylistic analysis of Keynes's most influential work in order to establish ways in which linguistic detail supports and sustains macro-aspects of textual organisation and patterning. Edgeworth's style has already been treated in an earlier chapter. The material presented here draws upon a similar method of analysis, i.e. the focus is on linguistic practice at the level of the sentence and of the paragraph. However, although Edgeworth and Keynes shared many research interests (Mirowski, 1994: 48), Keynes's writing follows, in detail, a different path from that of Edgeworth. Unlike Edgeworth, Keynes is very anxious to develop a direct relationship with target readers, widely defined, and to adopt, whilst manipulating classical rhetorical strategies, a 'natural' conversational tone. In adapting a colloquial phrase or by introducing a witticism, he establishes an intimacy that Edgeworth may have aspired to but rarely achieved. What they share in their writing is, however, an understanding of classical rhetorical devices and structures and an appreciation of the imaginative tradition of literary economics. Edgeworth has a reputation for stylistic obscurity (not always deserved) and Keynes for accessibility, issues of 'doctrinal fog' or bad writing not-withstanding (Fitzgibbons, 1988: 2; Leijonhufvud, 1968: 11). Both were concerned with engaging readers imaginatively in working out solutions to problems posed.

STYLE AND PERSUASION

Style is an abused term: I do not intend an appreciation of the beauty or even, to use a word lent from economics to literary criticism in the early years of the twentieth century, the *economy* of expression. No doubt, there will be occasion to point towards such expressions but such are not the focus of the research. What is of interest in the context of *The General Theory* is the way in which the work is structured linguistically. The focus is not the Keynesian biography, though this might help enhance the significance of typical features, but a given body of writing, from which the evidence concerning style is drawn and to which appeal can be made on a direct and immediate basis. Style implies choice and in some instances alternatives will need to be considered. By persuasion, I mean the stylistic devices used, in the words of Cicero, 'for the winning over, the instructing and the stirring of men's minds' (Cicero, 1942: 285).

The General Theory is a widely respected work and one which is regarded as conveying an important and significant scientific message. The context within which the work itself is being considered is 'persuasion': the interest is on how the text is structured in the details of its rhetoric to achieve ends, such as the delivery of a message, or messages, that are established within it. Unlike the recently published and interesting work edited by Marzola and Silva, the aim is not so much to evaluate the economic and epistemological arguments as to reveal micro-strategies of persuasion.[1] Micro-analysis of linguistic features will help reveal how Keynes constructed the target reader as well as the ways used to persuade the target reader of the validity of his approach. The approach to questions of style and rhetoric will be catholic and pragmatic.[2]

However in examining style, the interest remains in understanding how the text is constructed in order to persuade. The main problem is that of determining the typical linguistic and rhetorical devices employed in the text in order to convince readers that the story being told is more acceptable, more realistic and more general than that told in any alternative economic texts.[3] The focus of interest is not 'what is being argued' but 'how it is being argued through language'. Naturally, any consideration of the latter involves a reconsideration of the details of the former.

A CHARACTERISTIC PASSAGE

The first surprise of the book is the first chapter which consists of one paragraph and a footnote.[4] In terms of style and argumentation, Chapter 1 can be viewed, in one sense, as a miniature version of the rhetoric of *The General Theory* as a whole. It illustrates at the level of the chapter, the paragraph and the sentence, significant organisational features and textual detail that are common to most of the book as a whole. It is capable of contriving this by challenging assumptions about the nature of a chapter. In content, structure and length, Chapter 1 signals the dramatic nature of what is to follow. What it is not typical of is the longer-term stylistic influence of *The General Theory* which is to be found, not in the elegant argumentation but, as might be expected, in the technical aspects of the writing. The first section of Chapter 1 reads:

> I have called this book *The General Theory of Employment, Interest and Money*, placing the emphasis on the prefix general. The object of such a title is to contrast the character of my arguments and conclusions with those of the classical theory of the subject, upon which I was brought up and which dominates the economic thought, both practical and theoretical, of the governing and academic classes of this generation, as it has for a hundred years past. I shall argue that the postulates of the classical theory are applicable to a special case and not to the general case, the situation which it assumes being a limiting point of the possibilities of equilibrium. Moreover, the characteristics of the special case assumed by the classical theory happen not to be those of the economic society in which we actually live, with the result that its teaching is misleading and disastrous if we attempt to apply it to the facts of experience.
>
> (Keynes, 1936: 3)

The author is present in the text: 'I have called . . .'; 'my arguments'; 'I shall argue . . .' but the social experience and problems are shared: 'in which we actually live'; 'if we attempt to apply'. This shifting from 'I' to 'we' (and, by implication, from 'my' to 'our') is part of a wider strategy to point out contrasts, especially with 'them', the followers of 'the classical school'. The reader is incorporated into the text through this device: 'we', i.e. you and I reader, live in the same world, 'they', not used specifically in the passage (i.e. the governing and academic classes who have been bound by orthodoxy for a hundred years) do not. Throughout the work, Keynes's writing exhibits a high level of 'reader awareness', the 'I'/'we' switch being one of many devices. Others include meta-statements, e.g. 'Or look at the matter thus' as the initial sentence in a paragraph (Keynes, 1936: 105); colloquialisms; the occasional over-use of textual markers and twenty-two direct appeals or instructions to 'the reader'.

The authorial 'I' appeals directly to a reader who is assumed to be capable of working with the author against the interests of the established set of ideas. The radicalism of the text is established. The authorial 'I' establishes the point of view around which the narrative is to be developed. The target reader is one who identifies with the challenge to orthodoxy. This division of 'them' and 'us' is, of course, a continuation of a long-standing tradition in rhetoric which has its analytical origins in classical works, such as those of Cicero. By concentrating on the strengths of his own case and the weakness of 'the classical economics' Keynes is adopting Cicero's advice, offered through Antonius in the *De Oratore* (Cicero, 1942: 419). Keynes's approach is also shaped by his association with the literary ideas of the Bloomsbury group who tended to see nineteenth-century thinking as stuffy, hide-bound and out-dated, hence Keynes's specification of the governing classes and of the restricted nature of classical economics.

The structure of the narrative is hinted at: 'placing the emphasis on the prefix general. The object of such a title is to contrast the character of my arguments and conclusions with those of the classical theory.' This contrast is taken up in the second part of the paragraph where the contrast is developed: 'special' and 'general' and where 'a' special case is contrastively defined with respect to 'the' general case and to 'the economic society in which we actually live'.[5] This special case (there are others analysed) involves special assumptions (Keynes, 1936: 9, 16, 25, 30).

The text here is organised around the notion of oppositionals and contrasts. The words 'happen' and 'actually' are also worth noting in this context. The phrase 'happen not to be' (rather than 'do not happen to be') draws the reader's attention to the contrast (and perhaps irony) of the situation.[6] The use and location of 'happen not to be' adds a hint of what has been referred to as the 'academic sneer', another feature of the work which upset some of Keynes's contemporaries (McCloskey, 1985: 136; Dudley-Evans, 1993: 142–144). The word 'actual', in one form or another ('actual' is used eighty-four times and 'actually' thirty-eight) is used to reinforce the 'here and now' aspect of economic and social experience and perceptions. In various places in the text it stands for a number of accepted but often unspecified social experiences. The recurrent use of what, at first sight, seems a very obvious and somewhat shallow device as a way of incorporating a social reality beyond the text, into the discourse, is not to be dismissed lightly for it carries with it references to the philosophical ideas of Russell and, more especially, Moore. When taken together with the ideas of the 'ordinary man', or the 'instinctive' economic reasonableness of 'workers', the 'facts' of actual 'experience' carry the notion that experience yields proper economic knowledge about the world and hence justifies 'common observation' and 'common sense'. Keynes, through 'intuition' and the 'facts' of actual 'experience' is signalling his association with the non-sceptical empiricism of Moore with respect to the certainty of 'common-sensical' knowledge of the external world.[7] The strength of Moore's influence has, of course, been noted before, most interestingly by Mini (Mini, 1991: 76). The precise consequences for language use in Keynes has not. Whilst Keynes argues for the acute observations of the 'ordinary man' (Keynes, 1936: 33) he exits from *The General Theory* with an exciting hyperbole which inadvertently contradicts himself and declares that practical men are the slaves of defunct economists: their observations are theory-laden![8]

Within the context of the development of the ideas, another characteristic feature is also present: the use of the double or co-ordinated phrase (nouns, adjectives, adverbs) as in the following: 'my arguments and conclusions'; 'practical and theoretical'; 'misleading and disastrous'. The double elements, as will be shown below, can be contrastive but are more usually synonymous with respect to meaning and cumulative with respect to effect. Such devices are established characteristics of Ciceronian style, a fundamental part of formal oratory.

The next step is to illustrate that the rhetorical themes established in the first paragraph of the first chapter are embodied in the wider text in a significant way. The rhetorical pattern established in this small sample of text helps provide us with a way of looking at the wider work as a whole. The passage does not, however, reflect all of the complexities of the text of *The General Theory*. For example, Keynes's use of the long and complex clause, a stylistic feature which is in some ways reminiscent of Edgeworth, is found in the first chapter. The long sentences there are well executed but elsewhere in the text the craftsmanship can weaken and the clarity grow dim. Such sentences have a classical ancestry which also accounts for their presence in Edgeworth's work. Furthermore, the first chapter is devoid of any technical language, of ways of talking about complex processes. A significant feature of the development of Keynesian-type macro-economics is the emergence of a way of talking which involved complex nominal groups.

In the first part of this chapter a review is made of those aspects of the text revealed in Chapter 1 as significant. The order follows that of the section above and each aspect – the authorial presence, contrastive language and rhetoric, other rhetorical devices and the co-ordinated phrase – are examined in turn. The second, shorter, section deals with style and technical language and with aspects of the linguistic practices of the wider text not revealed in the first chapter.

The General Theory

AUTHOR, READERS AND OTHERS

The first step is to look at the authorial and reader presence in the text through the use of the personal pronouns and their associated possessives. Keynes switches point of view in order to develop and sustain established contrasts and to engage the target reader imaginatively in the text in a shared responsibility, recommended by Cicero as an effective persuasive device. The text is highly aware of the potentially active presence of the reader. The economic actor is also present and this adds to the conviction that the text is involved with the world even when the examples are highly stylised. The overall effect is to develop a sense of community, of psychological involvement and of purposeful, rather than anonymous, action. The (nearly) rounded human being is reintroduced into formal economic discussion.

The use of pronouns is interesting and varied. The following examples illustrate the range and context within which they are used. 'We' is used in *The General Theory* 687 times which is significantly greater than the number of times 'I' is used.[9] What follows is not an exhaustive analysis of the relationships signalled by 'we', or any of the other pronouns: it is merely indicative of the kinds of uses made.

1 'We' and characteristic phrases with 'we' as a signal for new terms

The relationship between the community's income and what it can be expected to spend on consumption, designated by d_1, will depend on the psychological characteristic of the community, which we shall call its *propensity to consume*.

(Keynes, 1936: 28)

We may call the former short-term expectation and the latter long-term expectation.

(p. 47)

'We' is often followed with an active verb: 'we subsume . . .'; 'we regard . . .'.

(p. 42)

2 'We' and 'our' as co-operation between the reader and the author

we shall find that the Theory of Price falls into its proper place as a matter which is subsidiary to our general theory. We shall discover, however, that Money plays an essential part in our theory of the

159

Rate of Interest; and we shall attempt to disentangle the peculiar characteristics of Money which distinguishes it from other things.

(p. 32)

It may well be that the classical theory represents the way in which we should like our Economy to behave. But to assume that it actually does so is to assume our difficulties away.

(p. 34)

If we examine any actual problem along the lines of the above schematism, we shall find it more manageable; and our practical intuition (which can . . .)

(p. 249)

The paragraph on pages 40–41 contains eight uses of 'we' in 29 lines. With respect to the wider use of 'we' in the text, an issue to be addressed is the complex switching from 'I' to 'we'.

A most striking example of the 'our', used 202 times in the work, is seen in the one-sentence paragraph which introduces Keynes's investigation of the theory of interest:'What, then, is our answer to the question?'(p. 166).

3 'You' as a direct appeal to the reader

'We' suggests an active reader. 'You' adds to the awareness of the activity, perhaps suggesting further tasks.

The great puzzle of Effective Demand with which Malthus had wrestled vanished from economic literature. You will not find it mentioned even once in the whole works of Marshall, Edgeworth and Professor Pigou, from whose hands the classical theory has received its most mature embodiment.

(p. 32)

Malthus is described in the past perfect. Marshall *et al.* are described in the perfect tense implying an undetermined but recent past. The grouping together of Marshall, Edgeworth and Professor Pigou (is the 'professor' ironic?), i.e. a grouping of the living and the dead, makes the implication of continuation forceful.

4 'Their' and 'they' as distancing devices

The celebrated optimism of traditional economic theory, which has led to economists being looked upon as Candides, who, having left this world for the cultivation of their gardens, teach that all is for the best in the best of all possible worlds, provided we will let well alone, is also to be traced, I think, to their having neglected to take

160

account of the drag on prosperity which can be exercised by an insufficiency of effective demand.

(p. 33)

This is a complex sentence of a pattern found frequently in the text. Technically, it is a 'classical' periodic sentence and suggests that Keynes undertook frequent Latin prose exercises when at school. Such sentence types would be common in such exercises at the time. By adopting the contrasting form Keynes is distancing himself and, indeed, his readers, from the Candides of this world. The 'I think' contrasts strongly with the 'their' which would have otherwise been a collective error, i.e. either a 'we' or an 'our' depending on choices later in the sentence. 'Their' is used 273 times in the work as a whole, the details of the language stressing the divisions between 'them' and 'us' in a variety of consistent and subtle ways. As is the case with other pieces of textual decoration, the entertainment is functional. Keynes is consistent in trying to look at the social world directly rather than through the lens of classical theory. The reference is, of course, faulty for it was Pangloss that taught that 'all is for the best in the best of all possible worlds' and Candide who suffered the consequences!

And as a way of manipulating vagueness

Those who have emphasised the social dangers of the hoarding of money have, of course, something similar to the above in mind. But they have overlooked the possibility that the phenomenon can occur without any change, or at least any commensurate change, in the hoarding of money.

(p. 161)

Vagueness, implied by broad contrasts, is further investigated below.

5 The complex uses of the 'I' (used 409 times)

Switching from 'we' to 'I':

In this and the next three chapters we shall be occupied with an attempt to clear up certain perplexities which have no particular or exclusive relevance to the problems which it is our special purpose to examine. Thus these chapters are in the nature of a digression, which will prevent us for a time from pursuing our main theme. Their subject-matter is only discussed here because it does not happen to have been already treated elsewhere in a way which I find adequate to the needs of my own particular enquiry.

The three perplexities which most impeded my progress in writing

this book so that I could not express myself conveniently until I
had found some solution for them, are . . .

(p. 37)

I would, however, ask the reader to note at once that neither the
knowledge of an asset's prospective yield nor the knowledge of
the marginal efficiency of the asset enables us to deduce either the
rate of interest or the present value of the asset. We must ascertain
the rate of interest from some other source, and only then can we
value the asset by 'capitalising' its prospective yield.

(p. 137)

6 'I' signalling a clear statement of personal opinion

Here the evidence is scattered throughout the text but a significant
chapter in which 'I' plays an important part is Chapter 7 and the examples
are taken from that chapter. The issue is the definition of investment.

But I see no object in excluding the play of other factors on their
decisions; and I prefer, therefore, to emphasise the total change of
effective demand and not merely that part of the change in effective
demand which reflects the increase or decrease of unsold stocks in
the previous period.

(p. 76)

My own use of terms . . . as I have explained . . . which I there
employed . . . I meant . . . I meant . . . As I now think . . . In my
Treatise on Money . . . I did not . . . I there argued . . .

(p. 77)

7 The 'I' and the 'we' are ever present in the text

They are frequently used in association with other features, such as
colloquialisms,[10] which, when taken together reinforce the conversational
quality, providing a sense of author and reader engaged in a discursive
conversation, in the context of an active community of interest, as in the
following examples:

The criterion must obviously correspond to where we draw the line
between the consumer and the entrepreneur.

(p. 62)

So far as I know, everyone agrees in meaning by Saving the excess
of income over what is spent on consumption. It would certainly be
very inconvenient and misleading not to mean this.

(p. 74)

However, when conversational aspects are blended with archaic and some-what 'donnish' (or even avuncular) use of language, the style is reminiscent of the Cambridge lecture/tutorial mode. Readers share more than the particular economic ideas that are being delivered.

8 Pronouns and agency

The General Theory, in stressing the psychological aspects of consumption and investment behaviour makes reference to individual economic agents. The agents are referred to and personalised, as 'he' or 'they'. The associated verbs tend to be active and in the present tense, and treated in the context of economic roles. Such strategies add to the sense in which the text is dealing with the world of actual social experience. The finest example, taken from pages 147–8, is difficult to summarise because of the length of text involved. The concern is with long-term expectations and the stylised economic agents, 'the consumer' and 'the producer' have been introduced earlier:

> We may sum up the state of psychological expectation which covers the latter as being the state of long-term expectation; – as distinguished from the short-term expectation upon the basis of which a producer estimates what he will get for a product when it is finished if he decides to begin producing it to-day with the existing plant, which we examined in chapter five.
>
> II
>
> It would be foolish, in forming our expectations, to attach great weight to matters which are uncertain . . .

The switching here is between an active, stylised producer ('he') and the reader as an economic agent ('our') capable of forming, and reflecting upon, expectations. In the twenty-two lines starting 'It would be foolish . . .', reference is made six times to 'our' and six times to 'we' in the context of making active economic judgements. This switching dramatically alters the relationship between a reader and the text and greatly assists in development of the partnership as well as a reader's sense of what is intended by 'expectations'. It is a device used by De Quincey in his *Logic of Political Economy* in developing an economic story which calls upon insights in consumer psychology. Keynes's use shares some similarities with De Quincey's device, for it also assists in the development of a relationship between the psychological subject matter of the text and the world of 'actual' experience to which Keynes is ever anxious to refer. Although not dealt with specifically in Chapter 1, the switching and the identification of the reader and the reader's experience of agency is consistent with the idea of 'the facts' of actual 'experience', for Keynes assumes (of necessity) that these facts are also (potentially) available to others. Cicero refers to the effective persuasive aspect of such strategies in terms of 'transference of responsibility' and 'consultation with one's audience' (Cicero, 1943: 163).

CONTRASTIVE LANGUAGE AND RHETORIC

1 The use of the definite and indefinite article

The pattern established in Chapter 1 is of a set of contrasts between Keynes's idea and what he chooses to call 'the classical theory' as well as between 'the classical theory' and 'the facts of experience'. Most commentators have dwelt upon Keynes's choice of the term 'classical theory'. The use of the term 'the' should also be commented upon. Glahe found 9,541 uses of 'the' but wisely decided not to list them. However, in the preface, he makes the following statement: 'while all the words used in *The General Theory* are cited and their frequency of use given, not all words are indexed. This was done to eliminate obviously uninteresting words such as "a," "an," "the," and "and" ' (Glahe, 1991: Preface). In normal circumstances this may be the case – though English offers a hierarchy of terms of increasing generality based on the articles, e.g. 'an unemployment . . .'; 'the unemployment . . .' and 'unemployment . . .' which lead to the possibility of easy distinctions between a specific and a technical use. Some uses of 'the' in *The General Theory* are very interesting and worthy of textual exploration. It is used in the context of 'The Classical Economics' and also of 'the Ricardian economics' (Keynes, 1936: 32). The word 'the' carries with it the idea of a single, indivisible entity or idea and has been described by Lord Russell as a 'monopolist', a vehicle for denying plurality of vision. The term is mainly used with the definite article though the precise phrasing differs: 'The classical conclusions are intended . . .' (p. 11); 'Thus writers in the classical tradition . . .' (p. 16); 'if the classical theory is only applicable . . .' (p. 16); 'of the classical doctrine . . .'; 'from the classical system . . .' (p. 17); 'the accepted classical theory . . .' (p. 378); 'the modern classical theory . . .' (p. 379). The term is not restricted to the Classical School, it appears later in the work as 'the traditional analysis' including on page 184 the interesting clauses, 'The traditional analysis has been aware that saving depends on income . . .'. The personification and verb form as well as the concession to 'classical' thinking is interesting and suggests that a study of the rhetoric of verb forms ought to be a significant part of any rhetorical reading of *The General Theory*.[11]

The monopolistic tendency with respect to portraying the Classical School is matched with a vagueness as to who precisely the living keepers of the classical tradition are: Pigou is mentioned in the footnote on page

3 and then several times in the text, though also with an element of vagueness: 'The conviction, which runs, for example, through almost all Professor Pigou's work, that money makes no real difference' (p. 19). 'Almost all'! The notion is that the work is concentrating on broad, theoretical issues, such exemplifications being the means whereby the broad sweep is realised. The question of exactness and vagueness must be approached not within the (prejudicial) understanding that science is concerned with exactness but within the notion of a contrastive rhetoric developed along Ciceronian lines. Only enough detail is supplied to achieve the communication ends set (Channell, 1990: 95). Keynes's insistence on the broad sweep requires that he ignore selected detail, especially when dealing with the views of 'some economists'. The outcome for those actively engaged in classical analysis is stereotyping!

An interesting concretisation merely serves to illustrate the extent of the vagueness with respect to the main actors:

> Thus writers in the classical tradition, overlooking the special assumption underlying their theory, have been driven inevitably to the conclusion, perfectly logical on their assumption, that apparent unemployment (apart from the admitted exceptions) must be due at bottom to a refusal by the unemployed factors to accept a reward which corresponds to their marginal productivity. A classical economist may sympathise with labour in refusing to accept a cut in its money-wage, and he will admit that it may not be wise to make it to meet conditions which are temporary; but scientific integrity forces him to declare that this refusal is, nevertheless, at the bottom of the trouble.
>
> (Keynes, 1936: 16)

Notice the switch from unspecified 'writers' to 'a classical economist', also unspecified, and the accompanying changes of tense. Is the professional insider meant to assume that the reference is to Pigou?

The rhetorical complexity and the attempt to provide concreteness whilst using an example founded upon generalisation are illustrated by a further passage:

> Even outside the field of finance, Americans are apt to be unduly interested in discovering what average opinion believes average opinion to be; and this national weakness finds its nemesis in the stock market. It is rare, one is told, for an American to invest, as many Englishmen still do, 'for income'; and he will not readily purchase an investment except in the hope of capital appreciation.
>
> (Keynes, 1936: 159)

The only evidence supplied is 'one is told': the switch from plural to singular and the use of the indefinite article, and the pronoun 'he', perhaps carry the conviction that this is meant to be an authentic rather than a hypothetical example. It is, of course, Keynes telling a story, and hence, a useful fiction.

The use of the definite article with 'economics' (as in the examples quoted above) is stylistically deviant with respect to the modern use of the term 'economics' as it would be with other singular and uncountable names of subjects ending in 'ics', viz. 'the Quantum mechanics'; 'the classical mathematics'; 'the solid state physics'.[12] It is not clear, to me, at what point 'economics' began to be used as the collective noun for the subject, thus resisting the use of the definite article. Sub-categories of the discipline sometimes carry the article, and sometimes do not: e.g. 'the economics of education' but not 'educational economics'. Does the expression 'the political economy' appear in nineteenth-century economics? Even in the 1930s, Keynes's usage must have been out of step with the use of the definite article in other economics texts. It gives to classical economics an antiquarian air and adds an ironic quality to the text. Furthermore, Keynes does not use an equivalent summarising noun phrase, 'the general economics', to refer to his ideas, though he does call his work *The General Theory*, perhaps drawing some modernistic strength from *The General Theory of Relativity*, whilst at the same time making use of a monopolistic tendency in language to fortify his case.[13] '*A General Theory*', carrying the implication of 'one amongst many', seems, somehow, less convincing. However, Mini points out that the sense of 'general' is methodological in the sense of capable of dealing with many changes in relationships rather than numerical quantity of cases (Mini, 1991: 155).

The use of the 'the' in conjunction with the term 'classical' has a distancing and dismissive effect, an interpretation which is fortified by the understanding that Virginia Woolf and other members of the Bloomsbury group were antithetical to that which is Victorian, classical, restrictive and dead. In the occasional use of archaic expressions, here perhaps suggesting archaic ideas, Keynes is again following Cicero.

2 Verbs and verb forms

In the example given on p. 164, the continuity of the tradition is emphasised in the verb forms. The move from the tradition in general to the stylised individual makes it possible to use emphatic verb form in the present tense as well as the general form of the present tense. This concretisation then emphasises the continuity of the tradition and its present status without providing individual evidence that what is said to be the case is in fact the case.

The verb forms, as the energising hearts of every sentence, are very important in building up the sense of continuity and contrast. The 'Candide' example has already established that the issue of teaching is one in which positioning is of potential textual significance, the illustrations below make use of forms of 'teach':

> For it is far from being consistent with the general tenor of the classical theory, which has taught us to believe that prices are governed by marginal prime cost.
>
> (p. 12)

This constructs the radical economist as victim.

> From the time of Say and Ricardo the classical economists have taught that supply creates its own demand; – meaning by this in some significant, but not clearly defined, sense that the whole of the costs of production must necessarily be spent on the aggregate, directly or indirectly, on purchasing the product.
>
> (p. 18)

Here continuous action in the past is carried by 'the classical economists have taught' and present consequences by the change to the present tense.

> The idea that we can safely neglect the aggregate demand function is fundamental to the Ricardian economics, which underlie what we have been taught for more than a century.
>
> (p. 32)

Notice that the first half of the sentence contains the present tense, stressing continuity, and the second half the phrase 'what we have been taught' (the present perfect passive) rather than 'what we have taught', i.e. the radical economist as victim, once again. The use of the term 'the classical theory' and of 'the Ricardian economics' greatly simplifies the task of building up a set of strong contrasts in the rest of the text. The selection of suitable verb forms greatly assists the development of the contrasts.

The continuity of 'the classical economists' is stressed by the use of the present perfect active tense, the process continues as it has done for the previous hundred years. The cumulative effect of the verb forms is to assist the emergence of the living presence of the classical economist as a relic, a perpetrator of outmoded thinking from the long nineteenth century.

It is not until page 175 that the fourth use refers to a shared responsibility: 'it is what I myself was brought up on and what I taught for many years to others'.[14] However with its next use, the original distancing is re-established: 'So long as economists are concerned with what is called the Theory of Value, they have been accustomed to teach that. ... If we reflect on what we are being taught...' (p. 292). A similar pattern of distancing can be found in Keynes's (infrequent) use of 'brought up':

'we were brought up to believe that . . .' (p. 335); 'amidst the discussions of which he had, of course, been brought up' (p. 364). When Keynes disliked someone's argument he complained that such a person had 'not been properly brought up'!

3 Other contrastive language

Though contrasts are an essential feature of Chapter 1 'but' is not itself used therein. However, as it is an implication of contrastive rhetoric that 'but', along with other contrastive language, will be used frequently, it is considered here. A striking feature is that 'but' is used 496 times, often in sentence-initial position. Another feature is the use of 'actual' and/or 'facts' (or some derivative) when contrasts are made with the Classical School. A final area examined here is the use of 'poetic' or rhetorical flourishes to highlight contrasts, or to stimulate excitement.

The use of 'but'

'But' is generally taken as a signal for reversing an argument or changing direction and this is certainly the case in *The General Theory*. Here is a typical example which illustrates two 'buts', vagueness, a hedge and the use of the co-ordinated phrase.[15]

> The question, also, of the volume of the available resources, in the sense of the size of the employable population, the extent of the natural wealth and the accumulated capital equipment, has often been treated descriptively. But the pure theory of what determines the actual employment of the available resources has seldom been examined in great detail. To say that it has not been examined at all would, of course, be absurd. For every discussion concerning fluctuations of employment, of which there have been many, has been concerned with it. I mean, not that the topic has been overlooked, but that the fundamental theory underlying it has been deemed so simple and obvious that it has received, at the most, bare attention.
>
> (Keynes, 1936: 4)

The 'but' changes the flow: notice that the two terms 'often' and 'seldom' are vague and that the modification of the view continues to make use of vague terms: 'every discussion, of which there have been many'. The conversational tone is reinforced by the vagueness, which here almost implies intimacy between the author and the reader in the sense of common knowledge about other 'discussion'. The contrast in the last sentence is forceful but the vagueness persists: 'at the most'. 'But' is about making objections and the term is very much in evidence in prominent positions throughout the first half of the book, even taking the sentence-initial position in the opening sentences of a number of paragraphs (e.g. pp. 10, 13, 31, 33, 97, 179, 248, 251, 253). If a sentence-initial 'but' is a strong argument reverser, then a paragraph-initial 'but' must count as an even stronger signal of a changed argument. The best example is 'But worse still' on page 31.[16]

As the text presents the argument in broad terms, so the contrasts tend to be strong. This can be seen in the use of another word in sentence-initial position:

Does it follow from this that the existing level of real wages accurately measures the marginal disutility of labour? Not necessarily. For, although a reduction in the existing money-wage would lead to a withdrawal of labour, it does not follow . . .

(p. 8)

'For' is not in itself contrastive: it is used rather to support and justify, a means for the continuation of the argument, sometimes within a chain of signalling terms, as in page 59, thus 'since . . . for', or, as on page 97, 'but . . . for'. The 'for' is associated with a prior contrast and usually provides a justification for it. The nicest example is seen with respect to the discussion of the theory of interest: 'But this is a nonsense theory. For the assumption that income is constant is inconsistent with the assumption that these two curves can shift independently of one another' (p. 179). The use of 'for' in sentence-initial position is to be found in philosophical writings such as those of John Locke. Again it is testimony to the argumentative and contrastive nature of the work that 'for' is used on 1,166 occasions.

The pattern 'but . . . for' is normally to be found close together (sometimes the 'but' and the 'for' are reversed). More complex chaining of contrasting ideas to be evaluated is to be found sometimes with fairly simple signalling such as 'on the one hand'. The chaining can be more demanding. A particularly complex example is found in the long paragraph on page 118 which is from the chapter dealing with the marginal propensity to consume. The signalling is as follows: 'It follows from the above that . . .'; 'but at the same time . . .'; 'If, on the other hand . . .'; 'but, at the same time . . .'; 'in the former case . . .'; 'In the latter case . . .'; 'In actual fact . . .'; it is significant that in this example the chain of reasoning terminates with the 'in actual fact' (see below).

'*Actual*', '*fact*' and '*experience*' as a means of highlighting contrasts with the Classical School

A good example is to be found in the series of paragraphs starting with the unbalanced sentence which constitutes the first paragraph on page 8:

> This calls for two observations, the first of which relates to the actual attitude of workers towards real wages and money-wages respectively and is not theoretically fundamental, but the second of which is fundamental.

The sentence is unbalanced because the referent of the second part is missing. It is not located in the text until six paragraphs later (second paragraph on page 10). Although the 'actual' suggests some direct real-world aspect the paragraph which follows commences with 'Let us assume'. The next begins with: 'Now ordinary experience tells us' and culminates with 'But, whether logical or illogical, experience shows that this is how labour in fact behaves'. The next paragraph ends with: 'These facts from experience are a *prima facie* ground for questioning the adequacy of the classical analysis' (p. 9).

An interesting point to be made about the series of paragraphs is that they are dealing with theoretical speculation and economics story-telling but there is nothing in the passages which would suggest 'facts' in the sense that the term is normally used.

On page 378, the following is to be found:

> Our criticisms of the accepted classical theory of economics has consisted not so much in finding logical flaws in its analysis as in pointing out that its tacit assumptions are seldom or never satisfied, with the result that it cannot solve the economic problems of the actual world.

Perhaps the most impressive use of the 'facts of experience' is to be found in the passage dealing with the propensity to consume:

> The fundamental psychological law, upon which we are entitled to depend with great confidence both *a priori* from our knowledge of human nature and from the detailed facts of experience is that men are disposed, as a rule and on the average, to increase their consumption as their income increases, but not by as much as the increase in their income.
>
> (p. 96)

The term 'actual' is used to reinforce the contrast between the world of the special theory and the world of *The General Theory*:

> Our final task might be to select those variables which can be deliberately controlled or managed by central authority in the kind of system in which we actually live.
>
> (p. 247)

Rhetorical flourishes

The occasional rhetorical flourish is made in contrastive terms, at the level of the sentence, again in figures of speech reminiscent of Edgeworth. Keynes had read Edgeworth, had commented on Edgeworth's style and shared an interest in the same economic problems. The similarities may have, of course, as much to do with a common understanding of classical rhetorical devices than with familiarity with Edgeworth.[17]

> We are reminded of the 'The Fable of the Bees' – the gay of tomorrow are absolutely indispensable to provide a *raison d'être* for the grave of to-day.
>
> (Keynes, 1936: 106)

This is just the type of linguistic playfulness that would have appealed to Edgeworth and which, with other examples, signals Keynes's appreciation of the literary tradition in economics. As would the light relief of a stylistically crowded sentence, complete with Edgeworthian colouring and tone and surprising reversals ('contain . . . when alive', 'shelter . . . after death') in the otherwise dry analysis of the 'Nature of Capital':

> In so far as millionaires find their satisfaction in building mighty mansions to contain their bodies when alive and pyramids to shelter them after death, or, repenting of their sins, erect cathedrals and endow monasteries or foreign missions, the day when abundance of capital will interfere with abundance of output may be postponed.
>
> (p. 220)

Rhetorical flourishes and the co-ordinated phrase

The structure and ornamentation of *The General Theory* makes it a part of literary cultural as well as a scientific document. Stylistically the various types of embellishments, figures of speech, the deliberate but not over-worked use of archaic phrases, the conversational but contrastive tone, realises much of the advice given by Cicero in the third part of the *De Oratore*. If the writing errs in its application of Ciceronian rhetoric, it is in its use of hyperbole. In the use of hyperbole, of references to English literature and of the recommendations of classical rhetoric, Keynes shares much with De Quincey, Ruskin (both much given to hyperbole) and F. Y. Edgeworth. Consideration of lengthier passages illustrates how the various elements of style, identified at the level of the sentence, interact in the paragraph, the next level of textual organisation.

Here is an extended example of the further use of the definite article, verb forms and subsequent rhetorical moves to reinforce the impression of completeness. The spectacular hyperbole well illustrates the structure of a self-consciously rhetorical paragraph specifically designed to reinforce the idea of a theoretical victory essential to setting up the novel nature of the ideas that Keynes will address later in the text. The Ricardian victory was not, of course, complete. Hyperbole is a figure of speech in which what is said is not literally what is meant.

> The completeness of the Ricardian victory is something of a curiosity and a mystery. It must have been due to a complex of suitabilities in the doctrine to the environment into which it was projected. That it reached conclusions quite different from what the ordinary uninstructed person would expect, added, I suppose, to its intellectual prestige. That its teaching, translated into practice was austere and often unpalatable, lent it virtue. That it was adapted to carry a vast and consistent logical superstructure, gave it beauty. That it could explain much social injustice and apparent cruelty as an inevitable incident in the scheme of progress, and the attempt to change such things as likely on the whole to do more harm than good, commended it to authority. That it afforded a measure of justification to the free activities of the individual capitalist attracted to it the support of the dominant social force behind authority.
>
> (Keynes, 1936: 32)

The rhetorical effort made in order to provide a sense of completeness is considerable. The repetition of the form 'That it' followed usually by an active verb and culminating in a short and concise clause, in a kind of contrasting parallelism, reinforces the notion of completeness. The repetition of a short opening phrase, in rhetorical analysis, is identified as anaphora, a device also used by Edgeworth in passages in which he was aiming for effect. Anaphora is a device frequently used in the context of political debate where its recurrence can quickly become tedious. The repetition of a demonstrative pronoun, in this case is of the phrase 'That it', is a distinctive literary device which can be found in the writings of Shakespeare.[18] As in some of the economics writings of Edgeworth, the references to literature other than economics can be very subtle. The phrase 'twice blessed', for example, taken from *The Merchant of Venice*, is used when referring to a national investment programme in the context of the international economy (p. 349). Here, anaphora is used within a section of the text that is polemical both in purpose and in tone. Its possible implications are also layered. The Keynesian challenge is, for example, ennobled and dramatised by the strength of the opposition. Mini's sense of *The General Theory* as an economic drama can be justified by reference to this sort of picture. Notice the move from a potential Keynesian hero, 'the ordinary uninstructed person' (and the almost weary 'I suppose') to the unreformed capitalist operating under nineteenth-century assumptions! Although the passage is a superb example of textual decoration, and certainly as vivid as any word picture painted by Ruskin or

Edgeworth, it is both dramatic and controlled. The passage is thoroughly informed by Keynes's notion of epistemology. Furthermore, it illustrates Keynes's conceptualisation of the elements of persuasion, economics argument needed to persuade at an emotional, intellectual, ethical and political level.

No further extended examples of anaphora have been found in *The General Theory* with quite the same literary flourish. On page 177, when rhetorical issues are to the fore (another attack upon 'the traditional theory') the device is once again in evidence at the level of the subordinate clause, though the rhetorical force is significantly weaker:

> Certainly the ordinary man – banker, civil servant or politician – brought up on the traditional theory, and the trained economist also, has carried away with him the idea that whenever an individual performs an act of saving he has done something which automatically brings down the rate of interest, that this automatically stimulates the output of capital, and that the fall in the rate of interest is just so much as is necessary to stimulate the output of capital to an extent which is equal to the increment of saving; and, further, that this is a self-regulatory process of adjustment which takes place without the necessity for any special intervention or grandmotherly care on the part of the monetary authority.

The exemplification of the 'ordinary man': banker, civil servant and politician says much about Keynes's own world. Notice also the co-ordinated phrases, 'a curiosity and a mystery', in the first passage above and 'any special intervention or grandmotherly care' in the second.

The co-ordinated phrase was identified in Chapter 1, and is used throughout the work: 'repeat and emphasise' (p. 381); 'uncontrollable and disobedient' (p. 317); 'dismay and uncertainty' (p. 316); 'organised and orderly' (p. 297); 'controlled or managed' (p. 247); 'of fundamental theoretical significance and of overwhelming practical importance' (p. 185); 'constant with, and agreeable to' (p. 146); 'confusion and misunderstanding' (p. 138); 'as a rule and on the average' (p. 96); 'in abnormal or revolutionary circumstances' (p. 91); 'more accurate and instructive' (p. 78); 'confusing and incomplete' (p. 78); 'inconvenient and misleading' (p. 74); 'subtleties or peculiarities' (p. 63); 'confused or interrupted' (p. 49); 'violent or rapid' (p. 48); 'more obvious and outrageous' (p. 31); 'simple and obvious' (twice on p. 5).[19]

Whenever the text becomes self-consciously elegant, the co-ordinated phrase is usually to be found. In this example, which as with other passages illustrates other features as well, such as the power and accuracy of direct experience, it is twice used:

> I remember Bonar Law's mingled rage and perplexity in the face

of the economists, because they were denying what was obvious. He was deeply troubled for an explanation. One recurs to the analogy between the sway of the classical school of economic theory and that of certain religions. For it is a far greater exercise of the potency of an idea to exorcise the obvious than to introduce into men's common notions the recondite and the remote.

(Keynes, 1936: 351)

Mini's statement that the work is an 'effort to convince economists, for nobody else needed convincing' is supported, in the above quote, by the reference to Bonar Law (Mini, 1991: 77). The dissonance between how the world is perceived by those who are not victims of the teachings of classical economics and those that are is dramatically encapsulated in the phrase 'rage and perplexity' and reinforced in the contrast between 'common notions' and 'the recondite and remote'. That the co-ordinated phrase is found in self-consciously oratorical passages ought to come as no surprise given the recommendations of classical oratory. Once again the textual decoration is best understood as the detailed realisation of a wider set of rhetorical purposes. The analogy, classical economics as religion, is extended by the reference to exorcism. Later in the chapter Keynes furthers the analogy by making reference to Douglas, Mandeville, Malthus, Gerell and Hobson as 'the brave army of heretics' (p. 371). Keynes is simply self-consciously exploiting an exaggeration made on page 32 where Ricardo's intellectual conquest of England is compared to the Holy Inquisition's conquest of Spain.

WHAT IS NOT TYPICAL

Enough evidence has been presented to illustrate the sense in which the first chapter can be taken stylistically as typical of the rest of *The General Theory*. In initiating an analysis of style and persuasion, it has proven to be a useful way into a rhetorically complex text. However, there are a number of ways in which it is not typical. In terms of the impact of the work on the way in which those convinced by it wrote economics, the work as a whole established a vocabulary and a set of definitions and terms that became standard for discussing macro-economic issues. The opening chapter contains little in the way of either technical vocabulary or analysis and it is these areas that constitute much of the work. Space, however, does not permit a detailed exploration of the sense in which Chapter 1 is not typical of the work as a whole. In the following example, what is striking is the use of nouns and groups of nouns:

It means that, with a given organisation, equipment and technique, real wages and the volume of output (and hence of employment) are uniquely correlated, so that in general, an increase in employ-

ment can only occur to the accompaniment of a decline in the rate
of real wages.

(p. 17)

Even here, in the second part of the sentence, the language has a slightly
exaggerated poetic turn. For a fuller example, using more complex nominal groups see the paragraph on page 77 starting with the phrase, 'As I
now think'. It is, of course, in language associated with the 'consumption
function' that Keynesian nominalisations were to find their fullest
expression. This language is in evidence in Chapter 1. Its development
in *The General Theory* and subsequent evolution, requires separate investigation.

Furthermore, although the structure of the opening chapter illustrates
the highly contrastive nature of the text, it cannot illustrate the macro-
strategy used to encourage the reader through the text.[20] A striking
feature is the complex patterns of repetition found in the work and
analysed by Marzola as part of the strategy of escaping from restrictive
classical thinking, a kind of spiral curriculum (Marzola, 1994: 219). Furthermore, in my judgement fifteen out of the twenty-four chapters end
with a dramatic rhetorical flourish, perhaps only hinted at in the last
sentence of Chapter 1. (Alternatively, it could be argued that Chapter 1
is all rhetorical flourish.) Such flourishes, when analysed in detail, are
marked by Keynes's sense of persuasion and epistemology. They no doubt
added to the sense of intellectual excitement and radicalism on the part
of the readership in which Keynes was interested. One contemporary
reader, Joan Robinson, noted that such passages came 'just at the right
points to keep one going' (Hession, 1994: 282). This is a judgement
about the work's construction in terms of features above the level of the
sentence and the paragraph. The clustering of the eloquent passages is
consistent with Cicero's advice on ornamentation:

> But further, in order to embellish it with flowers of language and
> gems of thought, it is not necessary for this ornamentation to be
> spread over the entire speech but it must be so distributed that
> they may be brilliant jewels placed at various points as a sort of
> decoration.

(Cicero, 1942: 77)

CONCLUSION

The argumentative framework and the rhetorical devices to be found
elsewhere in *The General Theory* are clearly and carefully signalled in the
provocative and unconventional Chapter 1. All of the elements both of
contrastive structure and of associated language used in the first chapter
are to be found at various places throughout the text. In many respects

175

Chapter 1 is a model, based upon Ciceronian contrastive rhetoric, and oratory more widely defined, buttressed, of course, by Cambridge philosophy and Bloomsbury, for the text as a whole. The cultural influences on the work and references to a wider intellectual culture within it are similar, ironically for some are classical influences, to those found in F. Y. Edgeworth or De Quincey. Chapter 1 illustrates in miniature the target reader and many of the persuasive techniques used to construct and reconstruct that reader that are in evidence elsewhere in the text. The contrastive rhetoric both helps and hinders for it carries with it an element of stereotyping, contrived by the vagueness that a broad sweep implies. Style is in the detail and the detail reveals how earnestly and consistently Keynes carried out his rhetorical project. Despite its importance as a turning point of twentieth-century technical economics, it has as much in common rhetorically with literary economics of the nineteenth century as it does with the technical and narrowed Keynesianism of the post-war world. Like the others, it was Keynes's intention to re-educate readers through persuasive writing. Literary analysis reveals, as we would expect, that *The General Theory* is (self-consciously) rhetorical from the bottom up: that choices made with respect to micro-features of the text reflect and reinforce in specific and consistent ways the rhetorical purpose expressed in the first chapter.

However, with respect to the stylistic impact of the text, i.e. its impact on how economics came to be written, Chapter 1 is less significant due to the absence of any technical analysis. The linguistics of the technical analysis differs, in detail, from that of the first chapter and it is some of these linguistic practices that have marked the development of the language of what has come to be known as 'macro'-economics. The influence and evolution of such language has yet to be traced in detail.

NOTES

1 Marzola and Silva (1994).
2 Possible motives for undertaking textual analysis of economics writing are set out in D. N. McCloskey, 1994: 319–342.
3 This is the Keynesian agenda as set out in Chapter 1.
4 Chapter 1 has been subjected to detailed technical linguistic analysis by Roncaglia and Favretti. The analysis provided here is non-technical. The analysis by Roncaglia and Favretti did, however, call my attention to the significance of the 'the' in the first chapter, though they see its role as providing cohesion within the paragraph. My use of the 'the' and of 'actual' is subjected to a different interpretation: theirs is linguistic, mine is rhetorical.
5 For more on the definite and indefinite article see below.
6 Irony is a significant element in the work but it will remain substantially unanalysed in this chapter.
7 For examples of his direct use of the term 'common sense' see pp. 54, 63, 66, 192, 349 and 350. However, other words such as 'obvious', 'actual' and

'experience', as well as the word 'practical', need to be examined to see the sort of company that they keep. Roncaglia and Favretti overlook the epistemological significance of the notion of 'actual circumstances' (Roncaglia and Favretti, 1989: 72).

8 Keynes's awareness of practice shares something with J. S. Mill:

> systematic enquiry into the modes of action of the powers of nature is the tardy product of a long course of efforts to use those powers for practical ends. The conception, accordingly, of Political Economy as a branch of science is extremely modern; but the subject with which its enquiries are conversant has in all ages necessarily constituted one of the chief practical interests of mankind, and, in some, a most unduly engrossing one.
>
> (Mill, 1929: 1)

9 See Glahe (1991). All word counts listed subsequently are derived from Glahe's concordance. I started this work using a method based upon close reading, before Glahe's concordance was published. Glahe's concordance proved a very useful alternative.

10 Colloquialisms are also to be found without the 'I' and are interesting in any discussion of authorial comment and of the relationship with the reader. See, for example, the first paragraph on p. 59 where the phrase 'are not going to be ruled out of the picture' is used.

11 It is important, however, not to over-emphasise the point. There are other points in the text in which the use of the definite and indefinite article stand in contrast to what we would expect in today's economics writing:

> so that a country secures for itself no larger a share in the stock of the precious metals than is fair and reasonable, but also that an immoderate policy may lead to a senseless international competition for a favourable balance.
>
> (p. 338)

'The' precious metals and 'a' senseless international competition would not be modern-day usage. Even here, however, I suspect that writing is deliberately old-fashioned and 'donnish'.

12 I am indebted to Tim Johns for this point.

13 Einstein produced two theories, 'The Special Theory of Relativity', designed to resolve an inconsistency between classical mechanics and classical electromagnetism and then, in 1916, his theory of gravitation or 'The General Theory of Relativity' which also included the Newtonian conditions but which was, in addition, capable of dealing with observations that Newtonian ideas could not account for. Keynes's justification for his use of the term 'classical economics' has to be read against a wider cultural background which includes the terminology of scientific discussion. I am indebted to Gron Tudor-Jones for an ongoing discussion on matters physical.

14 The example is illustrating the use of 'teach'. A contrite Keynes is to be found on page 61, but the contrition does not involve the verb 'teach'. Keynes's contrition does, however, lead him to take great care over questions of definition and conformity to 'common usage'. He seems to be taking Mill's advice on terminology:

> yet when employing terms which common usage has taken complete possession of, it seems advisable so to employ them as to do the least possible violence to usage; since any improvement in terminology

177

obtained by straining the received meaning of a popular phrase is generally purchased beyond its value, by the obscurity arising from the conflict between new and old association.

(Mill, 1929: 48)

15 The school-room prohibition on using 'but' in an initial position is probably of relatively recent origin. 'But' is used in the initial position by Bastaple in the *Economic Journal* in 1891 together with the long, elegant adjectival phrase and by J. S. Mill. Fowler (1926) does not mention it and *Collins/Cobuild English Usage*, which is based upon computer analysis of contemporary text, holds that: 'You do not normally put but at the beginning of a sentence, but you can do so when you are replying to someone, or writing in a conversational way' (112). Although the Cobuild work is referring to today's writing, the comments about replying and conversational writing ought to be kept in mind. I am indebted to Tim Johns for the Cobuild and Fowler references.

16 'But' is likely to be present in any argued text. However, it is heavily used in Keynes. Incidentally, Mill sometimes uses 'but' in paragraph-initial position; see Mill, 1929: 161.

17 Although the extra-textual Keynesian biography is not the focus of the analysis, Keynes had both read Edgeworth and worked with him. Both shared an interest in 'style' in the sense of 'grand style'.

18 Consider 'This royal home of kings, this sceptred isle . . .'.

19 The device, once identified, begins to lack charm. The examples given are merely a sample from a long list of possibilities.

20 The repetitive and cumulative nature of the writing, a kind of spiral curriculum, is analysed by Gotti and by Marzola in Chapters 5 and 6 of Marzola and Silva (1994).

REFERENCES

Channell, J. (1990) 'Precise and Vague Quantities in Writing on Economics', in Nash, W. (ed.) *The Writing Scholar: Studies in Academic Discourse*, London: Sage.

Cicero (1942) *De Oratore*, I and II, (trans. E. W. Sutton), The Loeb Classical Library.

Cicero (1943) *De Oratore*, III (trans. H. Rackham), The Loeb Classical Library.

Dudley-Evans, T. (1993) 'The Debate over Milton Friedman's Theoretical Framework: An Applied Linguist's View', in Henderson, W., Dudley-Evans, T., and Backhouse, R. (eds) *Economics and Language*, London: Routledge.

Fitzgibbons, A. (1988) *Keynes's Vision*, Oxford: Clarendon Press.

Fowler, E. (1926) *Modern English Usage*, Oxford: Oxford University Press.

Gerrard, B. (1991) 'Keynes's General Theory: Interpreting the Interpretations', *Economic Journal*, 101, 276–287.

Glahe, F. R. (1991) *Keynes's Theory of Employment, Interest and Money: A Concordance*, Savage, Maryland: Rowman and Littlefield.

Hession, C. H. (1984) *John Maynard Keynes*, London: Macmillan.

Keynes, J. M. (1936) *The General Theory of Employment, Interest and Money*, London: Macmillan.

Leijonhufvud, A. (1968) *On Keynesian Economics and the Economics of Keynes*, Oxford: Oxford University Press.

McCloskey, D. N. (1985) *The Rhetoric of Economics*, Brighton: Wheatsheaf Books.

McCloskey, D. N. (1994) 'How to Do a Rhetorical Analysis and Why', in Backhouse, R. (ed.) *New Directions in Economics Methodology*, London: Routledge, 319–342.

Marzola, A. and Silva, F. (eds) (1994) *John Maynard Keynes: Language and Method*, Aldershot: Edward Elgar.

Marzola, A. (1994) 'Rhetoric and Imagination in the Economic and Political Writings of J. M. Keynes', in *John Maynard Keynes: Language and Method*, Aldershot: Edward Elgar.

Mill, J. S. (1929) [1848] *Principles of Political Economy* (ed. W. J. Ashley), London: Longmans, Green and Co.

Mini, P. V. (1991) *Keynes, Bloomsbury and the General Theory*, London: Macmillan.

Mirowski, P. (1994) 'Marshalling the Unruly Atoms: Understanding Edgeworth's Career', in Mirowski, P. (ed.) *Edgeworth on Chance, Economic Hazard and Statistics*, Totowa, New Jersey: Rowman and Littlefield.

Roncaglia, R. and Favretti, Rossini, R. (1989) 'Reading *The General Theory*: A Linguistic Perspective', in Favretti, R. R. (ed.) *Il Linguaggio Della Teoria Generale: proposte di analisi*, Bologna: Pàtron.

179

Index

Index

Index

'fact', use of 169–70
Faraday, Michael 43
farmyard, parable of 123–5
Favretti, R.R. 176
figures of speech 134, 141–7; schemes
141–4; tropes 144–7
Fitzgibbons, A. 155
'for', use of 169
forced labour 83
Fox, Charles 69, 70
Fraser's Magazine 81–2, 85
free trade 82–3

Galton, Francis 132
Geddes, P. 112, 116–17, 119, 129
generalisation 118–19, 129
Gerrard, B. 154
Gide, C. 15
Glahe, F.R. 164, 177
Globe newspaper 66
'goodwill', reader's 95
Goulder, M.D. 123, 125
government: Martineau and reform 70,
82–3; Ruskin 122–3, 125, 126
Graves, R. 131
Greek 135–6, 152
Groenewegen, P.L. 98

Haldimand, A.F. 44, 45
Hare, A.J.C. 30
Heilbroner, R.L. 23
Heinzelman, K. 2, 13, 112, 123;
economics vocabulary 115, 117; Mill
16–17
Hession, C.H. 154, 175
hoarding 123
Hobson, J.A. 112, 116, 119
Hodgson, S.H. 96, 108, 109
household economy 123–5
Hume, David: dialogue 49, 62;
influence on M. Edgeworth 33, 34,
35, 36
Hundert, E.J. 33, 34, 35
hyperbole 171–2

idealism 51
illth 121–2
images, Ruskin and 115–27
imagination 31
income distribution 121; *see also*
distribution
indefinite article 164–6, 177

individualism: De Quincey 104; M.
Edgeworth 27
inequality: Marcet 58–9; Ruskin 120–1
Ingram, J.K. 97, 116–17
institutions 126
intrinsic value 125
investment, ethical 123
italics 134, 149

Jacobins 104
Jevons, William Stanley 108, 132
justice 118–19

Keynes, John Maynard 3, 4, 10, 18,
154–79; author 159–64;
characteristic passage 156–8;
contrastive language and rhetoric
164–74 ('actual', 'fact' and
'experience' 169–70; co-ordinated
phrases 158, 171–4, 178; definite and
indefinite article 164–6, 177;
rhetorical flourishes 171–4, 175; use
of 'but' 168–9; verbs/verb forms
166–8); F.Y. Edgeworth see
Edgeworth; Martineau 64;
pamphleteer 6; reader 13, 18, 95,
156–7, 159–64, 176; style and
persuasion 155–6
Knight, C. 68
knowledge: practical *see* experience;
previous and learning 54–5;
theoretical and practical 113; useful
5, 50–1
Kowaleski-Wallace, E. 22, 23, 24

labour: division of *see* division of
labour; forced 83; productive and
unproductive 74, 80; Ruskin
(management of labour 124–5;
work and 118–20); wage labour 75
laissez-faire 122; Martineau 63, 64, 82,
85
Lamb, R.B. 28
land, privatisation of 58–9
Latin 135–6
Law, Andrew Bonar 173–4
Lawless, E. 22, 31, 41
learning: active 53–5; experiential 31,
34–5, 37; *see also* education
Lee, A. 112, 113, 115, 117
Leijonhufvud, A. 155
lexical items 135–6; *see also* words
life, human 118, 119–20, 121–2

182

Index

Lincoln, A. 30

'literary economics' 1–20; literary reading of 10–14; Smith, Ricardo, Malthus and Mill 14–19

lithographs 125

Locke, John 24, 36

logic, De Quincey and 93, 105–6, 107, 108

Lunar Society 23, 24, 56

machine breaking 67

Maloney, J. 150

Malthus, Thomas Robert 3, 80, 160; De Quincey 95, 96, 97, 99, 110; M. Edgeworth 22–3; Marcet 45, 50; Martineau 15, 67, 73, 85

Marcet, Alexander 44, 45, 46, 47, 57

Marcet, Jane 4, 5, 13, 16, 40, 43–62; biographical background 44–8; comparison with De Quincey 91–2; comparison with Ruskin 114; *Conversations on Chemistry* 45, 46, 56; *Conversations on Political Economy* 45, 48–57, 60, 61, 67 (revisions 57–60); M. Edgeworth 27, 41, 46, 46–7, 56–7; education 21, 38, 39, 48–57; Marshall 5–6, 39–40, 43; reader 11; Schumpeter 64, 87; Smith 15–16; social implications 28; women's agency 8, 9

market: F.Y. Edgeworth 139–41; Ruskin 120, 125–6

market price 100, 108

Marshall, Alfred 60, 86, 113, 160; F.Y. Edgeworth 132, 151, 152 (comparison 149–50); Marcet 5–6, 39–40, 43; Martineau 5–6, 39–40, 64; public understanding 10

Martineau, Harriet 3, 4, 7, 13, 40, 63–90; agency 8, 41, 124; *Autobiography* 65, 70; *Berkeley the Banker* 65; biographical background 65–73; comparison with De Quincey 91–2; comparison with Ruskin 114, 122; *Demerara* 75, 76; M. Edgeworth 22, 24, 38–9; education 5, 21, 50, 70–3, 80, 85–6; 'Garveloch Tales' 80–1; *Illustrations of Political Economy* 63, 69–86 (contemporary reactions 78–84; as literature 76–7; as political economy 77–8); *Life in the Wilds* 73–5, 80; Malthus 15, 67, 73, 85; Marcet 46, 47–8, 56, 61; Marshall

5–6, 39–40, 64; *Moral of Many Fables* 76, 82–3; reader 11–12; Smith 15–16; social and economic life 28; *Tale of the Tyne* 83

Marzola, A. 155, 175

mathematical reasoning 145–6, 152

McCloskey, D.N. 2, 9, 19, 132–3, 157; allegory 152; reasons for rhetorical analysis 17

McCulloch, J.R. 66, 72, 73, 75, 92

McDonagh, J. 2, 4, 93, 103, 107, 110

McKail, J.W. 115

meaning of words *see* words

'mercantile economy' 116, 121, 125

meritocracy 74, 74–5

metaphor 139–40, 144–7, 149–50, 150

Mill, James 61, 72; Martineau 69, 73, 85; simplification 76

Mill, John Stuart 3, 4, 73, 86, 90, 91, 116; agency 119, 129; Coleridge 109; common usage 177–8; De Quincey 98, 108 (value 102, 107, 110); literary tradition 14, 16–17; Martineau 63–4, 68, 69, 77, 85 (response to Martineau's work 82–4); practical knowledge 177; Ruskin 16, 128; style 132; words 98, 117

Miller, Mrs Fenwick 76

Millhauser, M. 21, 40

Milton, John 94, 141

Mini, P.V. 154, 158, 166, 172, 174

Mirowski, P. 144, 150, 154

money 109, 120–1, 123

Moore, George Edward 157, 158

moral action 118; *see also* ethics

moral tales 52, 68, 76; *see also* economic principles, M. Edgeworth, Martineau

motivation 118–19; *see also* agency

Myers, G. 43, 48–9

Myers, M. 27, 28

national wealth 121

natural price 108

negative value 104–5, 108

New Poor Law 89

Newman, P. 131, 134

newspapers 66

obscurity 97–8

opium 93–4, 107

organicism 95

183

Index

Index